To: Bowling Green
Students + Friends.

Thank you for reading this book

I hope you enso... ...ing it a much
...

I enjoyed writing it.

Dr. Jox, Campbell, + Box

Go Turtles!

Joel Cutcher...

Valuable Disconnects
in Organizational Learning Systems

Valuable Disconnects
in Organizational Learning Systems

Integrating Bold Visions and Harsh Realities

Joel Cutcher-Gershenfeld
Massachusetts Institute of Technology

J. Kevin Ford
Michigan State University

New York   Oxford
OXFORD UNIVERSITY PRESS
2005

Oxford University Press

Oxford   New York
Auckland   Bangkok   Buenos Aires   Cape Town   Chennai
Dar es Salaam   Delhi   Hong Kong   Istanbul   Karachi   Kolkata
Kuala Lumpur   Madrid   Melbourne   Mexico City   Mumbai   Nairobi
São Paulo   Shanghai   Singapore   Taipei   Tokyo   Toronto

Published by Oxford University Press, Inc.
198 Madison Avenue, New York, New York, 10016
www.oup.com

Oxford is a registered trademark of Oxford University Press

Library of Congress Cataloging-in-Publication Data
Cutcher-Gershenfeld, Joel.
   Valuable disconnects in organizational learning systems : integrating bold visions and
harsh realities / Joel Cutcher-Gershenfeld and Kevin Ford
      p.   cm.
   Includes bibliographical references and index.
   ISBN-13 978-0-19-508906-6
   ISBN 0-19-508906-5 (cloth)
   1. Organizational learning.   2 Knowledge management.   I. Ford, Kevin.   II. Title.
   HD58.82.C88 2004
   658.4'038–dc22
                              2004057635

To Susan, Melanie, and our children—Gabe, Aaron, Kate, Tynan, Megyn, and Reilly—who have grown up with this continuing collaboration

CONTENTS

PREFACE

We begin this book with the core process by which learning happens: Data is interpreted to create knowledge, which is then applied to drive action. As action creates new data, the cycle continues and learning deepens. Various forms of this cycle are at the heart of most organizational initiatives around learning and knowledge. These Bold Visions for organizational learning systems have always been important, but they are now essential as the scale and scope of the "knowledge economy" reaches into virtually all types of work.

We then set these Bold Visions side by side with a second cycle, which is rooted in what we call the Harsh Realities of learning and knowledge. This second cycle involves the 3Ds—disconnects, dilemmas, and divergence. These are aspects of learning and knowledge that are too often treated with inaction, blame, or quick fixes. The result, predictably, is yet further disconnects and a downward cycle that undercuts learning and knowledge.

Our core thesis is that the disconnects are valuable—they provide a unique window into organizations that is essential for the success of any learning- or knowledge-based initiative. It is not easy to build the necessary skill sets and the mindsets to deal with disconnects, dilemmas, and divergence in constructive ways. Yet, learning depends on nothing less than the integration of Bold Visions with the Harsh Realities.

The book has been written as an extended essay. It is rooted in the scholarly literature and in field research. The analysis is rigorous, but the writing style is designed to be accessible. Our goal is to engage practitioners, scholars, and policy makers in new ways of thinking—helping readers see what was previously distorted, hidden, or undervalued.

This book builds on key insights from many leading thinkers on matters of quality, systems, organizations, transformation, and knowledge. The core cycle associated with the Bold Visions (data, knowledge, and action) that are introduced in chapter 1 builds on Dr. W. Edwards Deming's PDCA (plan, do, check, adjust) cycle and similar learning cycles dating back to John Dewey. Similarly, the use of the three-tiered framework, involving strategy, governance, and daily operations, derives from the work of Thomas Kochan, Henry Katz, and Robert McKersie on the *Transformation of American Industrial Relations.* Many parts of the book build on principles of organizational learning codified by Peter Senge in *The Fifth Discipline* and further developed in *The Dance of Change.* We add to these works a dialectic analysis of the interplay between the Bold Visions and the Harsh Realities that provides important insights into the challenges of implementing and sustaining organizational learning initiatives. We also build on much of our own work on training, knowledge-driven work, learning dynamics, negotiations, and new work systems. Certainly the core message of the book—that disconnects are valuable—is not a new idea. But we see the need for a systematic revitalization and integration of all of these ideas together, which we have attempted.

The book is organized into three parts. Part I, entitled "Bold Visions," introduces the importance and great potential associated with systems for learning, training, and knowledge. Part II, entitled "Harsh Realities," takes a deeper look at the dynamics of disconnects, divergence, and dilemmas. Finally, part III, entitled "Integration," brings together the Bold Visions and the Harsh Realities.

Chapters 1, 2, and, 3 compose part I. Chapter 1 begins with the many sources of pressure in the system associated with learning, training, and knowledge. This reflects a fundamental shift in the nature of markets and work—toward more of a knowledge-based model. However, the result of the pressure is too often a series of disconnects—gaps between the Bold Visions and the Harsh Realities. It is in this context that we introduce the two learning cycles that are at the heart of the book—one that reflects the Bold Visions for learning and one that reflects the Harsh Realities in most organizations. So much of the literature on learning, training, and knowledge involves efforts to drive the Bold Visions, without appreciating constructively the many ways that learning doesn't happen in organizations. Driving forces are overvalued, restraining forces are underappreciated, and successive waves of organizational learning initiatives stumble or fail.

Chapter 2 presents different illustrative examples of advanced learning, training, and knowledge initiatives in organizations. Five different cases are featured—each of which goes well beyond traditional notions of skill acquisition for narrowly defined jobs. These cases highlight training-the-trainers, integrating multiple stakeholders, forging external partnerships, investing in intellectual capital, and pursuing overall culture change. We see just how compelling the Bold Visions can be. Chapter 2 also introduces a key distinction between "routine" and "adaptive" capability—two very different aspects of learning that have different action implications.

Chapter 3 looks beyond the visible aspects of new models and presents the "story behind the story." We take a benchmark systems change initiative and trace its many successes, while also revealing the disconnects that are harder to see but equally important. Ultimately, the failure to attend to the disconnects takes this case down what we term a "slippery slope," which ends with the unexpected collapse of the organization itself.

Chapters 4, 5, and 6 compose part II. Chapter 4 makes the case that disconnects are inevitable. We identify typical disconnects, which can be classified in many ways, such as by the level at which they occur (disconnects at the strategic, governance, and frontline operations levels of organizations) and at what stage in the learning process (disconnects in the data, knowledge, and action parts of the Bold Vision). The litany of disconnects will be familiar to many—our hope is to illustrate ways to engage them constructively.

Chapter 5 takes the story a step further, introducing the underlying dilemmas that account for many of the disconnects. The concept of a dilemma is carefully defined and the power of this sort of deep insight is addressed. Dilemmas are often painful, but they are also liberating—pointing the way toward action, even if it involves hard choices.

Chapter 6 observes that disconnects and the dilemmas add up to divergence in most organizations. Six different types of learning are highlighted, with divergence possible within each and among them all. The six types of learning are derived by taking the distinction between "routine" and "adaptive" approaches (introduced in chapter 2) and pairing it with different configurations of stakeholder relations (loosely coupled, aligned, and opposed). This generates "incremental" and "continuous" learning, which are at the heart of the classic organizational theory and training literatures. It also generates "experimental" and "synergistic" learning, which are at the heart of the popular literatures on systems thinking, total quality, and lean transformation. Finally, this framework surfaces "entrenched" and "revolutionary" learning, which are rarely treated in the organizational learning literature, but are pervasive in organizations. Taken together, the dynamics of divergence create a picture of organizational learning that is both extensive and complicated—helping to explain the mixed experience with many learning- and knowledge-based initiatives.

Chapters 7, 8, and 9 compose part III. Chapter 7 is focused on the skill sets needed to value disconnects. These are the skills associated with interpreting data on disconnects, applying knowledge about disconnects, and assessing action taken with respect to disconnects. While none of these skills are particularly novel, many of them are missing across organizations—constraining the ability to value disconnects.

Chapter 8 focuses on the mindsets needed to value disconnects. These are less tangible, but no less important. We explore tools and techniques for increasing comfort and appreciation of disconnects, as well as the ways in which the skill sets and mindsets are interdependent.

Finally, in chapter 9 we examine the potential for the Bold Visions and Harsh Realities to be integrated around large-scale systems change. A generic change model is presented, along with the "story behind the story" for this model. Ultimately, bringing together the mindsets and skill sets associated with both learning cycles involves simultaneously showing passion for the Bold Visions for organizational learning and taking a nonblaming, constructive approach to the Harsh Realities. It is easy to say and hard to do.

Altogether, this book is designed to deepen appreciation for something that is both common and undervalued: disconnects. Ultimately, valuing disconnects represents a key missing ingredient in the full transformation of organizations based on learning and knowledge.

ACKNOWLEDGMENTS

We are deeply grateful to many colleagues and associates who have provided feedback on this manuscript, influence on our thinking, and inspiration through their efforts. For feedback and wisdom as readers of this manuscript, we would like to particularly thank Dave Binder, Steve Deneroff, Thomas Kochan, Robert McKersie, Steve Parry, Ed Schein, Anne Stevens, and Richard Walton. In this regard, we owe a particular dept of gratitude to Peter Senge for valuable dialogue and learning, as well as for calibration with respect to *The Dance of Change*. We cannot list all the practitioners who have enabled our learning through their leadership and actions, but we would at least like to express our appreciation to Deborah Fellman, Marsall Goldberg, Roger Komer, Nathaniel Lake, Jr., Chris Marlin, Larry Schultz, Chief Erv Portis, Marty Mulloy, Dennis Profitt, Ron Reeves, and Mona Rinehart. We would also like to acknowledge the influence of many additional colleagues, including Betty Barrett, Jerry Boles, John Carroll, Ray Friedman, Jan Klein, Irwin Goldwtein, Rich Klimoski, Nancy Leveson, William Nuttall, Wanda Orlikowski, and George Roth. We would also like to thank Georgette Rogers and Rita Berkeley for graphic design support. Finally, we are deeply appreciative of the editorial leadership and production support from Terry Vaughn and Leslie Anglin at Oxford University Press, as well as the initial support and leadership from Herb Addison and Joan Bossert—all have helped ensure the many "connects" needed to bring this book to completion. Of course, we take full responsibility for any inaccuracies or disconnects associated with the manuscript.

Valuable Disconnects
in Organizational Learning Systems

Pressure in the System

L earning . . . knowledge . . . skills . . . capability—these are emerging as leading sources of sustainable competitive advantage.[1] Organizations used to rely on factors such as natural resources, nearby transportation, readily available capital, new technology, or low-cost labor to ensure continued success, but substitutes for each of these factors are all too easy to find. Individuals used to graduate from high school, perhaps go on to earn a college degree or to complete an apprenticeship, and then they would enter the workforce. Now that model is incomplete.

Today, leading-edge organizations in public and private sectors are deriving ever greater value from employee insights, expertise, and capability. Work in these settings is becoming more knowledge driven. For individuals, the intrinsic value of learning is joined by a new sense of urgency around building the appropriate skills and capabilities—throughout a lifetime. So the question emerges: How can we create the organizational learning systems necessary for success in a knowledge economy? More to the point: How can we do this in ways that take into account the unintended and complicated consequences—not just the obvious beneficial outcomes?

New approaches to knowledge and learning are essential whenever an organization aspires to improve quality, to foster continuous improvement, and to achieve innovation in products or services. Improving quality requires the knowledge of frontline workers who interact directly with products and customers, so that quality is addressed at the source, rather than being inspected afterwards. Continuous improvement and innovation can occur just with inputs from top leadership or knowledge experts, but the potential is vastly increased when knowledge at every level focuses on these goals.

In this context, the importance of learning is elevated.[2] The strategic goals of countless organizations highlight the importance of investing in people. CEOs and other leaders are commonly quoted stating that "The only truly sustainable advantage that any company has is the quality, commitment, energy, and competitiveness of all its people."[3] In the United States alone, it is estimated that over $210 billion is spent every year on workplace training, with the fifty companies that lead the field in workplace training spending over $5.3 billion on it in 2000.[4] Bold Visions center on organizational learning.

Does this mean that most workplaces have suddenly become institutions of learning? That people everywhere are able to step back from the daily grind in order to reflect and grow? Does this mean that increased capability is truly valued by organizations as a resource to be preserved? Hardly. The reality is that most organizations have not even come close to realizing the Bold Visions.

We have had almost two decades of massive layoffs, downsizing initiatives, reengineering strategies, reorganizations, mergers, acquisitions, and privatization efforts. These are situations—examples of what we have termed "disconnects"—in which the knowledge and skills of all but a handful of leaders and experts is undervalued or even disregarded.[5] Budgets for learning activities are typically the first to be cut in a downturn, despite the human resource profession's continued efforts to quantify the gains for individuals or organizations associated with investments in people.[6] These disconnects continue to occur despite the ever-growing popularity of books, seminars, and speeches on organizational learning.

On the one hand, economic and social pressure builds for increased organizational learning. On the other, there are countless constraints on the development, delivery, and effectiveness of workplace learning activities. In part, the pressure for change is, itself, a factor driving the disconnects. As social theorist Kurt Lewin observed a half century ago, the forces driving change are as likely to generate resistance as they are to produce the intended change.[7] More recently, Peter Senge reiterated the point in his book, *The Fifth Discipline,* when he noted that the "harder you push, the harder the system pushes back."[8]

Today's reality is that organizational learning systems are simultaneously being driven by Bold Visions and undercut by Harsh Realities. The core thesis of this book is that the Harsh Realities are in fact a valuable and necessary complement to the Bold Visions.[9] These Harsh Realities, which are visible via countless disconnects, are increasingly being recognized as core challenges for learning organizations. For example, *The Dance of Change*, a 1999 book on the challenges of sustaining momentum in a learning organization, highlights the obstacles to initiating learning systems, including time shortages or staff shortages, issues of relevancy, and challenges around leaders walking the talk. The book also highlights challenges in sustaining and redesigning learning systems, including issues involving fear and anxiety, assessment and measurement, true believers and nonbelievers, governance, diffusion, strategy, and purpose.[10] To this life cycle of challenges, we add a key point, which is that all of the challenges represent valuable feedback loops in the system.

Properly valued, these disconnects enable learning systems to grow and adapt. Alternately, if the response is superficial or one of blame, the organizational learning systems will not be sustainable. The real leverage for sustaining a learning system lies in the way organizations approach and deal with the barriers to change.

Of course, the Bold Visions centered on the importance of learning, knowledge, skills, and capability are compelling. But just pushing harder on the Bold Visions will have limited impact, especially compared to taking an open and constructive approach to dealing with the Harsh Realities. Discounting the disconnects will not make them go away. Moving toward a learning perspective increases the pressure and anxiety of an organization's system. How leaders accept responsibility and set up systems to deal with this increased pressure is critical to the success of the effort.[11] Unfortunately, as noted by Chris Argyris, one of the pioneering scholars of organizational learning, many of the same leaders who are enthusiastic about continuous learning and improvement also prove to be among the biggest obstacles to its success.[12]

In our experience, the responses to disconnects are rarely constructive. First, someone is blamed for the disconnect. Second, a "Band Aid" solution is proposed. Third, statements on the importance of training and learning are repeated with even greater vigor. Fourth, nothing really changes. Fifth, cynicism deepens. Finally, since the need for knowledge to drive work systems is ever increasing in the present economy, the pressure builds.

Too many books on training, knowledge, and learning highlight the need for organizational learning and the many forces that justify the increased "pressure" for more learning activities.[13] Too many practitioners study the leading "learning organizations" assuming that the best practices will be directly transferable to their own organization. In our view, focusing on all the reasons for enhanced learning and all the "right" practices will not necessarily advance learning practices since these activities ignore the countervailing forces that are inevitable outcomes of this pressure.

This book lies at the intersection of the concepts of knowledge management, organizational learning, and continuous improvement—with a focus that simultaneously embraces the Bold Visions associated with attempts to enhance knowledge and learning, as well as the Harsh Realities that we all observe. This is not a book about ideal ways to conduct training or best practices for organizational learning. This is a book that takes an unblinking look at the realities—what actually happens on the ground in countless organizations. We do not do this to wallow in the many observed disconnects. We focus on disconnects because they are a necessary—and valuable—part of the path that leads to the Bold Visions. If knowledge is to truly become the primary source of sustainable competitive advantage in a global economy, it is necessary to appreciate disconnects and the opportunity they provide for examining more closely the realities of the organization.

A NEW LOOK AT DISCONNECTS

We urge a different and somewhat unconventional path. Data is embedded in each knowledge or learning disconnect. Disconnects are each a unique window into the current state of affairs in an organization. Disconnects illuminate operating assumptions and other parts of the culture that explain why old ways of doing things persist.[14] Scholars have long known that accidents and other cataclysmic events provide unique windows into how organizations actually function, including the creation of formal investigation reports that examine some of the most sensitive and otherwise inaccessible parts of organizations.[15] Our focus builds on this insight and extends it—so that the analysis of disconnects can be done on a more continuous and proactive basis—not waiting for cataclysmic events to take place.

For example, focusing on disconnects reveals forms of learning that are often overlooked—what might be called entrenched learning. Entrenched learning does not show up in many theories or seminars on organizational learning, but in most organizations it is ever present. It is the learning that happens when interests are opposed. Often survival in one form or another is perceived to be at stake. This includes learning how to cope with the frustration of canceled training, cut budgets, restructured assignments, and other disconnects. It is learning that leaders and new programs will come and go, and that enthusiasm for any new initiative should be tempered. This is the learning that success often comes to those who follow their narrow self-interest, rather than pursuing the greater good. It is learning about how to undermine new initiatives that threaten the status quo. We are certainly not celebrating entrenched learning, but we acknowledge that it takes place and we urge that it cannot be ignored. Indeed, this is just one of six distinct types of organizational learning highlighted in chapter 6, all of which are part of intertwined, divergent dynamics in organizations.[16]

There is great potential in building Bold Visions about organizational learning around concepts such as teamwork, collaboration, creativity, problem solving, and shared-knowledge processes. But the visions have little value if they are disconnected from everyday realities. All forms of organizational learning are part of the whole—learning that is constructive and oriented toward the greater good *and* learning that is in opposition to the system or even driven by a cynical disregard for the system. All types of learning are part of the picture. Without attention to Harsh Realities, the learning associated with Bold Visions is at risk of becoming one more passing fad. Without attention to the Bold Visions, the learning associated with the Harsh Realities lacks direction and purpose.

The implications of this point are far reaching. Consider situations where learning is not even on the agenda—situations where life is dominated by poverty, war, or disease. These are situations where learning is overshadowed by fundamental issues of survival. Yet, we would argue that even in these extreme cases there is learning taking place. It is a very complex kind of learning. It is the learning about how to inspire fear in others, how to avoid being caught by authorities, or how to cope with great loss. The task of bridging between these forms of learning and the learning necessary to reconstruct societies and social relations is daunting. Yet, this is precisely the work to be done if the Bold Visions around reconstruction are to have any hope for success.[17] Thus, even in the most extreme case we see Bold Visions for learning and Harsh Realities that include very different types of learning. We also see how large the gap is between them and we see just how important it is to bridge that gap.

PRESSURE TO LEARN AT EVERY LEVEL

The importance of learning plays itself out at many levels. Consider the sources of pressure at the individual level, and at the levels of work groups, organizations, institutions, regions, nations, and even global interactions. Each level is distinct, yet all are interrelated.[18]

For most working individuals—whether newly entering the workforce, experienced in the workplace, or on the verge of retirement—the pressure to learn is inescapable. What are the skills that I will need to get a worthy job? What are the skills that I need to keep my job? What knowledge is required to perform well on the job? In particular, what do I need to know about new technology? What should I know about e-commerce? How will I learn about the real strategies and plans of my employer? How will I properly understand the needs and requirements of my customers and suppliers? How do I figure out what I can do today or tomorrow that will increase my certainty or security about the future? These are some of the learning and knowledge-related questions that sit just below the surface for most people in most workplaces in most parts of the world.

For most people, there are too few chances for dialogue or action on such matters. As a result, these sorts of unanswered questions become a source of great pressure in the system. This is the pressure by individuals to learn what they really want or need to know on the job—whether by formal or informal means.

In most cases, people do not work in isolation—they are part of some kind of a group. This is an additional source of pressure for learning. There are questions about interpersonal relations, work operations, and links to the larger system. Why was this person rude to me? Why was that person nice? How can we act more like a team? Is there a way to make our work safer or easier or more interesting? Why can't we get the help we need? Doesn't anyone care about what we do? Are we really doing the right thing? Now that we finally have a decent boss, how can we keep her from leaving? Now that the leadership team is finally coming to a shared vision, how can we make this into a new reality? These are just some of the learning and knowledge-related questions that sit below the surface for most groups of people in workplaces around the world.

Learning at the group or team level is distinct from individual learning. These lessons require shared learning. In the absence of mechanisms to support this shared learning, there is yet further pressure in the system.

The pressure for learning also resides at the organizational level. Of course, it is not organizations that learn, but the people in them. In addition to their learning as individuals and as members of groups, there is also pressure to learn in their capacity as leaders and members of organizations. Are we on the right path, as an organization? What is it that makes this organization effective? What holds us back from even greater accomplishments? How should we be structured? Why do our roles keep changing? How should we measure performance? How should we reward contributions that improve performance? What about mistakes or flawed choices made by individuals and groups? Should we form learning partnerships with other organizations? These are all learning and knowledge-related questions that reside at the organizational level.

The pressure to learn at the organizational level can be deep and strong, though its expression is rarely very visible. Usually, these issues arise in a segmented way—among one or another groups or clusters of people—what we will term "stakeholder groups." There are many different stakeholder groups within and across organizations—sales, service, finance, quality, engineering, the day shift, the afternoon shift, high-seniority employees, new hires, first-line supervisors, local union leaders, senior managers, the troublemakers, men, women, minorities, people from that side of town, and so on. All of these groups are part of the organization and all have an interest in learning more about organizational matters. Sometimes, they engage in dialogue and learning that bridges across their different perspectives, but more often than not, things only occur within the bounds of the stakeholder group. This adds additional pressure to learn at the organizational level.

Similar pressures can be found at institutional or industry levels. There are many sets of people who choose to bear the mantle of responsibility for social and economic institutions. These include industry leaders, who have a mutual responsibility for the overall health of a given sector of the economy; customers and suppliers in a given industry, who have a shared responsibility for the supply chains and the economic markets in that industry; union and management negotiators, who have mutual responsibility for the institution of collective bargaining; religious leaders and members, who have a mutual responsibility for religious institutions; teachers, administrators, and students, who have a shared responsibility for educational institutions; as well as other such combinations. There are many questions driving learning at the institutional level. Is this institution adapting quickly enough to changing circumstances? Are we properly honoring the history and traditions associated with this institution? How do we prepare the next generation of institutional leaders? Are there alternative institutional arrangements that may come to dominate in the years to come? These are all learning and knowledge-related questions that reside at the institutional level—different from the organizational, group, or individual level.

For those sets of people who have assumed a shared responsibility for social and economic institutions, the pressure to learn depends on a curiously fragile and complex set of interactions. They all must work together to answer these questions, even though other roles pit them against one another as competitors or pull them in different directions. In the absence of institutional-level learning—and this is often lacking—there is yet more pressure in the system.

The pressure to learn doesn't end at the organizational and institutional levels. There is pressure to learn at community, regional, national, and even global levels. Members of communities or regions have many questions. How can we keep and attract "good" jobs to this area? Is the next generation ready for the demands of the workplace? How do we assess the capabilities and limitations of our community, region, or nation? Will there be economic growth in the years to come? Have we learned the proper lessons from past times of economic decline? Are we learning from innovations in other communities, regions, nations, or parts of the global economy? How can we promote learning partnerships—here or with people in other parts of the world? There are so many questions, each revealing sources of pressure for learning.

A close look at the many questions listed above reveals a set of common underlying forces. Some of the forces are economic, some are technical, and others are social. The economic forces driving many of the learning questions center on issues of economic survival and effectiveness. These issues may apply for individuals, groups, organizations, institutions, communities, regions, industries, and nations. Issues of economic survival come into play where there is a perceived competitive gap and a sense of urgency about closing that gap. Issues of economic effectiveness come into play where there is the potential for learning to drive innovation and thus create new competitive advantages.

There are also technological issues. Our lives are increasingly entwined in complex, engineered systems that require constant interpretation and learning. This may involve our interaction with new production systems in the workplace, new security systems as travelers, massive civil engineering systems in our communities, or new information technology in every aspect of our lives.[19] While there is a long history of scholarship around the concept of systems,[20] the particular application around learning systems takes on a new urgency in the face of growing technical complexity.

There are also social forces driving many of the questions, including the power of shared learning—where multiple perspectives bring new insights. There is the powerful intrinsic interest in learning that we all had as infants and as small children. This is an interest in solving puzzles, recognizing patterns, and making sense of our world. As well, there is the learning required for dealing with the social diversity that intersects our lives and the lives of others. As illustrated in table 1.1, these many questions reflect powerful social forces driving learning in workplaces around the world.

SUCCESS STORIES AT EVERY LEVEL

In the face of so much pressure, with such powerful drivers, it is no surprise to find that learning is in fact occurring in workplaces around the world. In-

TABLE 1.1 Sources of Pressure, by Level

Level	Sources of Pressure	Desired Outcomes
Individual	Push to build new knowledge, skills, and abilities	• Increased employability • Increased effectiveness on the job
Team	Push to increase team effectiveness	• Respectful, supportive work environment • Continuous improvement in operations
Organization	Push to increase organizational capabilities	• Flexibility and adaptability in a changing economic context • Ability to attract, retain, and motivate a capable workforce
Industry / Institutional	Push for industry or institutional revitalization	• Industry stability and growth • Institutional relevance and innovation
Societal	Push for societal success	• Social stability and economic progress • Fostering an increasingly knowledge-based culture and economy

deed, there are countless individuals who have begun to ask complicated questions and found their lives truly transformed. Consider the story of a colleague who we first met when he was a student.

Bill Mothersell began his working life as an autoworker in an assembly plant. He quickly determined that his pay and career prospects would be better if he learned a skilled trade, so he apprenticed himself in machine repair. At the same time, the drive to learn also took him to the nearby state university, where he completed an undergraduate degree by working off-shifts to accommodate classes and somehow fitting homework in during breaks, lunchtime, and other "free" moments. The link to the university continued as Bill went on to pursue a master's degree in labor relations and human resources. When informed of his accomplishments, however, his company in effect said that in their view he was still an hourly skilled trades worker—the two degrees were not seen as sufficient to enter the management ranks as a human resource professional. The response at a key competitor, the Ford Motor Company, was different. Bill was hired and quickly progressed to having significant responsibility for implementing team-based work systems across what was then the Plastic and Trim Products division of Ford. He eventually became part of the growing cohort of people developing what is known as the Ford Production System. In the meantime, Bill's interest in learning continued to grow, and he ultimately decided to pursue a Ph.D., studying the principles of large–scale system change and participating as a coauthor with one of us in a book entitled *Knowledge-Driven Work* that studied the cross-cultural diffusion of knowledge–based work systems.

Today, he is a professor at Grand Valley State University and is an active organizational consultant.

Bill's story is dramatic, but it is not unique. This is just one story among the tens of thousands of people who have begun to ask important questions on the job and who then found their lives transformed. The first steps are small. It might be that the member of a team is trained to use a six-step problem-solving model and this person then uses the same model to tackle problems in a church committee on which she serves. Or an individual who learned the principles of "kaizen"—roughly translated as continuous improvement based on knowledge—while working in a Japanese factory based in California and who now finds the same principles invaluable in raising his family. We have met these individuals and countless others for whom the learning process is changing their understanding of their daily work operations, their career path, and even the very nature of their approach to life.[21]

Above the individual level are organizations and institutions that are involved in transformations just as dramatic. These are often celebrated in the business press, and rightly so. When Lucent Corporation was spun off from what was then ATT, it was a collection of components factories, a research lab (Bell Labs), and various support functions (finance, human resources, information systems, and so on). Within a few years, it significantly improved the ratio of innovations that came to market from the research labs and acquired a number of small and mid-size entrepreneurial businesses that were well-positioned for the new economy. These changes were rewarded by large increases in the value of the company's stock, which reinforced the drive of many people within Lucent to make sure that such growth was sustained by ever-growing internal capabilities. A chief learning officer was appointed, with parallel leaders for learning in various functional and business units. When the value of the company's stock declined, however, it posed a fundamental challenge to the learning initiatives—with some that endured and some that were undercut—an issue that we will return to later in the book.

Lucent is but one of many organizations that have begun the complex journey toward becoming a "learning organization."[22] Organizational learning is increasingly embraced and new arrangements are emerging that more closely link businesses with educational institutions, including high schools, colleges, and universities.

Consider the case of Anderson Pattern in Muskegon, Michigan.[23] This company first contacted a local community college to develop various customized courses in topics such as reading blueprints and statistical quality control for the skilled "patternmakers" who design and build the metal dies that this company constructs for mass-production factories. The success of these courses led to the development of a two-year degree program that was customized for the workers in this firm, which was then followed by the development of a partnership with a nearby state college for a customized four-year degree involving both educational institutions and other area pattern-making firms. Meanwhile, Anderson Pattern has been able to grow its business substantially, based in part on the growing internal capabilities of its workforce.

The case of Anderson Pattern and the area colleges and universities is notable, but it is hardly unique. There are countless partnerships being forged between business and educational institutions, and entire regions of the United States have become valued sources of innovation based on such linkages. These include the Route 128 area around Boston, Silicon Valley in California, and the research triangle in North Carolina. Indeed, all around the world, there can be found examples of communities, regions, industries, and even nations that have embarked on journeys centered on learning and development.

There is, for example, the organization that has called itself the "Cluster Conocimiento" in the Basque region of Spain.[24] This is a consortium of over 150 businesses, universities, local governments, consultants, and other parties who have formed what they call a "Knowledge Cluster." Based in the town of Bilbao, Spain, with the bold image of the new Guggenheim Museum as a symbol of their efforts, they first organized themselves into working groups by different sectors of the economy. These sector clusters include, Machine Tools, Telecommunications, Aeronautics, Electrical Appliances, Automotive Supply, Paper Products, Environmental Services, Textiles, and the Port of Bilbao. Linking the sector clusters together is the knowledge cluster, which convenes annual conferences with invited speakers from around the world and in turn organizes a series of cluster teams investigating different topics of interest to the member organizations. Currently, there are about sixteen such teams focusing on e-commerce and other cross-cutting topics. Following a set of conference presentations on the concept of "intellectual capital," for example, they organized a team on this subject, which is now trying to better understand how to measure and account for the "intangibles" in the member organizations.

As notable as Cluster Conocimiento is, this is but one of many such transformational efforts. There are, in fact, traditions in Scandinavia, of consortia organized along these lines that have been in operation for thirty or forty years, now encompassing thousands of member organizations. In industries such as aerospace and textiles, industrial consortia bring together companies, unions, governments, and academic institutions with the not-so-modest aim of transforming a major sector of a nation's economy.[25] The nation of Singapore is an example of such transformation at a national level. Here is an entire country that has deliberately set out on a path defined by learning and capability. In the space of a single generation, it has transformed itself from a developing economy into a technology leader in the global economy, with one of the world's highest standards of living. The country of Israel recently commissioned a national assessment of its "intellectual capital," which included a wide range of measurements at the national level.[26] Looking around the world, there are learning success stories to be found at every level—individuals, organizations, institutions, communities, regions, industries, and even nations—all of which are embarking on learning journeys that are proving effective and transformational.

HARSH REALITIES AT EVERY LEVEL

Unfortunately, the learning journeys do not form an unbroken series of success stories. All along the way, including within each of the success stories, there are disconnects to be found—gaps between the aims sought and the realities achieved. Consider the case of a woman one of us met in a factory.[27] She had a statistical chart by her workstation and the discussion that followed went something like this: "I see you are doing SPC." (SPC stands for Statistical Process Control—a tool that allows workers to assess quality on a statistical sample rather than on all production—enabling them to be responsible for their own quality, rather than having outside inspectors.) She said, "No, I'm not." The response was, "What do you mean, clearly you have been filling in the chart on a regular basis, why do say you aren't doing SPC?" She said, "Look at the chart, what do you see?" Looking at the chart it was evident that most of the marks were within the acceptable range for quality, but some were outside, which was stated. She said, "Exactly, and what do you think happened when we went outside this range?" Of course, the response was, "I don't know, what happened when you went outside the range?" She said, "Nothing. Nothing happened. There was no root-cause analysis, no exploration in a quality circle, nothing." She said, "I'm not doing SPC, I'm just filling out a chart!"

This is, of course, just one of the many disconnects at the individual level. Take any group of people in any organization and ask them to list some of the learning disconnects they encounter in a typical day, week, or month— or ask them about the disconnects that will surface in the coming months. The precision and accuracy of the analysis is always startling. This can apply in manufacturing, service, retail, or government operations. Just ask yourself about learning that has fallen short of its potential—based on your own experience. Typical lists include training that was promised, but not delivered; failures met with blame, rather than with exploration; accomplishments attributed to an individual person, rather than to multiple inputs; and performance data that is collected, but not made available to the people being measured. The disconnects may be experienced at the individual level, but the implications cut across organizational, institutional, community, regional, industry, national, and even global levels.

The poignancy that comes with disconnects has become increasingly evident as organizations depend in greater degrees on the knowledge and skills of all employees—not just a small group of leaders and experts. This became vividly evident to one of us on a fateful day in 1987 during a visit to what was then the Fiero car factory. The small sports car had been an innovative learning experiment for the General Motors Corporation. It involved the idea of creating a relatively low-volume niche market, the use of composite technology in an auto body, the use of a team–based work system with in–station quality control in the factory, and the use of frontline workers for daily customer contact telephone calls with direct feedback to production and engineering design.

On all four dimensions the experiment at Fiero was a success. A niche market was identified for small sports cars that rapidly drew competition in the form of the Toyota MR2 and the Mazda Miata. A complete nonmetal composite plastic auto body was placed into volume production for the first time. The teams took on full responsibility for frontline quality and daily operations. And the rotating groups of workers calling customers on a daily basis found numerous quality improvements and product design adjustments to feed back to manufacturing and engineering. They also had a clear personal connection with their customers—a valuable end in itself. So what could be wrong with this picture?

The disconnect here became most visible on a day in 1987 when General Motors announced that it was canceling the Fiero car line. Some of the reasons given for the cancellation included that the car was no longer cost-effective given the new competition it had drawn into this niche market and that there were liability issues with some engines which had caught on fire. As always, the situation was more complicated. The people at the Fiero factory said that they could have met the competition if the power of the engine had been enhanced, but their perception was that this option was blocked by the people at Firebird (fearing it would erode their market share). As well, they wanted to offer a lifetime warranty against rust (not difficult with an all-plastic body!), but this was blocked by corporate officials fearful it would be expected on other products. The design issues with the engine fires had reportedly been addressed—so this should not have been a factor. Yet, despite all these powerful counterarguments, it was not these issues that dominated comments on the day of the announced product cancellation and plant closing.

Sitting in the factory on the day of the announced plant closing, the comments mostly centered on a combination of anger and confusion on why greater value wasn't being placed on their new capabilities—what we now term the intellectual capital. People said that they could live with the politics associated with canceling the product, but they couldn't understand the logic of taking the workforce and splitting it up among other General Motors operations. They said they now understood niche markets, composite technology, team-based operations, and customer feedback—why not keep them together and use these capabilities on another product? As it happened, the Human Resource Manager and the local union president did succeed in keeping some teams intact and sending them to the newly formed Saturn corporation. This reflected leadership and initiative, however, not a system designed to value these capabilities.

Of course, the Fiero story has been repeated countless times across all sectors of the economy. Whether it is the loss of knowledge when bank branches are merged[28] or when production facilities are moved to a new location,[29] what major corporation doesn't have its share of restructuring or redesign decisions in which there are disconnects in the way knowledge and skills are valued? The point is not to cast blame on these organizations, but to illustrate the huge untapped potential associated with these workplace disconnects.

Disconnects are not just at the individual, group, or organizational levels. Recently, for example, a commission was established to reexamine the accounting standards used by accounting professionals in Europe. At the time, there was an effort made to incorporate into the new standards, ways of tracking intellectual capital as an organizational resource. This is, of course, a very difficult challenge, but it is also a common underlying disconnect in many change initiatives—capability is built but not fully valued. Although there was debate on the issue, the final decision was in favor of a relatively conservative set of adjustments in the standards that did not fully address the issue of accounting for intellectual capital. This is an institutional disconnect that reveals the potential associated with disconnects when addressed at this level.[30]

This gap between what is possible and what actually occurs is not new. The implications of the gap are changing, however. At one time, disconnects were merely unfortunate, but accepted realities. Most work was organized around the principles of what Frederick Taylor called "scientific management" and what Max Weber termed "bureaucracies."[31] The resulting logic of mass production and hierarchical organizations promoted one kind of efficiency—that which was derived from the wisdom of top leaders and experts—while tolerating disconnects associated with the knowledge and capability of others.

Today, most public and private organizations have adopted goals that do not just center on increased volume of output or lower costs. Additionally, there are goals of improved quality, continuous improvement in operations, and innovation in products or services. Some have characterized this shift as a move toward "flexible specialization," others characterize the new work systems as based on "lean" manufacturing principles, while others highlight the increasing "knowledge-driven" nature of work.[32] Increasingly, it is these fundamental changes in the very nature of work that make such disconnects no longer acceptable. In particular, where such knowledge becomes integral to the goals of individuals, teams, organizations, and communities, disconnects are not just unfortunate, they are antithetical to the goals that have been identified. Thus, as we move toward more of a knowledge-driven economy—one where quality, continuous improvement, and innovation are the keys to success—disconnects must be properly engaged.

THE NEED FOR TWO PERSPECTIVES

Our approach to training, knowledge creation, and organizational learning does not just derive from a bold or ideal vision of what is possible. Our point of departure in this book examines both the pressures for becoming a learning organization and the countervailing forces against organizational learning. It is the combination of pressure for and against change that leads many organizations to experience "disconnects" in training, learning, and the management of knowledge. Disconnects refer to those situations where the reality of the situation does not match what people have articulated as the aims or expectations for learning. Disconnects exist where there is a gap between what people say or hope is occurring and what actually happens. These disconnects are both threats to success in the knowledge economy, and at the same time, essential for success.

Examining disconnects initially seems painful—especially in workplaces where a key cultural message is to "take risks, but don't fail." Yet, disconnects are critical windows into the operations of most organizations. Disconnects represent the cleavage points or splits in a system where controversy, frustration, cynicism, apathy, and opposition can be found. Disconnects are the lightning rods for people's energies, which can be channeled in constructive or unconstructive ways. The lessons in this book center on the journey toward building constructive capabilities to enact Bold Visions of a learning organization through an appreciation of and learning from the reality of organizational disconnects.

Throughout the journey in this book, we will be building on two deceptively simple perspectives. The Bold Visions for learning illustrates the key concepts for the visible and intentional process of workplace change. The Harsh Reality for learning illustrates the key concepts underlying the unintended, less visible consequences behind attempts to build learning systems.

The Bold Visions for learning consists of three elements—data, knowledge, and action. It is a reality-based approach in that it is driven by data, not unchecked assumptions. Data alone, however, does not represent learning—it must be classified and interpreted to create shared knowledge. Knowledge alone may be rewarding, but its full value comes through action. Indeed, some would argue that it is not even truly "knowledge" until it is manifest in action.[33] Action then generates new data and begins the cycle again, as illustrated in figure 1.1.

These elements underlying the Bold Vision for learning show up in many forms in the literature on organizational learning. It is adapted from W. Edwards Deming's classic "Plan, Do, Check, Adjust" (PDCA) cycle for quality-improvement efforts.[34] It is also at the heart of most problem solving models. There are five-step problem-solving models, as well as six-, seven-, or eight-step models—but all have steps that involve the collection of data, the analysis of data, and action based on data. Ultimately, the roots of all these learning cycles go back to the teachings of educational theorist John Dewey, who put forth the cycle: "Discover, Invent, Produce, Observe" and who specifically noted that knowledge is only fully generated with reflection and action.[35] We have distilled these and other such models down to these three core steps, which are then repeated over and over again—in a never-ending process of increasing convergence. This is the visible "front stage" or fore-

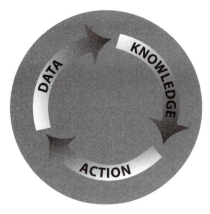

Figure 1.1   Core elements of Bold Visions for learning

ground of the learning process—used wherever active learning is encouraged. The aim is to use the data and knowledge to converge on action implications for individual, team, and organizational improvements.

The Harsh Realities for learning contains three elements—disconnects, dilemmas, and divergence—which we have termed the 3Ds. Here we find many disconnects, each of which is an indicator of ever-greater dilemmas embedded into the culture of the organization. The dilemmas, each of which involves hard choices, may be resolved in a variety of ways, but often create multiple, divergent types of learning within the organization. The result is often further disconnects—continuing the cycle. This is the "back stage" or background that is less visible, but no less important to the learning process. The cycle is presented below in figure 1.2.

In effect, the Bold Vision for learning portrays a simplified picture of the learning interventions that so many organizations are implementing—an in-

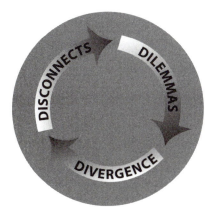

Figure 1.2   Harsh Realities of learning

tentional attempt to increase capability in response to the increased pressure to learn. The balance of part I of this book provides additional insights about the nature of this kind of intentional learning, including case examples, underlying theory, as well as the "slippery slope" that can be associated with only focusing on the front stage, visible, Bold Visions around convergent learning.[36]

The Harsh Reality for learning portrays a simplified picture of what is also taking place, though not usually through intentional interventions. The cycle of disconnects, dilemmas, and divergence—what we have termed the 3Ds—are driven by the pressure to learn just as much as the cycles of data, knowledge, and action. These concepts are not as well-developed—in field practice or in the literature—so we have devoted each of the three chapters in part II to the three elements of this second model. Disconnects, we note, are predictable, but they can also be treated as data and analyzed in systematic ways. Dilemmas are less visible, but represent core insights or what Dr. Deming termed "profound knowledge" around the underlying factors associated with the disconnects. Taken together, there is both convergent learning and divergent patterns of learning in organizations. This dynamic plays out in six distinct types of learning: incremental learning, experimental learning, continuous learning, synergistic learning, entrenched learning, and revolutionary learning.

In part III of the book, we bring the two perspectives together and focus on the way they interweave with one another. It is unfortunate that the linear format of a book forces us to construct the elements sequentially, before examining the learning dynamics of both taken together. Our approach is what is known as a dialectic argument, where there is a thesis—centered on Bold Visions for learning systems—an antithesis—centered on Harsh Realities—and a synthesis, which is presented in part III.[37]

Simply put, Bold Visions for organizational learning that use the concepts of data, knowledge, and action, are powerful, wonderful, and essential. There is great joy in interpreting data, generating knowledge, and seeing it applied. The unintended Harsh Reality of disconnects, dilemmas, and divergence are often complicated, painful, and also essential. Most important of all, the two are interdependent—accounting for many of the different types of learning that are found in most organizations. Valuing disconnects, divergences, and dilemmas increases the capability to drive data, knowledge, and action.[38] This increased capability reveals new connections between the Bold Vision and Harsh Realities and the interdependency deepens. Becoming a genuine learning organization is a journey that involves the appreciation of all forms of learning—connected and disconnected.

Taken together, we are describing a process in which disconnects are valued as the key to a learning dynamic that is essential for survival in a knowledge-driven economy. This is a fundamentally different mindset which requires different skill sets for most individuals and organizations. Ultimately, however, it is hard to imagine anything less. To put it simply, the reality of learning involves connections and disconnects. This reality is something we have to deal with, but it is also something to value and appreciate.

Notes

1. There are a number of books on viewing people as the key to competitive advantage including, Ikujiro Nonaka and Hirotaka Takeuchi, *The Knowledge-Creating Company* (New York: Oxford University Press, 1995); Michael E. Porter, *Competitive Advantage: Creating and Sustaining Superior Performance* (New York: Free Press, 1998); Thomas Stewart, *Intellectual Capital: The New Wealth of Organizations* (New York: Currency, 1997); Lester C. Thurow, *Building Wealth: The New Rules for Individuals, Companies, and Nations in a Knowledge-Based Economy* (New York: HarperCollins, 1999); and Sultan Kermally, *Effective Knowledge Management* (New York: John Wiley, 2002).

2. For example, the value of U.S. exports of royalties and licenses now exceeds the value of airplane mainframe and parts sales. And, these knowledge "products" are a small part of the entire knowledge economy (Airplanes and Airplane parts totaled $41.4 billion in 2002, while royalties and licenses totaled $43.2 billion. Sources: U.S. International Trade in Goods and Services—Current, Prior, and Compressed. Report FT900 (03) (CB-03-93), U.S. Census Bureau, Foreign Trade Division, FINAL 2002.

3. This quote, for example, is from Alex Trotman, then CEO, Ford Motor Company. Special advertisement section, Fortune, May 1999.

Similarly, consider the following statement by Scott McNealy, CEO, Sun Microsystems: "Hiring, retaining and developing great people is the biggest challenge and the single greatest key to success of any business." Source: Women in Management. Comments. September 1995.

4. See Anthony P. Carnevale, Leila J. Gainer, and Janice Villet, *Training in America: The Organization and Strategic Role of Training* (San Francisco: Jossey-Bass, and T. Galvin, 1990); "Training Top 50," *Training* (March 2001): 57–79 for data on training investments.

5. The effects of downsizing on individuals within an organization are emphasized in a chapter by Steve W. J. Kozlowski, Georgia T. Chao, Eleanor M. Smith, and Jennifer Hedlund, "Organizational Downsizing: Strategies, Interventions, and Research Implications" in *International Review of Industrial and Organizational Psychology,* ed. C. L. Cooper and I. T. Robertson. Vol. 8. (New York: John Wiley & Sons, Ltd, 1993).

6. See Laurie J. Bassi and Daniel P. McMurrer, "Training Investment Can Mean Financial Performance" (Alexandria, VA: American Society for Training and Development, 1999), for one approach for linking training and results.

7. See Kurt Lewin, *Field Theory in Social Science* (New York: Harper, 1951); and A. J. Marrow, *The Practical Theorist: The Life and Work of Kurt Lewin* (New York: Basic Books, 1969).

8. Peter Senge, *The Fifth Discipline: The Art and Practice of the Learning Organization* (New York: Doubleday, 1990).

9. We are taking a dialectic approach to change here—with the Bold Visions being the "thesis," the Harsh Reality being the "antithesis," and the integrated approach being the "synthesis."

10. See Peter Senge, Art Kleiner, Charlotte Roberts, Richard Ross, George Roth, and Bryan Smith, *The Dance of Change: The Challenges to Sustaining Momentum in Learning Organizations* (New York: Doubleday, 1999).

11. See the intriguing interview with Edgar Schein (by Diane L. Coutu) on the anxiety of learning in the *Harvard Business Review*, March 2002, 100–108.

12. See Chris Argyris, "Teaching Smart People How to Learn," *Harvard Business Review*, 69 (May–June 1991): 99–109.

13. Even the growth in training providers produces a barrage of brochures and promotional materials without much guidance in identifying which programs will best add value.

14. See Edgar Schein, "Three Cultures of Management: The Key to Organizational Learning," *Sloan Management Review*, 38 (1997): 9–20 for an interesting discussion of subcultures within an organization that can impact organizational learning initiatives.

15. Comment at MIT Engineering Systems Division Offsite, David Mindell (May 2003). The space shuttle Columbia disaster provides an example of this intensive look at the realities of the organization, such as actual management practices separate from formal roles, which might otherwise be hard to observe.

16. The six types of organizational learning are noted at the end of this chapter and presented in more detail in chapter 6. These are: incremental, experimental, continuous, synergistic, entrenched, and revolutionary learning.

17. See, for example William Ury, *Getting to Peace: Transforming Conflict at Home, at Work, and in the World* (New York: Viking Press, 1999).

18. For further information on levels of analysis issues see J. Kevin Ford and Sandra Fisher, "The Transfer of Safety Training in Work Organizations: A Systems Perspective to Continuous Learning," *Journal of Occupational Medicine: State of the Art Reviews*, 9 (1994): 241–260; and a recent book by K. Klein and Steve W. J. Kozlowski, *Multilevel Theory, Research, and Methods in Organizations* (San Francisco: Jossey-Bass, 2002). For an examination of how levels issues can be applied specifically to training-needs assessment, see Cheri Ostroff and J. Kevin Ford, "Introducing a Levels Perspective to Training Needs Assessment: Implications for Research and Practice," in *Training and Career Development,* ed. I. Goldstein (New York: Jossey-Bass, 1989). For an update on training innovations at an institutional level, see Joel Cutcher-Gershenfeld, "Union-Management Investments in Training and Capability in the United States," OECD Project on: *Collective Bargaining and Worker Participation in Continuing Vocational Training* (Paris: OECD, 2002).

19. These are just some of the examples motivating the newly formed Engineering Systems Division at MIT, which is helping to pioneer "Engineering Systems" as a field of study. For a historical context, see Thomas Hughes, *Rescuing Prometheus: Four Monumental Projects that Changed the Modern World* (New York: Vintage Books, 1998). Also, see Benjamin S. Blanchard and Walter J. Fabrycky (1981), *Systems Engineering and Analysis*; and Vladimir Hubka and W. Ernst Eder (1988), *Theory of Technical Systems.*

20. For a sampling of relevant literature, see Ludwig von Bertalanffy, *General System Theory: Foundations, Development, and Applications* (New York: George Braziller, 1968); Fred E. Emery and Eric L. Trist, *Towards A Social Ecology: Contextual Appreciation of the Future in the Present* (Plenum: London, 1972); Johh D. Sterman, "Learning In and About Complex Systems," *System Dynamics Review* 10 (1994), 2–3: 291–330; M. Mitchell Waldrop, *Complexity: The Emerging Science at the Edge of Order and Chaos;*

and Marie Csete and John Doyle, "Reverse Engineering of Biological Complexity," *Science* 295, 5560 (March 1, 2002): 1664–1669.

21. See a discussion of this issue in Joel Cutcher-Gershenfeld, Michio Nitta, Betty Barrett, Nejib Belhedi, Simon Chow, Takashi Inaba, Iwao Ishino, Wen-Jeng Lin, Michael Moore, William Mothersell, Jennifer Palthe, Shobha Ramanand, Mark Strolle, and Arthur Wheaton, with Cheryl Coutchie, Seepa Lee, and Stacia Rabine, *Knowledge-Driven Work: Unexpected Lessons from Japanese and U.S. Work Practices* (New York: Oxford University Press, 1998).

22. Business books on the subject, such as Peter Senge's *The Fifth Discipline*, have become best sellers. The membership of the American Society for Training and Development (ASTD) has increased dramatically since its founding in 1944 to include more than 70,000 members working in over 100 countries worldwide across 15,000 multinational corporations, small and medium-size businesses, governmental agencies, and universities. ASTD states that its learning manifesto is: "The focus on our profession on developing people, in the light of the knowledge economy, is the key to competitive advantage. There is a new world of learning emerging—one that links people, learning, and performance—and a new community growing around it" See American Society of Training and Development Web site at http://www.astd.org for information on this society.

23. For a discussion of linkages of businesses with other stakeholder groups such as colleges, see Joel Cutcher-Gershenfeld and J. Kevin Ford, "Worker Training in Michigan: A Framework for Public Policy," in *Policy Choices: Framing the Debate for Michigan's Future*, Tim S. Bynum and associates (East Lansing: Michigan State University Press, 1992). See also, Richard Walton, Joel Cutcher-Gershenfeld, and Robert McKersie, *Strategic Negotiations: A Theory of Change in Labor-Management Relations*. (Boston: Harvard Business School Press, 1994).

24. "Las Sociedades del Conocimiento," Cluster Conocimiento, Annual Conference, (Bilbao, Spain, 1999).

25. Murman, Earll, Tom Allen, Kirkor Bozdogan, Joel Cutcher-Gershenfeld, Hugh McManus, Debbie Nightingale, Eric Rebentisch, Tom Shields, Fred Stahl Myles Walton, Joyce Warmkessel, Stanley Weiss, and Sheila Widnall, *Lean Enterprise Value: Insights from MIT's Lean Aerospace Initiative* (New York: Palgrave/Macmillan, 2002).

26. Edna Pasher, "The Intellectual Capital of the Country of Israel," Las Sociedades del Conocimiento, Cluster Conocimiento, Annual Conference, Bilbao, Spain, (presentation, 1999).

27. Cutcher-Gershenfeld, et al. *Knowledge-Driven Work.*

28. Hunter, Lawrence W., Annette Bernhardt, Katherine L. Hughes, and Eva Skuratowicz, "It's Not Just the ATMs: Firm Strategies, Jobs, and Earnings in Retail Banking," *Industrial and Labor Relations Review*, 2001, 54 (2A): 402–424.

29. Consider the case of the Pratt and Whitney jet and rocket engine facility in West Palm Beach, Florida. Most of the jet engine work in that factory was recently shifted to the home facility of that corporation in Connecticut. While people working in the facility were upset about the loss of the work and the threat to their livelihoods, there was an additional dimension to the story that is increasingly common in organizations that have forged new workplace partnerships around quality and innovation. The people who had been involved in partnership and workplace improvement activity in this facility asked a simple question: Why wasn't a value placed on these new capabilities when the decision was made to move the work? Was it that the current efforts were deemed insufficient or were they not even fully appre-

ciated at the highest levels? Even if the work was to be moved, why wasn't a greater effort made to ensure the knowledge and skills of the continuous improvement teams moved with the work? The point is not to castigate Pratt and Whitney for this disconnect, but to recognize the challenges facing any organization such as this.

30. See Baruch Lev, *Intangibles: Management, Measurement, and Reporting* (Washington, D.C.: The Brookings Institution, and also see ongoing debates in the *European Accounting Review* and the proceedings of the first conference on "Intellectual Capital/Intangible Investments" held in Helsinki, Finland, 1999.

31. See Fredrick W. Taylor, *Principles of Scientific Management* (New York: Harper & Row, 1911) and Max Weber, *The Theory of Social and Economic Organization* (London: Oxford University Press, 1947).

32. Richard Locke, Thomas Kochan, and Michael J. Piore, *Employment Relations in a Changing World Economy* (Cambridge, MA: MIT Press, 1995); Michael J. Piore and Charles F. Sabel, *The Second Industrial Divide: Possiblities for Prosperity* (New York: Basic Books, 1984); James P. Womack, Daniel T. Jones, and Daniel Roos, *The Machine that Changed the World* (New York: Macmillan, 1990).

33. Indeed, some would argue that knowledge doesn't really exist independent of action or "doing." "All learning integrates thinking and doing," observe Peter Senge, C. Otto Scharmer, Joseph Jaworski, and Betty Sue Flowers in their new book, *Presence: Human Purpose and the Field of the Future* (Cambridge, MA: Society of Organizational Learning, 2004), 9. Although it could be argued that the entire cycle is therefore about knowledge, we use the term here in a more limited way as the bridge connecting data with action. In this sense, our interest is in knowledge acquisition and application—the connection between what some term "know-what" and "know-how." We use "learning" as the overarching term, treating the entire cycle as a Bold Vision for organizational learning. We are grateful to Peter Senge for the time spent exploring these different ways to use language to convey the sometimes subtle and sometimes substantial spectrum of meaning around the terms learning and knowledge. Our experience with field applications of the cycle suggests that it can be useful, but we also recognize that alternative formulations are possible.

34. This derivative of the PDCA cycle was initially developed in response to observed difficulty in retaining and utilizing PDCA by a broad cross-section of people. We still value the powerful way in which PDCA drives deep learning—a theme that is developed more fully in chapter 8. It is our hope that this model is a valuable complement—reducing learning down to its simplest elements.

35. John Dewey, *Essays in Experimental Logic* (Chicago: University of Chicago, 1916), 1–74.

36. These learning elements should be familiar to most readers. In many ways we are just codifying what is already well developed in field practice and in the literature.

37. It has been pointed out that either part II or part III of the book can be read first—so these too are options for the enterprising reader.

38. Michael Lewis's recent book on baseball *Moneyball: The Art of Winning an Unfair Game* by (New York: W.W. Norton, 2003) explores the issues of what is overvalued and undervalued in baseball organizations when it comes to evaluating talent. We take a similar perspective to organizational learning where pushing on the Bold Vision is often overvalued by leaders as the key to success, while working on the Harsh Realities is undervalued when it comes to sustaining organizational learning initiatives.

2

Building Capability

B uilding capability" is today drawing the attention of scholars and prac- titioners in ways comparable to how "improving morale" used to do so. Morale is still important—organizations have countless surveys to take the pulse of the workforce—but the investments here are dwarfed when compared to the investments in building capability. This reflects the in- creasing evidence of a clear connection between investment in skills and or- ganizational performance outcomes.[1] In order to thrive, leaders at all levels have concluded that their organizations will need to learn at an increasingly rapid rate, made possible by the growing capabilities of the workforce[2] It also reflects a shift in labor markets, where skills and capability represent the primary way that individuals ensure continued employability.

What does it mean to build capability? Bold Visions centered on learning and capability have many different elements including,[3]

- Learning and diffusing knowledge in the workplace
- Deploying knowledge and demonstrable skills in novel ways—to re- spond flexibly to new challenges
- Bridging across traditional organizational boundaries to solve problems and to create innovative solutions
- Learning from whatever resources are available; converting individual information into organizational knowledge
- Establishing shared meaning and consistent processes around team- work, collaboration, and creativity
- Supporting training and problem solving across the organization
- Building organizational cultures that value investments in capability
- Strengthening training across local, regional, national, and international boundaries

Underlying each of these elements is the common process of analyzing data to generate knowledge, which guides individual and collective action.

The process begins with the collection of data. The information generated includes charting activities, survey results, identifying normative beliefs, and countless other types of data. All of these types of data can lend insight into organizational operations, processes, and goals. Data is the point of departure in the learning process—the more focused and targeted the data, the more focused and targeted the learning can become for individuals, teams, and the organization.

However, as we noted in chapter 1, data is not the same thing as knowledge. Data must be classified, interpreted, and shared in order to contribute to an expanding knowledge base within an organization. The interpretation of data can lead to hypotheses and theories designed to account for the patterns or trends observed in the data. The data can also be used to drive discussions of what the data "really" mean. When it is possible to make sense of the data, knowledge about organizational operations has been generated.

In the Bold Vision, some degree of consensus should be reached among people across relevant organizational levels and functions about the meaning of the data. Then, action is required if this collective power is to be tapped. Actions may include experiments or pilot tests, policy changes, redeployment of resources, or other tangible moves. These actions require new rounds of data collection, analysis, and interpretation to monitor and adapt to changing realities. Therefore, continuous learning and long-lasting changes can be achieved through a never-ending cycle of action steps beginning with data, guided by knowledge, and rooted in action. Interpreting data to generate knowledge, which then guides action, is at the core of the Bold Vision for fostering organizational learning. The specific words may be different and the number of steps in the process may vary, but the principle is the same—systematic mechanisms to support intentional learning are taking place and being encouraged.

Although disconnects are less visible, it is also clear that they pose dilemmas for key stakeholders that can lead to divergence in what is actually learned and retained. Although rarely recognized as such, these Harsh Realities are also at the core of any formal attempt to foster organizational learning.

But as can be seen from the Bold Vision statements above, these core elements are not, in themselves, systems of organizational learning—they are only aspects of a learning process. To understand the systems for organizational learning, it will be helpful to first take a historical perspective and then examine five illustrative examples of organizational learning innovations that have emerged over the last fifteen years.[4]

CAPABILITY IN A KNOWLEDGE ECONOMY

Learning has been occurring in workplaces since the beginning of recorded time. For many centuries, the primary mode of learning was the apprenticeship model. This model is central to the craft mode of production, where a skilled artisan is the master of a given trade and is generally responsible for completing an entire task. This model is very much with us. Training in many professions is still organized in this way, including the training of scientists, scholars, musicians, actors, chefs, and technical specialists in professions such as law, medicine, and engineering. This model dominates the development process for many skilled trades, including masonry, carpentry, metal work, tool and die making, electrical work, plumbing, and hydraulics.[5] In all these cases, there are important skills to be learned in schools, colleges, and universities, but mastery depends on having a mentor or master in the trade, who takes on responsibility for completing your development.[6] Where the craft economy is dominant, this apprenticeship mode of learning is integral to it. In this model, learning takes place on the job, which is primarily focused on the mastery of craft.

The rise of the industrial revolution and the bureaucratic organizational form brought forth a different model for learning on the job. The early hints of this model can be found in the works of Frederick Taylor and Max Weber. Taylor based what he called "scientific management" on the assumption that people could be trained in specific elements of a job without needing to acquire the knowledge and skills to do the entire job. He advocated the scientific study of jobs so as to identify the best approach for completing the job and then training workers to perform exactly according to those job requirements.[7] As noted by Taylor, "you are not supposed to think. There are other people paid for thinking around here."[8] Weber, writing half a century earlier, identified the segmentation of work into bureaucracies as a much more efficient model compared to the craft approach.[9]

Both the industrial revolution and the newly developed bureaucracies required a segmented form of learning, focusing on a narrowly defined set of tasks. This mode of learning has been just as integral to a mass-production economy as the apprenticeship mode was integral to the craft economy.

In the emerging knowledge economy, we see a new form of learning also taking shape. Here the learning is focused both on the task at hand and on the systems or context within which it occurs. This more systemic learning is just as integral to the knowledge economy as earlier types of learning were in prior eras.

Both the production economy and the knowledge economy require the achievement of consistent and superior performance. Nevertheless, the move from the production economy to the knowledge economy has important implications for the development of the capabilities of employees.

Routine Capability   The production economy placed value on developing what is commonly referred to as routine capabilities or expertise.[10] Routine capability is defined as applying solutions or strategies to well-known and familiar contexts.[11] Routine capabilities involve tasks that require the application of the same method to a set of similar situations. An example would be a machinist who has learned how to set up a particular type of lathe or troubleshoot a particular type of electrical problem. Routine capabilities are evident when an individual can generalize the problem and apply the solution to another, similar situation.

Individuals can quickly recognize that a situation falls within the range of those they have experienced before. They can then retrieve and apply the appropriate method to solve the problem. While individuals with routine response capabilities can solve familiar problems quickly and accurately, they may have difficulty with new or novel problems or issues that involve multiple causes and larger contextual factors. Routine capability was at the heart of the mass-production model and the standardization associated with routine capability is still relevant in many knowledge-driven operations.

Adaptive Capability The concept of adaptive capability has emerged in the literature as a counterpoint to routine capability. Adaptive capabilities are the skills required to integrate simultaneously multiple sources of knowledge for use in addressing a given issue or problem. Adaptive responses involve inventing new procedures based on an individual's knowledge and making new predictions.[12] The key to adapting to novel problems is a deeper conceptual understanding of the situation. This allows individuals to recognize when current procedures must be changed to respond to novel circumstances. What would be a threat to someone with routine capability might be seen as an opportunity for those with adaptive capability. Thus, individuals with adaptive capabilities can adjust their knowledge and skills in the face of novel situations or requirements—adapting different methods from those previously learned and using existing knowledge to generate new approaches and strategies. An adaptive person would recognize when methods are not appropriate or effective, new methods must be learned, and new strategies must be considered, given increasing levels of task complexity.

To build adaptive capabilities, people must learn from a variety of methods, as well as learn how to select and combine them in order to perform in new situations. It is equally important to identify when an existing strategy is not sufficient, as well as how to create a new and more appropriate one. Building adaptive capabilities requires creating a learning environment in which the learner engages in more active and exploratory activities. The learning processes lead to a deeper understanding of the tasks and help build hypothesis-testing and problem-solving capabilities that are, in themselves, necessary for adaptive capabilities.

What can we learn from this journey into routine and adaptive capabilities? First, a learning organization is one where both routine and adapative capabilities are being built at every level. Second, the process for building such expertise requires a mix of instruction, practice, coaching, and mistakes—it doesn't happen all at once. Third, the nature of the learning process is very different for routine capabilities compared to adaptive capabilities—with adaptive capabilities requiring much more of a change in the organizational operations.

Bold Visions may extol learning in general, but that is not sufficiently precise. It should already be evident that routine and adaptive capabilities introduce the Harsh Reality of multiple, concurrent modes of learning, each requiring different forms of administration, different levels of funding, and different expected outcomes. Beyond this core distinction, we see many different ways in which organizations are investing in capability. The following examples are illustrative.

FIVE EXAMPLES OF INVESTMENT IN CAPABILITY

Each of these five vignettes illustrates the establishment of organizational learning systems in ways that contrast with the earlier, mass-production, bureaucratic models. Each is a window into a story that is still unfolding—with Bold Visions that have been articulated and enacted to some degree. The examples range from a focus on "training trainers," "stakeholders," "partnerships," "intellectual capital," and "culture change." No one approach is a pure type—each has elements of the others in it.

In each example, real organizations are cited, with the change activities extending back over the past fifteen years. In all cases, we focus on just one aspect of the organization and one particular point in time. The Lucent case, for example, marks changes that took place prior to the spin off of major parts of the organization and a subsequent devaluing of high-technology stocks, which was particularly hard on this organization. New developments have not diminished the need for learning in any way, though the way these organizations are pursuing such learning will continue to evolve. These cases are not pure successes or failures—they are illustrative of different types of learning journeys, each of which is instructive for showing the value organizations are placing on knowledge-creation and continuous-improvement strategies and developing the adaptive capabilities of the workforce.

Training Trainers Weyerhaeuser Structurwood, a wood products company located in Grayling, Michigan, was envisioned in the 1980s as a new type of plant that would become a benchmark for how to more fully utilize human resources through a team-based work approach. A key component of this effort was the systematic application of the train-the-trainer approach and a knowledge mastery program.

From the outset, the plant built its human resource system around the "train-the-trainer" concept. Workers trained one another in technical skills as part of a pay-for-knowledge mastery program. Workers were also the lead trainers around group process and personal development skills training. Management emphasized that both process/developmental training and technical training were critical to the plant running effectively. Major portions of these training programs focused on improving quality and customer satisfaction.

Managers, including the human resources manager, were all involved in designing the business plan for the plant. Once the plan had been established, all employees in the plant became involved in the operationalization of the plan. Training needs, linked to the plan, were identified both formally and informally through a number of mechanisms—from employee attitude surveys to task forces and improvement teams. Most significantly, the plans came from the teams themselves. Both management and operators initiated training and participated in decisions regarding training. With all the training that was occurring, trying to maintain continuous production and schedule training was a constant challenge for the plant. Training was therefore a complex, decentralized function.

The training philosophy at Grayling was well-articulated in the plant's mission, which reads (in part):

> Training will develop the skills and knowledge necessary to operate the mill efficiently and will contribute to individual and organizational growth.

The train-the-trainer focus of learning at Weyerhaeuser was especially clear in the context of the plant's commitment to quality. The quality statement of the plant stated:

> We are committed to providing the necessary education and training for continuous improvement.

In explaining the strategic importance of the train-the-trainer approach, the plant manager highlighted his belief that building internal capability is the only way to be able to adapt to changing customer needs. For example, customers are increasingly looking for small runs of specialty products. This demands increased flexibility on the shop floor.

At the core of Weyerhaeuser's train-the-trainer system was a training philosophy entitled LUTI—Learn, Use, Teach, and Inspect. This philosophy stressed that each person who receives training should learn the material well enough to use it and then be able to teach it to others. Employees were encouraged to teach training seminars on topics which they were masters or experts. It was seen to be more effective to have insiders teach and train since they could serve as constant reminders for maintaining the skills and information learned.

A pay-for-knowledge mastery program served as the major driver for technical training at the plant. Individuals were cross-trained and taught how to master various production processes by other experienced masters. The mastery program allowed individuals and teams to set goals for what needed to be learned and how it was learned. Training manuals used to familiarize new production workers with the various production processes were written by masters of those functions.

To support the pay-for-knowledge mastery program, 100% of the mill was trained in peer-performance appraisal. The eight-hour sessions trained people in how to give appropriate feedback to one another. This skill was critical to the teams' interactions and the pay-for-knowledge system. In a system premised on the train-the-trainer model, the ability of workers to give one another feedback was essential. Indeed, the plant found that after two to three "generations" of trainers training others, the core message has shifted in a way that required this self-correcting feedback capability.

By the early 1990s, there was a wide range of training activities that took place around technical and developmental skills at Weyerhaeuser. Woven throughout all of the training was a core philosophy centered on what we have termed a "train-the-trainer" approach, where internal capability, which was seen as a core organizational strategy, enabling the plant to adapt to ever-changing business realities.

Stakeholder Integration By the mid-1990s, Thomas Design and Engineering Service, Inc. was a rapidly growing design, engineering, and manufacturing firm. The firm had made a strong commitment to developing the technical expertise of its engineers and the developmental needs of their supervisors and managers. This commitment was seen as essential for attracting highly talented applicants to the firm. In addition, the company saw a fully trained engineer or manager as a highly valued resource who might even be hired away by their customers. Rather than viewing this with alarm, the company had decided to embrace this relationship with customers as a way of helping to solidify their partnerships. Training and development, then, was truly an integral part of the organization's strategic business plan.

At that time, Thomas Design primarily served the automotive industry, with over 90% of its business tied to various divisions of General Motors. Although it is still under the leadership of its founder and president, Bruce Thomas, the establishment of systems, procedures, and training policies marked its movement from an entrepreneurial start-up toward a larger, well-established business. The company's core strategy centered on positioning itself as a full-service supplier to its customers, starting with design ideas, giving engineering support, and constructing product prototypes. The firm has multiple facilities with over 150 employees.

The Thomas Design strategy reflected two key aspects of the business: a rapidly changing technological context and a strong commitment to building human resources. Technical training, such as geometric tolerancing, was geared primarily to meet client-driven expansion in new equipment and technology, as well as to meet the traditional need for professional development among design engineers. Process/developmental training in skills such as problem solving, health and safety, career development, and personal effectiveness was available to all employees. The developmental training was seen as key to organizational flexibility, individual growth, and the transition into a more established business.

There were four primary stakeholder groups that influenced decisions on training. First, were the customers, whose product and service needs directly defined the content of training programs. They often participated actively in framing the decision-making on training (such as by insisting on mastery of a particular kind of computer design software). Employees were a second stakeholder group whose repertoire of skills and career progression was ultimately defined by the learning activities each of them pursued. The third set of stakeholders was supervisory personnel, who were responsible not only for task accomplishment, but also for the career development

of their employees, either acting as trainers or as coordinators of training experiences. The last set of stakeholders was the executive committee, headed
by the president. They defined the general objectives of the firm and provided guidelines for learning activities in accordance with the general business strategy. In emphasizing the importance of learning for the business—
especially at the managerial level, the president stated:

> The traditional problem for entrepreneurs is growing the business to the
> point that it can run on its own. Training broadens the knowledge base so
> that there can be a real managerial team. My interest is in expanding into
> new business areas, but I can only do that after the management team is
> sufficiently trained to keep things running here.

The relationship with customers as a stakeholder group was quite unique.
Customers not only shaped the training agenda through the technologies
they used, but also hired away many of the best-trained Thomas Design employees. This would seem to be an outright loss, limiting return upon the
training investment. But, there was a key countervailing factor that lead to
a broader understanding of the return on investment in human capital. Many
of the employees who left were hired by the firm's primary customer, General Motors. Over time, there formed a tacit understanding between Thomas
Design and its major customer that recognized the human resource development costs borne by Thomas Design. This recognition came in the form
of continued contracts for work and even closer partnering on projects.

In this sense, Thomas Design was a supplier to General Motors not just
of engineering and design products, but also of trained design employees.
Such practices, while increasing the short-term cost of training, led to a
highly trained workforce that was an additional "product" provided to customers in exchange for continued business contracts. An additional benefit
of pursuing this strategy was that the company could now attract some of
the best and brightest engineers out of college. Although the starting salaries
at Thomas Design were lower than could be obtained elsewhere, new employees were aware that they would be well trained and become expert in
their field, increasing their marketability in three to five years. Thus, training and learning activities were not only a business enabler, they were a
product in themselves, a product that led to a positive, productive, human
resource cycle for Thomas Design.

External Partnerships   As a small organization in a manufacturing design business that was being transformed by computer technologies, Anderson Pattern had to educate its highly skilled workforce but did not have
the trainers or expertise on staff to do so. As noted in chapter 1, the story
begins with a selection of highly technical courses that a local community
college developed specifically for the organization. Over time, a unique set
of public-private partnerships emerged. With funding from state government, the community college expanded course offerings into a full two-year
degree program available to Anderson Pattern employees. Additionally,

Western Michigan University agreed to accept the two-year degree toward a four-year degree program. For a facility with about 130 people, there was now a level of education and training available that rivaled some of the largest multinational corporations.

Anderson Pattern's plant in Muskegon, Michigan, makes three-dimensional models for automobile wheels and other components. These form the basis for mass-production operations in auto supply plants. The entire workforce consists of skilled trades employees who command relatively high wages.

In the late 1980s, the Patternmaker's association was approached with a proposal from management. The proposal focused on management's willingness to invest heavily in a new computer-controlled machining system if the union would be willing to grant flexibility on a work rule that limited employees' assignments to "one man per one machine." Though the rule was a hard-won vehicle providing a measure of job security, the promise of new investment also represented job security in a different form.

In order to come to a decision on this issue, the workforce had to be educated about the technology. Toward this end, top management announced that any employee who wanted to, was welcome to take time off work and travel by bus to a trade show in Chicago where the proposed new equipment could be seen. Over one hundred employees chose to make the trip, and seeing the equipment, provided essential data for the employees and the union to negotiate with management over the change. They were persuaded that the new equipment would substantially increase the company's capacity to bring in new work, but they were still concerned that there could be a negative impact on employment. Ultimately, they agreed to suspend the contractual work rule on a one-time basis as an experiment.

Once the new equipment arrived, the employees needed to be trained to operate the computer and build other technical skills related to the equipment. Although the vendor provided some training, Muskegon Community College was approached to develop what proved to be a number of courses in specific skills targeted to this equipment in this location. At the time, there was a state program to support workplace-specific curriculum development, which provided funds to the community college.

The popularity of this program led Anderson Pattern to request the development of courses in other more general skills, such as blueprint reading. As more employees took these courses, the community college approached Anderson Pattern with a unique proposal. They pointed out that some employees had taken enough courses that they only needed some English, math, and elective courses in order to qualify for a two-year degree. Anderson Pattern modified its policy on what college courses were reimbursable and encouraged its employees to pursue the full two-year degree if they were interested. In essence, a custom degree program had been developed for Anderson Pattern employees.

After a few emloyees completed the two-year degree, a further set of conversations unfolded with Western Michigan University. The university indicated that it would accept all of the credits in the two-year degree toward a four-year degree. Some employees have followed this path, achieving educational goals that previously would have been much more difficult and much less applicable to their jobs.

As more employees became involved in the training and as the new equipment proved effective in increasing work (rather than eliminating jobs), the union was approached about setting aside the work rule permanently in exchange for investment in four more computer-controlled work centers. After extensive negotiations, this agreement was reached and the business doubled in volume in a relatively short time frame.

There were some complications with the arrangement, however. In particular, the company reached the point where there were substantially more people trained to use the new technology than needed. The employees and the union were interested in providing all trained employees with a chance to apply their skills via a rotational series of assignments. The company was reluctant to do this, however, since it could introduce variation and impact quality and since the employees were substantially more marketable to other organizations after they had operated the equipment. There was not an easy answer to this situation and, at the time we were studying the organization, the issue had been resolved in favor of keeping a smaller pool of people who were being used to operate the new equipment.

The experiences at Anderson Pattern illustrate the ways in which various external public-private partnerships can substantially increase the range of education and training opportunities available to employees. These experiences also illustrate the degree to which there was a close interrelationship between external learning partnerships, new technology, and internal employment relations dynamics. In this case, the initial learning at the Chicago trade show was an external educational event that helped reinforce internal dialogue about change. At the same time, the external technical training served to create opportunities for people to apply what they had learned in classes at the community college. In the end, realizing the full potential of the new technology required a fundamental rethinking of the way learning was taking place at Anderson Pattern—not learning as a one-time event, but as an ongoing process of adjustment.

Intellectual Capital Investment   The chief financial officer and chief information officer, as well as their senior leadership teams at Lucent Technologies, faced a difficult challenge. They had found a great way to recruit new finance and information systems professionals by offering a three-year set of rotating assignments, interspersed with custom-developed courses offered through Babson College. At the end of the three years, the new employees had a masters degree and exposure to key aspects of the finance and information systems function. Although this was a great way to draw in new talent, there were two complications. First, a small number of these individuals ended up being recruited away. Second, and more seriously, a large number of these individuals completed the process only to find themselves assigned to positions where they were given few opportunities to apply what they had learned in the preceding three years.

Whether people were being recruited away or underutilized (and at risk of being recruited away), the issue was the same. Valuable intellectual capital had been created through substantial investment on the part of the organization and the individuals involved—a three-year investment in course work, field assignments, and related activities. Yet this investment was at risk of being underutilized or even squandered with the subsequent work experience.

The initial response centered on the students. First, periodic networking and feedback sessions were established to foster peer learning across the students. Second, each student was assigned to a mentor in his respective function, finance or information systems, to help him while in the program. Third, increased attention was placed on the subsequent assignments given to the students.

A deeper response centered on the larger organization. Cohorts of middle- and higher-level managers from within the finance and information systems were offered the chance to receive a total of seven advanced sessions. Included in the cohorts were controllers, managers in charge of Enterprise Resource Planning (ERP) implementations, and other such leaders. Each of the seven sessions were two to three days in length and featured focused training in a summary of the student's degree work (new finance and information systems principles), as well as additional course work in the principles of entrepreneurship, coaching, and mentoring. In essence, the goal was to train the leaders in skills that would allow them to more fully value the intellectual capital being created.

Built into the curriculum were chances for the managers to undertake systems change initiatives—to understand systems change dynamics and to directly address barriers to the full appreciation of the investment being made in what was seen as the organization's next generation of leaders. One such project, led by Elaine Smith, involved the development of a formal mentor-matching system across the information systems function. The goal was not just to preserve the intellectual capital associated with the new hires coming through the fast-track rotational/masters degree program, but to value similar capabilities across the information systems function. In effect, mentoring was being transformed from a limited form of learning for the lucky elite, into something much broader in impact. Now, mentoring would be a system-wide mechanism for cross-level learning on careers, strategies for dealing with systems barriers, integration of new acquisitions, as well as the application of lessons learned in various degree programs.

Although this set of activities at Lucent was undoubtedly affected by the split of the company into two different operations, there are many lessons from the story so far. First, we see that investment in intellectual capital must be managed if the full value is to be gained. Second, interventions at multiple levels of the organization are required. Third, the implications associated with any one target population can have parallel implications for much broader groups of people.

Culture Change   Since 1999, the Jackson, Michigan, Police Department has embarked on a transformational change to redefine how the agency operates. This effort has focused on the adoption of a community policing philosophy. The change was championed by a new chief and has been emerging over the last five years. Community policing is the delivery of police services through a customer-focused approach.[13] This customer-based approach leads to the development of partnership arrangements with the community to better meet community needs and to enhance police effectiveness. Partnerships also include efforts to better integrate the internal functions of the police organization to be consistent with the transformation to a customer-focused approach. Underlying this move to community policing is the recognition by the department of the need to continuously learn about and improve their policing efforts. This requires the department to work with the community in new ways to develop and implement unified, information-based efforts to solve problems in the community rather than only to react to events or incidents when they occur. This approach utilizes community partnerships to maximize problem solving, reduce the fear of crime, and improve the community's quality of life.

The culture change is from police as reactors to police as proactive contributors to the quality of life in the community. The change effort includes the generation of large amounts of data to create shared knowledge and drive action. Early on in the process, the top leadership attended a one-week transformational change workshop that focused on systems thinking, empowerment, and continuous learning. Early efforts to build momentum for the change were spent developing a new vision and value for the department. Based on the community policing philosophy, the core values the department aspired to included issues of professionalism, community, ethics, excellence, respect, and justice. For example, in terms of the values of the community:

> We believe in enhancement of our community through service and ownership, therefore: we are involved in our community, we take pride in the community we serve, we promote cooperative efforts to enhance quality-of-life issues, and we recognize that our authority is derived from the community.

A cross section of police personnel helped to identify what a "victory" would look like (how the department would be different). These suggestions then became drivers of the planning and implementation process that was based on the principle of a high degree of involvement across all levels and functions. A cross section of police personnel specified that if the department is successful in the transformation to community policing, the following things should occur,

- A majority of the citizens will know the names of the officers assigned to their area.
- Citizens will actively identify and prioritize problems and work with officers to resolve them.
- The entire department will feel that community policing contributes to solving problems.
- All section officers will have a neighborhood watch group of their own.
- Officers will routinely take time to pull up timely data and use it in problem solving.
- Citizens will have access to crime information in their neighborhoods.
- A standardized, accurate evaluation process will be in place that lets officers know how they are doing in relation to personal and departmental goals. This process will enable the individual officer to take responsibility for his or her success in the department by recognizing what needs to happen and making changes.
- Every employee will be able to identify two or three community partnerships that are important to successful police work.
- Community policing will be integrated into the entire department. This will be indicated by the elimination of the need for special inducements to get officers to participate in community policing activities.

A guidance committee of twenty-two officers and administrators that cut across levels and functions was formed to develop the strategic plan for the transformation. The committee members were exposed to the concepts of systems thinking with the focus on a roadmap for change that included twenty-two different systems within the department which needed to be aligned to the new philosophy. From this perspective, the committee initially focused on identifying the geographic division of the city, identifying key partners, and identifying a problem-solving model for the department. The team members were trained on how to run effective meetings and on how to incorporate problem-solving methods into their team meetings.

Prior to implementing the new team-based work system, all officers and administrators attended classes on the philosophy behind the change as well as received specific training in problem solving. In addition, a training committee identified a three-year training plan to facilitate the transformation to community policing. The plan focused on developing skills relevant to using new technology, gathering and analyzing data, solving advanced problems, and improving presentation skills and team-building skills.

These efforts have lead to the development of new reporting systems within the department, new methods of crime analysis, neighborhood teams within geographical sectors, new ways of responding to and interacting with the community, new approaches for reporting and disseminating information to neighborhoods, new systems for collecting and disseminating data to aid problem-solving activities, and new call-for-service protocols and processes for allocating officer time. These efforts have required the reengineering of operating systems to support the move to community policing. For example, the records department has had to be restructured from a centralized-processing facility that generates monthly reports on crime for leaders and governmental agencies to a new technology-based system that allows for decentralized access by all officers to crime and problem-solving data in real (within twenty-four hours) time. The hierarchy has been restructured to increase empowerment and accountability of police personnel. Managing human resources (selection, training) has had to change to align them with the philosophy and goals of community policing.

This move to community policing is still unfolding. The transformation has been very complex and has presented many challenges and pitfalls. For example, it became clear that the initial training in developing a problem-oriented perspective at a police department, while necessary, was not sufficient for an effective problem-solving system. The department came to realize that, to better meet the needs of the community, problem solving required more than individual or team activity; it required an organizational system. Therefore, the department has embarked on the path of valuing knowledge management and the creation of systems in an organization to facilitate the creation, transfer, and sharing of knowledge. The police department is merging advances in information technology with the advancement of organizational knowledge. This merging of technology and knowledge allows for organizational learning to occur. It also is leading to a future where officers on the street are able to access in real time, information on problem-solving strategies and root-cause analyses conducted by other teams in the city in order to benchmark and to learn from the actions of others.

Throughout the process, data has been collected (for example, employee surveys) that point to areas for improvement. The top leadership has had the resolve to use data to consistently push for the change, devoting more resources to the effort and allowing the officers and administrators affected by the change to be the key planners and implementers of the change process. As an example, an internal "learning history team" has been formed to monitor the change process, generate lessons learned from the efforts so far, and to recommend the next steps to keep the momentum going. The internal team has members from across organizational levels. The team has recently examined over one hundred recommendations that have been made over the last three years by various ad hoc committees to help drive the culture change. The internal team analyzed why certain recommendations were not acted upon and whether it deserved a new priority. The review revealed that many of the recommendations had been enacted but as one team member put it "we need to share with members of the department what has been done, as a lot of people do not know what we now know." Developing new norms or a climate for innovation continues to be a challenge to change the status quo. Training has been used as leverage for moving the change process along, but attempts are being made to capture experiences in the field so as to learn from the change process. Oftentimes, the change seems to be adding more things for police personnel to do rather than streamlining what is already being done (for example, types of information/reports to file). In addition, there are many turf issues (for example, courts, schools, social agencies) that continue to need monitoring and resolutions. The current leadership challenge is how to build upon some initial successes so that new adaptive behavior patterns and new norms and values become institutionalized across individuals, teams, and functions within the police department.[14] All of the learning initiatives discussed above have elements that are quite compelling.

COMMON THEMES

Elements of all of the above learning initiatives are quite compelling. Who would not want a workforce that is capable of managing its own learning as takes place in Weyerhaueser's Structurewood plant? Who would not want to see training take on the strategic role that it occupies in Thomas Design—linking the business to its customers? Is not the partnership between Anderson Pattern and area educational institutions the sort of "out-of-the-box" thinking that opens up new possibilities for everyone involved? What is not to like about a large organization that is making hard-won progress through training, technology, and leadership in the transformation of an entire work system? Can we not learn lessons about constancy of purpose in the large-scale systems change taking place in a traditionally mechanistic and para-military organization like the Jackson, Michigan, Police Department?

In reading these models, it is temping to want to schedule a benchmarking trip as soon as possible to better learn about their successes. Indeed, there is much to learn from these organizations about how they generated data, interpreted that data to acquire knowledge about their organizational systems, and analyzed the root-cause issues to drive actions that enhanced knowledge and built deeper capabilities into the organizations. From these examples, learning can occur that is relevant to how to construct a vision, how to develop structures to coordinate efforts in translating the vision into a learning system, and how to support the learning system within the day-to-day realities of the company. In addition, some learning can occur regarding how to involve internal and external stakeholders in the process of creating a learning system, how to develop team-based work systems, how to develop a shared mental model of the future, and how to view events within a larger organizational framework.

However, the learning can not come solely from any attempt to copy or replicate the models. First, there is no one right model for building capability. In fact, the highlighted elements of any one of the five examples can be found in many the other cases. For example, Lucent was presented as an "intellectual capital" example, but the company is involved in numerous strategic partnerships with colleges, universities, and other organizations.

Second, each of these examples represents a snapshot of an evolving and dynamic process. What is important about the cases is not the elements that we have highlighted, but the process by which these elements came to be. Benchmarking can help highlight the outline of a learning organization but can not provide the process or "guts" of a learning organization. In fact, the hallmark of a learning organization is that the learning emerges over time and that the system is continually being reshaped and reinvented. The learning processes that take place are the key to building an effective continuous learning system.

Consequently, a mere copying of these cases, or even a combination of them, will generate a flurry of activity that attempts to create a positive convergent learning cycle. It might even lead to specific accomplishments, such as large numbers of people trained in a given set of principles. It would not, however, necessarily result in a learning organization that is actively improving the way it operates as an organization.

Most organizations that have launched initiatives involving various aspects of learning do not become learning organizations. In fact, in a number of highly visible cases, and many less visible ones, the exact opposite seems to have happened. While adaptive capabilities of some individuals have been enhanced, the overall effect is that people in these organizations have become more frustrated, more cynical, and more confused about the direction of the organizations and less clear about their roles. Sadly, the people are also less engaged in the learning process that fuels a downward cycle toward the status quo.

What separates organizations that have effectively become learning organizations from those that do not? Each organization creates a Bold Vision with knowledge as the key to competitive advantage. Each organization generates data in order to enhance knowledge and to drive action. Each organization empowers workers to design and implement the Bold Vision.

From our experience, it has become clear that the successful organizations also develop mechanisms to learn from the experiences that are *not* consistent with the Bold Vision that the organization is trying to implement. These organizations build capacity to identify key problems and are not afraid of addressing them. Disconnects, dilemmas, and divergence are not seen by leaders as key threats. These organizations even welcome the gaps between the realities and the Bold Vision in order to learn more about the organization and where it needs to focus attention to continue to change and evolve. This form of learning from Harsh Realities is not as well developed—in field practice or in the literature. Chapter 3 presents a case study of an organization that began down the Bold Vision path, but fell well short of its potential as a learning organization. The organization created many of the ingredients that could have led to a learning organization. In fact, this organization was seen by others during implementation as a model or benchmark for other agencies. Nevertheless, the seeds of failure or the slippery slope can be seen, as the organization ultimately failed due to its lack of efforts to develop approaches for dealing with the realities of the three Ds—disconnects, divergences, and dilemmas.

Notes

1. There is evidence that organizations with stronger learning orientations demonstrate greater organizational effectiveness. For example, a recent survey by the American Society for Training and Development found evidence that leading-edge organizations spent approximately 4.39% of training expenditures as a percent of payroll or $1,956 per employee. Training expenditures for other firms were 1.81% as a percent of payroll for an average of $649 per employee (see L. J. Bassi and M. E. Van Buren, *The 1998 ASTD State of the Industry Report, Training and Development*, 52 (1998), 21–43. In a study of manufacturing firms, it was found that those organizations that implemented more training programs increased productivity by an average of 17% (See K. M. Kapp, "Transforming Your Manufacturing Organization into a Learning Organization," in *Hospital Material Management Quarterly*, 20 (1998): 46–54. A study by the Brookings Institute suggested that 60% of an organization's competitive advantage is derived from internal advancements in knowledge, innovation, and learning. See also, Joel Cutcher-Gershenfeld, "The Impact on Economic Performance of a Transformation in Workplace Relations," *Industrial and Labor Relations Review*, 44, no. 2 (January 1991): 241–260; and Casey Ichniowski, Katherine Shaw, and G. Prennusi, "The Effects of Human Resource Management Practices on Productivity," *American Economic Review* 87(3): 291–313.

2. Scott Tannenbaum, "Enhancing Continuous Learning: Diagnostic Findings form Multiple Companies," in *Human Resource Management*, 36 (1997): 437–452. D. Ulrich , M. Von Glinow, and T. Jick, "High Impact Learning. Building and Diffusing Learning Capability," in *Organizational Dynamics*, 22 (1993): 52–66.

3. The vision statements for organizational learning come from the following sources (in order of presentation in the text):

Denise M. Rouseau, "Organizational Behavior in the New Organizational Era," *Annual Review of Psychology*, 48 (1997): 515–546.

Chris Argyris and Don A. Schön, *Organizational Learning* (Reading, MA: Addison-Wesley, 1996).

Karl M. Kapp, "Transforming Your Manufacturing Organization into a Learning Organization," *Hospital Material Management Quarterly*, 20 (1998): 46–54.

Ikujiro Nonaka and Hirotaka Takeuchi, *The Knowledge-Creating Company* (Oxford, England: Oxford University Press, 1995).

Sharon J. Confessore and William Kops, "Self-Directed Learning and the Learning Organization: Examining the Connection Between the Individual and the Learning Environment," *Human Resource Developoment Quarterly*, 9 (1998): 365–375.

Irwin Goldstein and J. Kevin Ford, *Training in Organizations*, 4th ed. (Belmont, CA: Wadsworth, 2002).

Joel Cutcher-Gershenfeld, "Union-Management Investments in Training and Capability In the United States," OECD Project on: *Collective Bargaining and Worker Participation in Continuing Vocational Training* (Paris: OECD, 2002).

4. The case studies were drawn from research conducted under grants from the state of Michigan, as well as from our own consulting work with some of the organizations.

5. For example, General Motors operates over five hundred apprenticeship programs involving two-year colleges. See Jeffrey Cantor, "The Auto Industry's New Model: Car Companies and Community Colleges Collaborate to Provide High Technology Training, *Vocational Education Journal*, 66 (1991): 26–29.

6. Federal and state guidelines specify that registered apprenticeship programs must include at least 144 hours of classroom instruction and one year (about 2000 hours) of on-the-job experience under a master.

7. Frederick W. Taylor, *Principles of Scientific Management* (New York: Harper & Row, 1911).

8. Quote of Taylor cited by Gareth Morgan in his book *Images of Organizations* (Oaks, CA: Sage Publications, 1997).

9. Max Weber, *The Theory of Social and Economic Organization* (London: Oxford University Press, 1997).

10. We use the terms capabilities and expertise interchangeably—focusing on the definition of expertise associated with ability to accomplish tasks, rather than the connotation of being an expert.

11. See Eleanor M. Smith, J. Kevin Ford, and Steve W. J. Kozlowski, "Building Adaptive Expertise: Implications for Training Design," in *Training for the 21st Century: Applications of Psychological Research,* M. A. Quiñones and A. Ehrenstein (Washington, D.C.: 1997) American Psychological Association.

12. For a discussion of the differences between routine and adaptive expertise see Giyoo Hatano and K. Inagaki, "Two Courses of Expertise" in H. W. Stevenson (New York: W. H. Freeman, 1986), K. J. Holyoak, "Symbolic Connectinonism: Toward Third Generation Theories of Expertise," in *Toward a General Theory of Experitise: Prospects and Limits.* K. A. Ericsson and J. Smith (Cambridge, England: Cambridge University Press) Research on the components of adaptablity in the workplace can be found by examining a study by Elaine Pulakos, Sharon Arad, Michelle Donovan, and Kevin Plamondon, on "Adaptability in the Workplace: Development of a Taxonomy of Adaptive Performance," in *Journal of Applied Psychology*, 85 (2000), 612–624.

13. See a set of readings from Merry Morash and J. Kevin Ford, *The Move to Community Policing* (Thousand Oaks, CA: Sage Publications, 2002) for more information about community policing efforts and the key issues for changing established police organizations.

14. For example, see James M. Kouzes and Barry Z. Posner, *The Leadership Challenge* (San Francisco: Jossey-Bass, 1995) for a discussion of key leadership challenges and strategies for dealing with those challenges.

3

The Slippery Slope

T here are many possible innovative responses to the pressure for change in organizational learning systems. Organizations have attempted to duplicate innovations, such as those presented in chapter 2 (and related success stories), generating a flurry of activities to transform themselves into a learning organization. Many of the people in organizations who have attempted to move to a learning perspective, however, have found the path a difficult one to travel. This is due to the Harsh Realities of disconnects, not necessarily any inherent flaws in the Bold Visions.

Disconnects will continually arise and pose problems for any organizational learning or change-related effort. Further, the disconnects are indicators of underlying dilemmas that are not easily discussed or addressed. The dilemmas, regardless of how they are addressed, will inevitably lead to divergence in what is learned and how new disconnects are handled. Consequently, it is not surprising that once on the road to organizational learning, it is easy for leaders to feel lonely and vulnerable—regardless of the success stories they have used as benchmarks. It is easy to feel that each step forward is matched by two that are sideways or even backward. While the first sideways and backward steps don't seem particularly problematic, the implications increase over time. This is what we refer to as the "slippery slope."[1]

No organization sets out to travel down a slippery slope. No one wants to lose ground on an initiative. Moreover, even if ground is to be lost, no one wants to come away without having learned any lessons from the experience. So why is it that there are so often backward twists and turns, that increase in intensity and ultimately undermine organizational learning?

In this chapter, we will follow one case example as it began to head down the slippery slope. This is the case of a large-scale quality initiative—premised on harnessing the knowledge of employees at all levels. First, we examine the case at the very outset of what was termed "a continuous quality-improvement initiative," at which time an initial vision for the initiative was crafted. Then, we will pick up the case at the planning stage, where issues of coordination of efforts were addressed. Finally, we will examine the case at the point of implementation, where the initiative was both reaching into daily operations and being undercut in ways that reach all the way back to the early steps down the slippery slope. Even while going down the slippery slope, learning was taking place. Indeed, many accomplishments were celebrated as leading benchmarks—and rightly so. Unfortunately, as the change effort evolved, the learning became more and more fragmented. Travel with us alongside this organization as it creates a common vision, coordinates structures for learning and improvement, and trains the workforce in new skills.

As background, this is a state-level department that embarked on a quality-improvement initiative. We have masked the name of this department and are calling it the Department of Valuable Services (DVS). The DVS included over three thousand employees at the time of this case. The agency had operations in over two hundred offices and field facilities within a structure of twenty divisions. It provided public services and administered a variety of regulations involving natural resources and environmental protection, much of which involved high levels of technical expertise.

There are relatively few detailed case examples in the literature of large-scale systems change initiatives that have gone awry.[2] Most published reports are on success stories. The DVS case is a mixture—with notable accomplishments and seemingly minor initial mistakes that ultimately undermined the entire initiative.

CONSTRUCTING A VISION

Most change initiatives begin with the construction of a future vision. This is usually a highly energizing process. People often leave these sessions motivated to share the vision with others so that all may work toward it. But, just as likely, embedded in this process is the first step down the slippery slope.

At DVS, the process began with the establishment of a Management Review Committee, appointed by the director of the agency to investigate what was then termed total quality management. The group included ten midlevel and senior managers from a cross-section of different divisions in the agency—including field operations and central administration. After reviewing public and private sector benchmark cases, the group issued a report strongly recommending that the agency begin a quality initiative.

Based on this recommendation, one of the top three managers in the agency—the head of central administration—was given the assignment to develop a strategy for introducing total quality principles into the DVS. This individual then identified a number of potential external consultants, a subset of which was interviewed by a team of four managers from the Management Review Committee. Ultimately a team of faculty from a large state university was selected.[3] At the same time, a thirteen-member Total Quality Management (TQM) Planning and Design Team was appointed that included many of the initial committee members and a few additional senior managers.

The faculty team then met with the full TQM Planning and Design Team. The sessions were highly energized. It was agreed that the term "total quality management" did not fit the state government context—even though it was part of the title of the team. In particular, the word "management" was seen as too limiting. After extended brainstorming, the term "continuous quality improvement" (CQI) was selected. A timeline was developed and a plan generated for presentation to the DVS leadership team. At the first meeting with the agency's top management leaders, it was recommended that a shared vision be constructed.

The meeting took place at a nearby hotel and began with an ambitious agenda. The full Planning and Design Team and the full leadership team were in attendance. As the session began, a number of dynamics became evident. First, it was clear that the Planning and Design Team members were by far the most enthusiastic people in the room. From others, there were many questions and concerns raised. The issues focused on feasibility and logistics. Responses from the committee members all centered on the substance of these issues—making the case for a major quality initiative.

The external consultants played a dual role, beginning the meeting with a presentation on quality principles, and then shifting into a facilitation role as the group explored the ideas. For example, the group engaged in brainstorming about hopes and fears. It also revisited the label of CQI and reviewed alternatives before agreeing to the Planning and Design Team recommendation. At one point, the group was asked if these were the appropriate people to be in the room and there was a general nodding of heads that this was a representative group. At the end of the session, everyone agreed that they had learned more about the topic and that it made sense to meet again.

At the following session, the vision and the development of coordinating structures were the main agenda items. The group engaged in extensive brainstorming on potential elements of a vision. A sample vision statement from a parallel federal agency was reviewed and the potential elements were narrowed down to a core set of points. In addition, a set of eight potential task forces was identified to focus on issues such as training, communication, stakeholder involvement, and other implementation issues. There was also discussion around the establishment of a quality office in the agency, with a senior management position to be created that would signal the importance of the initiative.

Following the session, the external consultants worked with the elements from the brainstorming session and prepared draft vision language. This language was brought to a third session, during which adjustments were made and a set of core guiding principles were also added. The session included all Planning and Design Team members and most of the Leadership Team— though a few key managers had schedule conflicts and were not there. At the end of the session, a vision statement was approved, a quality office was announced with a director of quality designated, a budget was established with funds from each of the twenty divisions in the agency, and a set of seven task forces were convened. The final text of the vision was as follows,

> CQI in the DVS is aimed at continuous improvement in conservation, protection, and enhancement of natural resources, through a participative, team-oriented and customer-focused approach that builds on people's talents and creativity.

In addition to drafting the vision statement, an effort was made to communicate the meaning behind the vision. This involved drafting and agreeing on a statement of what CQI is and is not. The group agreed on the following:

The CQI framework focuses on:
What do you do?
How well does that serve customer/stakeholder needs?
What can you do to improve?

What is CQI?
- CQI is a *participative* process that recognizes and encourages the contributions of every employee.
- CQI is a *management philosophy* to serve as a guide in carrying out department activities.
- CQI is a process that generates *measurable results*, where appropriate.
- CQI is a process that utilizes teams and encourages *teamwork*, wherever appropriate.
- CQI is a *customer-focused* process to provide better service to current and future generations.
- CQI is a process for *continuous improvement*.
- CQI is a responsive approach for interacting with *internal and external stakeholder* groups.
- CQI is an approach that moves *decision-making* to the appropriate level.
- CQI is a flexible way to *remove barriers* that keep people from doing the best job they can possibly do.

What CQI is not or should not be?
- CQI is not a quick fix or a smoke screen.
- CQI should not be used to threaten or intimidate people.
- CQI should not be a waste of time or effort.
- CQI should not be a mechanical process.
- CQI is not an end in itself.

This statement reflected extended dialogue among a cross-section of managers. Note that each point is carefully worded. For example, the CQI is not described just as moving decision-making down to lower levels, but as "an approach that moves decision-making to the appropriate level"—a subtle but critical difference. Together, the vision statement and supporting materials represent a potentially powerful framework for continuous improvement, which could apply in many public- or private-sector organizations.

THE STORY BEHIND THE VISION STORY

At this point many key agreements were reached and some forward momentum had begun. In contrast to the launch of many initiatives, this looked like a strong start. So where is the slippery slope? Let's take a close look at what we might call the story behind the story.

In the senior manager who was given the task of exploring the quality principles, we have an individual with a reputation for being a tough manager, who had recently been brought into the agency based on his track record of cutting budgets and restructuring operations. Thus, when he established the Management Review Committee and gave initial support to the idea, it was taken seriously. The story behind the story, however, is that it may have been taken seriously because no one wanted to speak against this individual (nicknamed by some, "the hatchet man").

Turning to the Planning and Design Team, a key strength of the group was that it spanned many different divisions of the agency, cut across multiple levels of the hierarchy, and even included managers in different "camps" within the organization. Still, there were key stakeholders not in the room, including front-line employees, representatives from the five unions representing employees in that agency, and representatives from the external public advisory groups affiliated with the agency. In fact, the absence of the unions surfaced in the planning sessions and it was observed that management was too internally divided on these issues at this stage.

While it might not have been feasible to have an even more diverse task force, there are a couple of key disconnects suggested. First, if management was so deeply divided, perhaps there was a need to better understand these internal splits. Second, there should have at least been a way to formally give a "heads up" and gauge the interest of these stakeholder groups. This did occur informally with the unions, but not with the other groups.

Once the Planning and Design Team and the Leadership Team began to engage the substance of the vision, there were many issues and concerns raised. One issue that was mentioned, but not discussed in great detail, was a controversial reorganization that had recently taken place in the agency. Privately, people said that too much had been done too fast and that there were many hard feelings in the field offices. If fact, some of the more aggressive aspects of the reorganization had been quickly scaled back in the face of field resistance. The agency leaders emphasized the importance of "putting the past behind us." The story behind the story is that many people in the agency were not yet ready to forget about the reorganization—even if top leaders wanted people to forget it. As a result, at later briefing sessions throughout the agency, cynicism about the reorganization constantly surfaced—with CQI being seen as just a further attempt to pursue the more aggressive parts of the reorganization agenda that were put on "hold" earlier.

In retrospect, the reorganization represented a lost opportunity. Consider the alternative possibility where the director of the agency might have publicly stated that the reorganization was a mistake. He might have said that he had failed to solicit sufficient employee input or involve key stakeholders in the change process. Then, he could say that the quality initiative was being undertaken in ways that reflected his having learned from the experience. This was true, but it was never said publicly. If it had been said publicly, it might have taken some of the edge off of the reception to CQI.

During the early discussions of the vision, there were also many positive statements made about the importance of embracing quality principles. On the surface, these were encouraging endorsements. Looking behind the story, however, we see that many of the statements may have reflected a sophisticated reading of the politics of the situation. Many of these managers knew that the governor's office would look positively on an agency taking a lead role on quality issues and they knew that these issues were also on the agenda in sister agencies in other states and at the federal level. Thus, some of the positive contributions may have had as much to do with fostering a perception of progress on the quality issue as they had to do with embracing quality or learning principles.

The key lesson here is that many of these managers had not wrestled with the underlying assumptions about whether learning and continuous improvements in their specific operations could be driven by front-line employee knowledge and a team-based work system—as was contemplated by the visioning process. By not looking behind their endorsements, the front–stage learning cycle was set for what could be considered a superficial consensus on the vision. In fact, the cynicism among front-line employees had a measure of truth to it, given their experience with some managers.

The superficial nature of the consensus was evident later, when feedback around this cynicism was brought back to the Leadership Team. The response from the Leadership Team was to redouble the intensity of the messages proclaiming top management support, rather than confronting the realities of the issue and engaging in what we call *learning from disconnects*. For example, a summary of the CQI vision statement and an introduction to the process was distributed in a special flyer that was included in the pay envelopes for all employees. Top managers were also urged to meet with their staffs and emphasize the importance of the initiative. This was all a rapid response, but that's not what people were looking for. This was another case where an opportunity was lost. If there had been public acknowledgment of the work that needed to be done within the management team, the message would have been accurate, more credible, and a source of legitimacy when people were later asked to work on their issues.

Finally, let's take a close look at the vision itself. The language conveys the image of a unified agency bound together by a common purpose. Certainly this is what the director of the agency and many of the managers desired. As later became evident, however, this view was not shared by all managers. Indeed, as we will discuss shortly, one of the divisional heads who participated in some of the discussions had a very different conception of CQI that ultimately led to a great divide in the organization. The focus on unity of purpose failed to acknowledge the inherent divergence in the organization—again this reality was ignored so that mechanisms to support learning from harsh realities were not set up or encouraged.

We will never know if the forces driving the split within the agency were as intense during the visioning process. We do know, however, that the tensions and distrust between this divisional head and the director of the agency was one of the critical dynamics during the sessions. People would often look from one to the other when controversial issues were on the table, and any agreements reached, when one or the other was absent, were suspect. It is possible that surfacing these issues more directly in the early sessions would have led to the demise of the initiative rather than any constructive engagement of the issues, but there should have at least been some consideration for how to anticipate this vulnerability.

GOVERNANCE AND COORDINATING STRUCTURES FOR PLANNING AND IMPLEMENTATION

Once the leadership of the DVS had established a network of task forces, created the quality office, appointed the director of quality, and agreed on a statement of mission and principles, there was the challenge of planning and implementation. Lead responsibility for planning and implementation was given to a central CQI Coordination Team, combined with the newly created Quality Office. The Quality Office involved a director of quality, an administrative assistant, and a portion of the operating funds for the quality initiative.

The first part of planning involved constituting the task forces, which took place in the space of two to three months. Initially there were seven task forces and the central CQI Coordination Team. The task forces were as follows:

- Communications
- Training
- Strategic Planning
- Recognition
- Quality Action Team (QAT) Model
- Evaluation and Feedback
- Stakeholder Coordination

Each task force featured a cross-section of members including members of the initial exploratory task force, members of the leadership team, and people from various parts of the agencies with appropriate skills or knowledge of quality principles. For example, the Training Task Force included staff members from the Human Resource function with training responsibilities, the head of one of the agency's divisions, two staff members who had been trained as quality facilitators in a program being run by a federal agency with parallel responsibilities, and a staff member with prior work experience in secondary education.

The experience of each task force was shaped by the nature of its mandate. The Communications Task Force, for example, had a substantial agenda from the outset since there was a steady stream of issues and developments to communicate and the existing infrastructure was incomplete (not everyone had e-mail, some offices were geographically remote, and so on). There was also a high level of urgency facing the task force on Quality Action Teams (QATs), but the task was very different. Here the challenge was to sort through the many structural and policy issues associated with having QATs. For example, this group ultimately received policy support for QATs to be convened by employees at any level, provided they had a senior management sponsor; for QAT members to receive release time from work to serve on the team; for a common seven–step process improvement model to be adopted throughout the agency; and for a network of facilitators to be created with each having a minimum of four hours' release time per month to support one or more QATs.

Given the overlapping nature of the work, many of the task forces had to coordinate activities. For example, once the QAT task force received leadership agreement to have a network of part-time facilitators, then the training task force worked with the consultants in establishing the curriculum for a week-long facilitator institute. Then, the communications task force helped to send out notices inviting people to apply for training and a special review subcommittee was established in conjunction with the Human Resource office to select candidates for training. Ultimately, over one hundred facilitators were trained and the facilitators' network that they established became a key source of coordination and innovation as the implementation unfolded.

As the task forces began to operate, it became clear that many parts of the organization featured innovative activities by individuals that were consistent with CQI principles. Rather than reject these existing innovations or force them into a cookie-cutter model, the Coordination Team decided to establish an eighth task force entitled the "Council of Existing Innovations." The aim was for this group to identify existing innovations, learn from these experiences, and integrate them into the CQI framework.

After the first two groups of facilitators were trained, their first assignment was not the facilitation of QATs. Instead, they were paired up and given an aggressive schedule to provide all employees with a briefing on quality principles and the CQI initiative. Each of these sessions featured the generation of a list of perceived driving and restraining forces associated with the initiative. These lists were tallied and analyzed by the consulting team. In a report based on the data, the top five hopes and fears prioritized by the session participants were as follows (in priority order):

Hopes about CQI

1. Positive results such as efficiency, effectiveness, productivity, quality improvement, and better decision-making.
2. Participation and empowerment of all employees leading to job enrichment, rather than merely job enlargement.
3. Public service and public image improvements
4. Management commitment to the CQI process through participating, delegating decision-making, and following through on team recommendations
5. Increased teamwork and cooperation between divisions, between central administration and the field offices, and between levels in the organization.

Fears about CQI[4]

1. Management will not be fully committed to the CQI process, they will not follow through on recommendations, and there will be variation in support across managers.
2. The CQI process will not last and will be a short-term fad like previous programs.
3. CQI will not be consistently implemented across the organization due to individual agendas, predetermined decisions, and the selection of particular people to teams.
4. CQI will result in negative outcomes such as no change, slower decision-making, more workload, more meetings, more paperwork, and more duplication of effort.

At the same time that the data was collected on hopes and fears, a brief attitude survey was administered at the end of each session. When asked what response would best describe their feelings about CQI at DVS, the participants revealed neither great enthusiasm, nor deep opposition. In particular, among 859 respondents, the distribution was as follows:

Enthusiastic:	9%
Interested:	37%
Skeptical:	48%
Waste of Time:	5%

Among the 140 managers who were also at these sessions, the responses were slightly more favorable, but similarly split:

Enthusiastic:	16%
Interested:	59%
Skeptical:	23%
Waste of Time:	2%

In order to address the implications of the data, a special meeting was convened involving the Coordination Team, the full Leadership Team, and all division managers (who were not on one or the other of the two top-level teams). In reacting to the lists, there was a shared sense that the hopes and fears were realistic and required a response. In particular, it was agreed that top management needed to better convey its commitment to CQI. An example of how this was done involved plans to produce a videotape of the director and some of the division directors to candidly address questions that had come up in the briefing sessions. As well, all division directors and managers were urged to meet with their staffs and reiterate their support for the CQI initiative.

Some task forces had mandates that involved a longer time horizon. For example, the Stakeholders Task Force had identified the five unions representing agency employees as the first and most critical stakeholder group to address. The issue of union involvement had come up right at the outset of the initiative, but the top management leadership had indicated that they had to reach their own consensus on these issues before they would be able to discuss them with the unions. Given the tensions that were evident within the leadership team, the request was honored. However, once notification about the initiative began to roll out, the unions were understandably vocal about not having been included.

Interestingly, when the Stakeholders Task Force approached the unions, the reception was not the same in each case. Some unions, such as the union representing scientists and engineers at the agency, saw the quality initiative as a strategic priority and were quick to embrace it. Others, such as the union representing clerical employees, were openly critical of the initiative for its potential to generate improvements that would result in the elimination of jobs held by their members.

Following a series of briefings, off-line meetings among the union leaders, and internal union dialogue with constituents, all five unions came to a consensus that it was important to be involved in the quality initiative. This set the stage for a key test event. The unions made a formal request that the Coordination Team responsible for the initiative within the agency include five seats—one for each union. Though some managers initially balked at this, preferring a smaller number of seats, they were eventually persuaded that each union had a legitimate and independent role that justified a separate seat. It is important to note that this idea elevated the profile of the unions within the agency—none had been involved in any prior joint activities with DVS management.

If according new status to the unions was a challenge for management, the unions faced an immediate challenge in response. Management also proposed that the committee include two representatives from the underrepresented, nonmanagerial portion of the workforce. There ensued great debate over just how to select such employees, with the ultimate decision being to do so through an open nomination process in the agency and selection by a subgroup from the Coordination Team. In the end, a new "Guidance Committee" was established and, over time, the unions proved to be a key driving force for the initiative.

As these activities were unfolding at the DVS, other state agencies began to call the quality office. There was great interest in the structure of the task forces, the policy issues that had been resolved, the facilitators who had been trained, and the involvement of the five unions. Increasingly, the DVS came to be seen as one of the benchmark state agencies on quality and as *the* lead agency on joint governance issues with the unions.

THE STORY BEHIND THE GOVERNANCE STORY

When the quality office was established, funds were allocated based on what was essentially a tax on the various divisions in the agency. Publicly, little was said by the divisional managers about the loss of these funds, but privately it was an ongoing sore point in the context of continued budget cuts from the legislature. The issue was not only the loss of funds (which were relatively minor), but more the fact that this was a unilateral decision by the director of the agency.

In retrospect, it would have been possible to have some advance dialogue with the managers on this issue. Even if the contribution was mandatory, there may have been different preferences in how to make the contribution. Moreover, there might have been the development of explicit understandings of what the division directors might expect in return for their investment. Their focus was just on the short-term loss of funds and it might have been possible to reframe the issue around a long-term investment in which they could expect various forms of support—positioning them more explicitly as internal customers.

Since the amount of money was not large relative to each division's budget, the responses of the division directors were also indicators of the degree to which they valued the continuous improvement initiative. At the time, the director of quality responded by holding one-on-one meetings with each division director to demonstrate his commitment to the initiative. This was a more promising response than just trying to address these issues in group meetings or not addressing these issues. However, it placed the director of quality in an awkward role. Either he had to make twenty-six bilateral deals or apologize in twenty-six different ways for the unilateral budget cut. In retrospect, this was a responsibility that resided with all of the senior managers—if not to manage the change differently, at least to take the time to interpret the data. In this case that data was clearly providing further evidence for splits in management and surfacing a deep cultural issue around unilateral decisions.

While the Quality Office was establishing itself, most of the task forces were actively meeting. Many of the task force members found these meetings to be very productive and highly engaging. The Quality Office ensured that facilitation assistance was provided at the meetings, tangible products were being generated, and there were linkages across teams. Altogether, people had the experience of being part of something large and meaningful.

At the same time, these task force members were only serving in this capacity for about four to eight work hours a week (though many would work on their assignments on their personal time as well). For the balance of their time, they were working in traditional jobs, set in fairly rigid hierarchies. Further, many of them had managers who did not fully value or appreciate the time they were spending on the quality initiative. Thus, many of these people had the experience of doing excellent work, but not being recognized or supported for doing so. This reveals the degree to which the task forces were successful in spite of the system, rather than because of the way the system was changing to support quality principles.

The emergence of the Council of Existing Innovations had great potential, but fell short of this ideal. The reality was that the council consisted of people who themselves were directly part of major initiatives that qualified as existing innovations. As such, they were under great time constraints, not trained in quality principles (so they didn't have a common language), and did not have a process established to collect data about the existing innovations in a way that would facilitate learning from these experiences. Further, they were primarily given leadership signals to complete the initiatives, without support for the additional time and training that would be required to bring them into alignment with CQI.

The disconnect between the experiences on the quality initiative and regular work experiences were most acute for the successive people trained as facilitators. The people attending the facilitator institute were drawn from a broad cross-section of the organization and they formed many close bonds by the end of an intensive week of training. The groups included anywhere from sixteen to twenty-five facilitators who were trained in intervals of approximately three to six months. For the first two groups to graduate from the facilitator institute, however, there were relatively few opportunities to support Quality Action Teams since all of the policy decisions on QATs had not been made. In addition, the communications process educating all employees about QATs had not fully taken place.

When their energies were instead directed to delivering the orientation sessions, a subtle disconnect was revealed. The data from the sessions did prompt top leadership to deliver messages of support with new intensity, via management meetings with staff and a videotape. Unfortunately, both messages had an effect opposite what was desired. The managers who were ambivalent about CQI did not change their behaviors, so any statement of support delivered in a staff meeting did not ring true. Further, there were endless battles over the script and casting for the video tape, with the result being a watered-down message that really didn't say much at all. For example, it had been planned that the tape would feature a focus group meeting of the director with a cross-section of employees, but it was decided that this was too risky.

Perhaps most important of all, the top leadership reaction to the data centered on the first two fears—that management was not committed and that

CQI was just a fad. They did not engage the deeper issues around divergence within the agency and the need for consistency of implementation and the minimization of political dynamics. At the time, the CQI director, the outside consultants, and a few key management leaders concluded that it was at least a good thing that people were starting to deal with reality. In addition, there was also discomfort around the deeper issues or dilemmas that had not been discussed. The deeper issues didn't go away and came back to haunt the initiative in countless ways.

This deeper problem was vividly illustrated when the first group of facilitators was graduating from the weeklong training session. A senior manager from the agency gave a rousing speech about how each one was a very special individual. They were told that they had been carefully picked and that, in essence, they were the hope for the future. After this talk, there was a long silence. The group had just spent five days learning to focus on improving the system, rather than on just trying to motivate individuals. Finally, one of the consultants apologized to the senior manager and indicated that the group had been trained in the exact opposite principles. Success should not depend on these individuals doing a heroic job, but rather on the systems being put in place for them to do a good job using the skills in which they had been trained.

Sadly, the system took almost two years to begin to emerge. Eventually, there were quite a few QATs calling for facilitation assistance. In the meantime, the facilitators were largely saddled with the heroic task of facilitating quality improvement in an organization that had not yet made the commitment to becoming a learning organization. This experience posed an interesting dilemma. Should facilitators be trained for the kind of setting that does not yet exist or should they be trained to do battle in an organization that is still very much rooted in hierarchical and bureaucratic assumptions?

SUPPORTING WORKPLACE OPERATIONS

The application of quality principles took many different forms at DVS. In some divisions there were employee briefings, but little else. In others, one or two Quality Action Teams were established and that represented the scope of activity. In a few cases, there were large-scale redesign initiatives undertaken around the creation of cross-functional teams for service delivery. As well, at an agencywide level, the implementation of a new management information system was linked in some ways to the quality initiative.

One of the first QATs to be established was in administrative operations and was named the "Time and Attendance Team," which is illustrative of the learning and improvement process associated with this type of off-line team. The problem facing this team seemed simple—employee paychecks would be issued quickly in some divisions and with a range of different delays in others. The group undertook constructing a process map of the way payroll checks were generated.

Beginning with employee time cards, they traced the paper trail all the way through to the issuance of checks. They found that the paperwork made this journey in some divisions in about seventeen steps, while others took more than twice as many steps. As they probed deeper into why this might be the case, they found that additional steps were added to the process in many of the divisions where problems occurred and additional checks or audit procedures were added. After talking to a variety of stakeholders, the group began to surface improvement options and new insights into some of the root causes. The group worked with its sponsor and generated a clear presentation highlighting the nature of the problem and recommended options for streamlining and coordinating operations.

Altogether, Quality Action Teams were established on a wide range of topics. Most met for four hours once a week. They all followed a six-step process-improvement model developed by the consulting team. A process-improvement model was utilized since most existing problem-solving models required defining a problem and many processes were being addressed that were not necessarily problems, though they could still be improved. The model was termed the "ARRIVE" model, with a step corresponding to each letter of the word:

1. **A**im (What is the aim of the process?)
2. **R**eality (What is the present reality for this process?)
3. **R**oot Causes (What are the root causes of any gaps between aim and reality?)
4. **I**mprovement Options (What options might be considered for improvement?)
5. **V**alue Added Implementation (For those options that are likely to add value, what are the elements of an implementation plan?)
6. **E**valuation and Continuous Improvement (How will we evaluate whether we have made an improvement and how do we continue the process?)

Most QATs found the model useful, because it helped them to systematically surface ideas about how to improve operations. Many also reported being engaged in the learning itself—something that did not happen enough as part of their regular jobs.

There were at least two divisions where the concept of continuous improvement was defined more broadly to include the design of the jobs themselves. In these settings, there were initial discussions and pilot initiatives on establishing various types of cross-functional service delivery teams. For example, in one of the divisions, a variety of technical specialists would each be interacting with a given factory or other business operation. They would be conducting inspections, collecting data, and issuing reports under a mix of state and federal laws and regulations governing air quality, water quality, and other factors. Separate files would be maintained and inspection visits would be uncoordinated.

In this case, there was a pilot initiative aimed at maintaining a single, common set of shared files on each facility—with site visits coordinated within a cross-functional team. Unfortunately, the pilot experiment with cross-functional service delivery proved short lived. The DVS learned that the shared files and the common team structure made it impossible to maintain audit trails for the mix of state and federal funding associated with the different inspection and monitoring activity. Still, the agency did learn that the model itself was a potentially viable alternate way to deliver service that had great potential for improving quality and efficiency.

THE STORY BEHIND THE WORKPLACE OPERATIONS STORY

Despite creative problem solving and well-developed recommendations, the majority of the Quality Action Teams did not see their recommendations implemented. Take the Time and Attendance QAT, for example. Their analysis was presented to the top leadership team, which asked many excellent questions and concluded that the recommendations were sound. It was recommended that implementation go forward. However, the QAT and its champion (a division chief) found that there were no funds available for the implementation. Since it cut across all divisions of the agency, no single division was willing to take on the task.

At that same time, central administration was involved in the implementation of an agencywide information system. At first, it was suggested that the new payroll procedures should be integrated into the new information system. When it became apparent that this would not happen in a way that was consistent with the QAT recommendations, there were again efforts to surface the issue. Ultimately, however, the split in the agency occurred before this was ever resolved. The recommendation became "lost" in the sea of issues facing the agency.

The funding barriers encountered by the pilot experiment having separate audit trails for integrated service delivery teams did not seem insurmountable at the outset. This looked like a bureaucratic barrier that might be tackled by a committed champion. In fact, the lead manager driving this initiative was both highly capable and powerful within the agency. Yet, despite a number of attempts to address the issue, he concluded that it would require systemwide attention—throughout state government and even with some federal agencies.

Interestingly, this issue was raised with quality officials at the state level, but was seen as too complex and still quite remote from their focus at the time, which was on clarifying the quality framework, training facilitators, and communicating the concepts to employees throughout state government. In other words, the statewide initiative was preoccupied with precisely the issues that had preoccupied the DVS earlier in its efforts. In retrospect, the state-level initiative was being offered data that would help it prepare for future challenges, but it did not have support for this sort of learning.

INTEGRATION AND ALIGNMENT

As the CQI activity was unfolding, it became increasingly clear that the central Coordination Team did not have the right composition. It had been designed to coordinate the activity of eight task forces, which it had done well. As we saw earlier, the work of the Stakeholder Task Force surfaced the absence of union representation, which led to the reconfiguration of the group as the CQI Guidance Committee. The primary work of the Guidance Committee was to facilitate integration across the three levels—strategy, governance, and daily operations.

After about two years experience with the CQI initiative, discussions began in earnest at the top leadership level about an entirely new way to organize agency operations. Historically, the agency was set up along functional lines. Each of the twenty divisions represented a different set of technical task or topic areas, about half of which were regulatory in nature and about half of which were focused on delivering public services. The alternative that surfaced represented a bold rethinking of agency operations around the concept of what was termed "Watershed Management." This would link daily operations to strategy and governance.

Under this concept, many of the different divisions would work in distinct geographic areas, characterized by different degrees of population concentration, natural watersheds, and other defining characteristics. It was proposed that the services of the agency be organized around these different common defining features, rather than around functional tasks.[5] In essence, this represented a restructuring similar to the service delivery teams, but at the level of the full agency. It meant that the organization would be aligning operations to match the natural phenomena for which it was responsible.

While the proposed reorganization of operations was highly consistent with the direction and focus of the CQI initiative, the discussions were swamped by a larger set of political considerations. The lead manager advocating for the concept of watershed management was one of the three associate directors of the agency, not the director of the agency. This was seen by the director as a threat to his power and he resisted. In response, the associate director made a bold and controversial move. He took the issue directly to the governor—going around his boss.

In response, the governor decided to split the agency into two separate organizations—a regulatory agency and a service delivery agency. The stated logic of the split was to ensure a more integrated approach to both important tasks. The manager who went to the governor became the head of the new regulatory agency and the former director remained in charge of the agency responsible for services.

In the split, the Quality Office was disbanded and the head of quality became the personnel director for the new regulatory agency. A majority of the facilitators were also in divisions that became part of the new regulatory agency, though many were also in the service operations. Neither organization continued CQI as an initiative, though both continued to form special teams and task forces that used the facilitators and followed the CQI process-improvement model.

THE STORY BEHIND THE INTEGRATION AND ALIGNMENT STORY

The Guidance Committee bonded and became a very effective group in terms of managing its agenda and feeling cohesive. It did not, however, fully manage the challenge of integration and alignment. For example, one of the associate directors was seen by many employees and managers as a dedicated champion of CQI. This manager served on the Guidance Committee and did an excellent job of carrying out ideas and pilot initiatives in her operations. However, this same manager ran into great resistance when trying to extend these ideas into the operations of other divisions.

In retrospect, there was not a mechanism established to link the Guidance Committee into to regular top-level decision-making operations. It was not sufficient to have some individuals serving on both groups. When the logical link was made to the very structure and operation of the entire agency, the splits among leaders proved more compelling than any vision of integrated operations. At the session where there was the most engaged dialogue on the concept of "Watershed Management" the key manager who ultimately led the split was absent.

At the next meeting, which was just a few weeks later, the governor had announced a major statewide downsizing initiative aimed at cutting the budget. When a top manager began to challenge elements of the definition of "Watershed Management" it triggered a discussion of whether this would just become a vehicle for cutting operations. By the end of this session, the entire concept was in a shambles—with no clear sense for CQI, Watershed Management, or even the entire agency.

Ultimately, this suggests that the learning process in organizations is vulnerable to political and power dynamics. The interesting challenge is to consider how to harness or redirect these energies. The challenge is to engage in what might almost be thought of as a form of organizational judo—taking disconnects as data and converting them into learning opportunities. Throughout this story, it is clear that the agency was resistant to using data on disconnects to better understand the divergence in the agency and how that divergence needed to be addressed. Instead, various opportunities for learning from disconnects were missed with repercussions felt throughout the length of the change initiative.

CONCLUSION

In comparison to most organizational change initiatives, the experiences at DVS featured many notable successes. In particular, a large amount of energy went into building the infrastructure for the change initiative:

- The initiative began with broad input from a cross-section of managers
- It featured a well-crafted vision and educational process
- It involved top leadership from the beginning
- The activity was centered on bottom-up innovation
- There was a well-developed set of process improvement methods, including the ARRIVE model—appropriate to the many different kinds of work taking place in the agency
- The initiative was staffed with well-trained facilitators
- A five-day facilitator institute had been established, with over one hundred facilitators training in the first two years of operations
- An integrated governance structure was established, involving five unions
- A common vision emerged around the entire realignment of the organization

These are powerful drivers for meeting the Bold Vision. In these respects, the story could have been told in such a way that others would want to "benchmark" one or more of the many innovations at DVS. In fact, many public agencies from this state and others did just that, as well as some private-sector organizations.

These successes alone do not help us to understand how the organization simultaneously was heading down what now looks like a slippery slope. It has required us to look beyond the surface and attempt to present the story behind the story. In the process, we saw the reality of the organization was that successes either masked tensions or created pressures that served to later undermine the learning process.

Examining the story behind the story can be troubling on many levels. We urge, however, that these stories not diminish the successes. Rather, we suspect that the reality of all success stories involves a more complicated tale if you look at what happens behind the scenes. We have sought to present the many positive elements of the case with full appreciation of the effort involved and the many successes along the way. At the same time, we have presented the "story behind the story." It is rare to be close enough to an initiative to see this story, yet to also be sufficiently separate from it to be able to share it with others.

In following this path, we have identified many key insights that were not fully evident as events were unfolding. The challenge posed by this story—which is, in many ways, part of the motivation for this book—is to be able to foster continuous learning in a way that is attentive to the story behind the story as it is unfolding. Our aim is to legitimize an approach to continuous learning and organizational change that can simultaneously value success in moving toward the Bold Vision but also deal with the Harsh Realities behind the scenes.

In part II of the book, we devote a chapter to each of the three elements of this Harsh Reality, the three Ds—disconnects, dilemmas, and divergence. In part III of the book, we bring the Bold Vision and Harsh Reality perspectives together and focus on their many interdependencies. While the ideas are presented in sequential chapters, the interrelationships are as important as the separate ideas.

However the ideas are engaged, the core thesis should be clear: learning cycles that take data, generate new knowledge, and then use this knowledge to take action are often powerful, wonderful, and essential. Undesirable issues of disconnects, dilemmas, and divergence are often complicated, painful, and also essential. Most important of all, the two are interdependent—accounting for many of the different types of learning that are found in organizations today. Appreciating disconnects, dilemmas, and divergence increases the capability of organizations to drive data, knowledge, and action. This increased capability reveals new disconnects and the interdependency deepens. Becoming a genuine learning organization is a journey that involves the appreciation of all forms of learning.

Taken together, we are describing a process in which disconnects are appreciated as the key to a learning dynamic that is essential for survival in a knowledge-driven economy. This is a fundamentally different mindset for most individuals and organizations. Ultimately, however, it is hard to imagine anything less. This is reality—so we have to deal with it—but it is a reality to be valued and appreciated.

Notes

1. The slippery slope argues that once some action is carried out it causes a second event that in turn can cause a sequence of events that lead to bad consequences. Lawyers are known for using the slippery slope argument to point out logical problems with a line of argument. Philosophers have long debated the validity or facility of slippery slope arguments. For example, see Douglas Walton, Slippery Slope Arguments (New York: Oxford University Press, 1992) or an article by Eugene Volokh and David Newman "In Defense of the Slippery Slope," *Legal Affairs* (March/June 2003). We are not trying to weigh into the debate so much as to use this phrase as a metaphor for people stepping off the edge of a slope and having a difficult time coming back up once headed down.

2. The classic text, Phillip Mirvis and David Berg, *Failures in Organizational Development and Change* (New York: John Wiley & Sons, 1977), is a notable exception. Our analysis here is presented in the same spirit—a constructive examination of initiatives that proved to be flawed in order to identify enduring lessons. For a recent chapter on learning from both successes and failures, see William H. Starbuck and Bo Hedberg, "How Organizations Learn from Successes and Failures," in *The Hand-*

book of Organizational Learning and Knowledge, ed. M. Dierkes, A. Antal, J. Child and I. Nonaka (Oxford, England: Oxford University Press, 2001).

3. As co-leads for this team we were uniquely able to observe the many learning dynamics. We were also direct participants in the change process, which must be considered by the reader in evaluating the various elements of this account. Note that this account of the story has been reviewed by the person who served as our key point of contact throughout the engagement.

4. Note that the fourth item on this list is from a parallel set of barriers that were brainstormed in addition to the fears. It is included here since it was discussed as a barrier and as a fear.

5. Note that we are being deliberately vague about the exact defining features in order to preserve the masking of the case.

4

Predictable Disconnects

L earning disconnects are pervasive. Oftentimes, disconnects—which we defined in chapter 1 as the gap between what was intended (the aim) and what actually occurred (the reality)—seem more common than learning "connections." Of course, there is a long history of organizational change experts surfacing disconnects in change initiatives during leadership retreats or through the use of focus groups. It is easy—perhaps too easy—for people to identify areas where the aims do not meet reality. The key question centers on whether this is an isolated activity or part of a larger strategy for organizational learning.

The development of a strategy begins with the fact that disconnects are not only easily observed, but also predictable. We are continually impressed by the capacity of people to predict accurately the many disconnects that will be encountered, *prior* to any major change initiative. For example, one goal of a police agency was to improve problem solving with community members around long-standing issues. The officers and sergeants at the meeting needed only a little prodding from us to predict the gaps that were likely to occur relevant to this new organizational strategy for improvement. These predictable disconnects can undermine the success of any change initiative and undermine other parts of the organization that depend on skills, knowledge, and capability. But again, predicting disconnects is not the same as learning from them and understanding them prior to taking action.

The core thesis of this chapter is that disconnects are not "good" or "bad." Disconnects are data. They can and should be recorded, analyzed for patterns, and addressed. Better still, they can be anticipated. The identification of disconnects can lead to a dialogue that can lead to shared knowledge of an issue or sets of issues. This can only occur when the gaps are not avoided, discounted, or feared. As noted by Peter Senge, the gap between vision and reality can lead to constructive tensions. These tensions, if harnessed properly, can facilitate the creative process.[1] The first step in leading to a more creative process is to identify and frame the disconnects that one typically finds in organizational settings in order to build shared understandings.[2]

MANY TYPES OF DISCONNECTS

There are many types of disconnects in learning systems—some minor and some cataclysmic. Sometimes disconnects are unintended and sometimes they are a product of intentional resistance to change.[3] Too often, as we have noted, they are greeted with inaction, blame, or "Band Aid" solutions—none of which are particularly constructive.[4]

We have selected what might be called a baker's dozen of particularly common and important disconnects to present as "data" in this chapter. These disconnects arise out of our experience with organizational learning initiatives in a wide range of public- and private-sector organizational initiatives. Indeed, disconnects are generalizable to most major change efforts that focus on people as a key source of competitive advantage. Many more disconnects could be listed, but what might also be termed our "dirty dozen" listed here should be sufficiently illustrative of the concept.[5] Most of these problems will be familiar, just by their labels alone.

Labels for Selected Disconnects in Learning Systems

- *If it ain't broke, don't fix it*
- *Do as I say, not as I do*
- *Ready, fire, aim*
- *The emperor's new clothes*
- *The train has left the station*
- *Dropping the baton*
- *The left hand doesn't care what the right hand is doing*
- *A mile wide and an inch deep*
- *All dressed up and no place to go*
- *You can't get there from here*
- *It doesn't take a weatherman to know which way the wind is blowing*
- *I've cut this board twice and it's still not long enough*
- *Flavor of the month*

In labeling these problems, we have deliberately chosen the common language of organizational life—where disconnects get labeled in ways that are ironic, humorous, or particularly telling.[6] Although these are serious matters, we suspect that a bit of levity is appropriate to open up discussion on these matters—especially in organizations where there are cultures of blame and inaction. Though the labels may seem self-evident, it is helpful to examine them in a bit more detail to highlight the dynamics of each in the context of learning systems.

Disconnect 1: If It Ain't Broke, Don't Fix It   Advocates of organizational learning systems frequently encounter this disconnect. In early stages of exploring the concept of organizational learning, some people will be engaged and enthusiastic, while others will be silent and even resistant. With further probing on the silence or resistance, the response is often the phrase we have highlighted: "If it ain't broke, don't fix it." Similar comments include, "Why now?" "Why change?" This defense of the status quo is most common where there is an intensified focus on learning in existing organizations (rather than at start-up operations).

This disconnect arises as people are beginning to gather data around what are proving to be the increasingly complicated implications of making a shift in favor of an organizational learning perspective. At this point there is a temptation to placate the critics and indicate that organizational learning will not involve a major shift in emphasis for the organization or they will be told that their concerns will be addressed at a later time. An alternate temptation, advocated by the reengineering community, is to silence these critics by turning the words against them. Here the new motto is "If it ain't broke, then break it." Either response—downplaying the potential impact of a learning initiative or discounting any value associated with existing operations—sets the stage for predictable disconnects.

In reality, there are always aspects of existing operations where constructive learning does already take place—where things are not "broke." There are also opportunities worthy of deeper exploration and there are almost certainly aspects of existing operations where things are "broken." Instead of opening up dialogue on such matters, this disconnect serves to shut down dialogue and action.

Disconnect 2: Do as I Say, Not as I Do   This disconnect, which is also known as not "walking the talk," is predicable whenever leaders make bold assertions about new learning initiatives, such as pronouncements that: "We are deeply committed to continuous learning" or "We are a learning organization" or "Continuous learning is at the core of our transformation strategy."

Too often, the statements are not made with attention to other concurrent business strategies or capability across levels of the organization. As a result, the leaders come across as insincere, disingenuous, or worse, as soon as a major cost-cutting initiative is announced or when unilateral leadership behaviors persist following the bold announcements.[7] Suddenly there is a gap between what was promised by leaders and what is actually experienced by the workforce.

To counteract this problem, learning initiatives are often accompanied by published lists of expected leadership behaviors—often with special training sessions on these behaviors. Unfortunately, the lists of behaviors and the training—sometimes derisively referred to as "management charm school"—can actually make matters worse. While potentially valuable, the lists and the training alone will rarely be sufficient to prevent the disconnects, which makes that gap between what was promised and what is experienced even more visible.

There is a related set of behaviors that come together in a sequence that includes the "hand on the shoulder," followed by the "run for cover," and then the disconnect best known for its technical abbreviation, "CYA." This sequence involves a task or action requirement for certain leaders (hence the "hand on the shoulder"), with an avoidance response ("run for cover"), and then an attempt to hide any evidence that action was expected ("CYA"). The net result is right back to not "walking the talk," but it may be harder to see.[8]

Disconnect 3: Ready, Fire, Aim
This disconnect involves making decisions with inadequate or incomplete data. Once a strategy and philosophy about organizational learning begins to emerge, pressure for action builds in the system. Staff professionals are handed policy and training mandates. They are in effect told, "now go do this." A problem can arise when people follow such orders. They are then proceeding to action without first constructing the necessary infrastructure for decision-making and coordinating the multitude of efforts that will be necessary to move forward.

Many stakeholders within the organization have interests that will be affected by an organizational learning initiative. In most organizations there are not well-defined ways to attend to these many stakeholder interests. Given the action-oriented nature of most organizational cultures, there is also not much patience for the time it takes to construct the needed support systems (such as a reorienting of the training staff to "just-in-time" needs assessment, targeted delivery of training modules, the facilitation of learning dialogue, and many other such capabilities). Nor is there much tolerance for the ambiguity that new decision-making structures create. Hence, top leadership is ready and they push staff to fire off new rounds of activities without the calibration or aim that can come with full stakeholder input and the appropriate supporting infrastructure. Time invested in the establishment of effective social infrastructure pays large dividends later on. Relying solely on existing mechanisms, which are usually tied to existing hierarchies and long-established ways of operating, can seriously constrain subsequent efforts—producing *"ready, fire, aim"* disconnects.

Disconnect 4: The Emperor's New Clothes
In certain respects, the concept of organizational learning is deceptive. It is often presented as inherently good—who would object to the idea of learning and developing your human resources? In fact, to take the concept seriously is to anticipate substantial contention, as the existing organizational culture is unfrozen. Conflict and resistance to learning principles and processes should be supported as central to the process of becoming a continuous learning organization. Typically, the opposite occurs.

People who challenge the activities associated with organizational learning are criticized for not being team players. Often the first people making the criticisms have a reputation for griping already—so the issues they surface are just disregarded as more negativism. When legitimate issues surfaced by individuals are disregarded, it sends a signal to everyone else. As a result, tensions among leaders at all levels regarding their level of commitment to a learning perspective are not voiced or addressed in concrete ways. This is especially common where the initiative is a pet project of a highly influential manager or leader.

In the absence of honest feedback through experimenting, testing out new ideas, and discussing differences, it is just like the story of the emperor and the tailor. The emperor was sold a bill of goods but no one raised the questions that would lead to closer inspection of the situation. Leaders who are attempting to create a learning organization are too often sold a bill of goods that all will go well, conflict will be minimal, and teamwork will increase. The focus is just on good things that can happen, without the concurrent willingness to detail all the painful issues that must be thought through when cascading a continuous learning system throughout the organization. At stake here, is an unrealistically positive framing of the issue that closes off any negative feedback that is quite essential to the initiative's learning, adapting, and growing.

Disconnect 5: The Train Has Left the Station

Some very large organizations maintain corporate universities that have a detailed course catalogue of offerings. In most organizations, it is common to have only a small core of regular offerings (such as new-employee orientation). Then, there will be successive waves of training on whatever topic is most pressing. This creates disconnects for employees who are not able to be part of a given wave of training. For them, the train has already left the station.

This problem is most common in new, start-up initiatives or for the launch of a new product. In these cases, there is often a great investment made in training the lead groups, but nothing comparable for successive groups of employees. The later groups are essentially being asked to jump on a moving train. The resolution is not that the same offering needs to be maintained indefinitely, but that the situation should be anticipated at the outset and the training adapted or adjusted over time to match the changing circumstance.

There is a related situation that might be labeled, "who will not be invited to the wedding?" This situation concerns who will be involved in initial decision-making about the scale, scope, and content of learning activities. Implementing and sustaining learning systems often brings together groups of people who do not usually interact with each other. Or, at least, it should. But this raises many complex issues around who is and who is not a legitimate representative for each set of stakeholders.

The process is not unlike sending invitations for a wedding or another fancy party—if you invite one person, then protocol dictates three others also be invited. And these are just threshold issues. After the invitation list is sorted out, then everyone has to deal with the reality that they are all going to be in a room together on a regular basis and they will be expected to generate wise decisions and to effectively coordinate often-conflicting aspects of the organizational-learning initiative. So here too, the train will have left the station around the governance of organizational learning—with some stakeholders on board and others not. This can lead to people resenting being left out of the process or to uniform decisions being made because of missing data inputs.[9]

Disconnect 6: Dropping the Baton   There is an old adage that a camel is a horse designed by a committee. This reflects the all-too-common negative experience that people have with decision-making processes and coordination efforts that are derived from team meetings. In fact, many people from a very early age are not provided with strong models for effective group decision-making. Students in school and children in families are too often given rewards for compliance rather than for participation.

As stakeholders come together under the auspices of new governance structures for organizational learning, there are countless disconnects that can arise around the decision-making processes. Sometimes, effective meeting procedures are not established—agendas are not set, interruptions are common, decisions are not clarified and recorded, due dates are not set, and so on.[10] The bottom line is that decisions critical to organizational learning are not made or are poorly made.

Even where meeting procedures are established, representatives may just go through the motions to finish a meeting, sidestepping difficult or controversial issues. Alternatively, the difficult or controversial issues are brought to the table, but not surfaced or addressed in a constructive fashion.[11] This may take the form of escalating conflicts, withdrawal of a key party, or neverending debate. Whether the sin is one of omission or commission, a breakdown in the decision-making process means that key individuals have dropped the baton supporting learning and training activities.

A breakdown in any of the procedures can lead to a bottleneck in the decision-making and coordination processes. The challenges are most complex where there are many stakeholders with highly divergent interests. However, even a small set of stakeholders with relatively common interests can get hung up with ineffective decision-making processes.

One lesson that has emerged with particular clarity from the literature on systems dynamics is that, in the absence of feedback, systems will spin out of control.[12] Dropping the baton in the governance of organizational-learning systems means that feedback is constrained and the learning systems are at risk of spinning out of control.

Disconnect 7: The Left Hand Doesn't Care What the Right Hand Is Doing   This disconnect involves incentives in organizations to conceal, shade, or otherwise misrepresent data on what is and is not happening with front-line operations. Too often, the people who are developing, delivering, and receiving training or otherwise learning are acting independent of, and sometimes, in opposition to, decisions that are experienced as mandates from above. For example, a corporate headquarters or division may start a major new program initiative on quality that includes mandated training for select leaders, followed by a training rollout for all organizational members. Sometimes, local facilities will go through the motions but minimize the degree to which the mandated training effort impacts daily operations and their own local training priorities. As a result, for example, it might be requested that intact work groups from a given area be trained together with their supervisor, but the reality might be piecemeal training, pulling a sample of people from different areas. At the extreme, plants and offices have been known to even distort data to demonstrate progress against such mandates.

The key point is that the actual behavior at the front lines is not driven by the same data and priorities driving action at higher levels.[13] To make matters worse, there are incentives to misrepresent data on what is actually happening on the ground.

A related concern involves what is indelicately termed, "running out of spit."[14] This occurs when senior leaders are called upon to provide briefings, updates, or justifications for what is happening on the front lines. Leaders will provide brief overview statements consistent with the original vision. When probed for more details, however, they quickly "run out of spit" and can't speak to the important details of what is taking place. This further feeds the downward spiral.

Disconnect 8: A Mile Wide and an Inch Deep   This disconnect involves knowledge generation that is so superficial or poorly timed so as to be useless. Organizational life is full of training mandates, which can trigger the expenditure of vast resources in order to hit established deadlines for training hundreds or thousands of people. The same is true of mandated benchmarking trips, with forced learning at a given time and with a mandated focus. In these cases, however, there may be a bias toward thinly spreading a given set of training resources across a target population. Sometimes referred to as "peanut-butter training," these thinly spread learning activities are rife with potential problems.

First, people may not need the training at that moment, but the resources are already spent when they do need the training a year or two later. For example, work groups may be given training in how to conduct effective team meetings, but may not have started meeting. By the time they do start, they have forgotten what they were taught. Second, where the training was delivered before there was a perceived need, the attempt to apply the principles will generate frustration and cynicism more often than positive results. Staying with the work group example, those groups that demonstrated initiative and did attempt to apply the principles would likely encounter a larger organization that is not supportive of their meeting efforts, which calls into question the original training. Third, some work areas and operations may need more or less detail, but the delivery is restricted to a uniform model. There are many other possible disconnects, all of which occur at the operational level, where knowledge is not matched to need or opportunity for application. Essentially, leaders are making assumptions about what is appropriate, but these assumptions are not based on data and are not connected to any feedback loops.

A corollary set of concerns exist around training that is "a mile deep and an inch wide." Here, deep technical expertise is built, but it exists in a separate "chimney" or "silo" that hampers the integration of the training with other aspects of the organization's operations. This is less problematic where the work tasks are not highly interdependent. Unfortunately, most work these days involves many interdependencies.

Fostering either "mile-wide" or "mile-deep" learning casts a long shadow over the delivery and impact of training.[15] Poorly informed choices along these lines lead to a misguided use of scarce resources, which then fuels suboptimal results and cynicism.

Disconnect 9: All Dressed Up and No Place to Go

Evaluations of training programs often lead to the impression that training has been successful. Many employees enjoy the opportunity to increase their knowledge base, to learn new tasks, or to improve skills. Consequently, at the end of a reasonably well-designed and well-delivered training program, there will be feedback that the training was worthwhile. The ultimate goal of training, though, is not that trainees like the experience or see it as useful, but that they actually use the knowledge and skills gained to improve effectiveness on the job.[16]

Regardless of the quality of the training program itself, there are a number of barriers that make it difficult for the aims or objectives of the training to be realized on the job. These barriers include, (1) companies often invest heavily in technical training but there is little attempt to understand how the skills can be effectively used on the job and what systems must be put in place to support the use of new skills, (2) supervisors do not see coaching and development as part of their job (usually due to day-to-day pressures) and therefore do not take the time to understand the training their employees are undergoing or take the steps necessary to support the continued development of new knowledge and skills, and (3) people are trained in new skills but managers stick to people with established competence.[17]

These are all disconnects relevant to the feedback system at the workplace level. Despite training having occurred, it is not utilized. In that sense, the effort associated with producing the output is not well harnessed—people are all dressed up with no place to go. The result is more than just a waste of effort. The image of training and the larger principles of organizational learning are compromised.

Disconnect 10: You Can't Get There from Here

This disconnect concerns the actual design and delivery of training and learning in front-line operations—the action of making learning a part of the daily operations, or as we highlight here, the failure to do so. Even where there is a clearly identified need for training and decisions that support learning efforts to address that need, there is no guarantee the training delivered will accomplish the intended purpose. In essence the design, materials, delivery, and other aspects of the training are not well matched to the training goals and objectives. There are many factors that can serve as barriers to "getting from here to there." Each of these is its own mini disconnect. Just focusing on training, we see that these include many familiar ways in which training falls short of what is hoped for it, such as (1) rather than engaging individuals in active learning, the training primarily consists of telling people what they should do; (2) providing concepts but not the tools to apply the concepts; (3) selecting trainers who do not have content credibility or who do not have delivery skills, which includes not training potential trainers to be effective; and (4) goals and objectives are not serving as a useful guide for the training design and delivery, leading to training that falls short of objectives or even training that produces opposite outcomes. Similar operational disconnects exist for other forms of front-line learning.

All of these situations lead to the same disconnect, in which effort and resources are expended in the form or actions but without the expected yield. These are all barriers to effective training and learning—each will keep a training program from being a driver for organizational learning. The situations all concern the critical task of developing the knowledge base or foundations of continuous learning throughout the organization to drive the change initiative.

Disconnect 11: It Doesn't Take a Weatherman to Know Which Way the Wind Is Blowing

When disconnects arise in the delivery of training or other learning efforts, they are usually highly visible. People quickly learn about poorly developed materials, "crash and burn" deliveries, low enrollments, poor facilities, and lack of support on the job for the use of new skills. Hence, it doesn't take a great deal of sophistication to know that there are problems with organizational-learning systems.

There are many consequences of this type of situation. First, training and related learning activities become an easy target for criticism and cynicism. Second, people who are working on efforts to address these problems have to worry about having their reputations tarnished. Indeed, the many disconnects almost become part of a self-fulfilling prophesy or a downward cycle, where they confirm the view that "an ill wind is blowing" and everyone "runs for cover," which then further undercuts the initiatives.

A related aim and reality gap is to "take risks, but don't fail." Like the rhetoric of learning, there is a constant rhetoric exhorting people to "take risks," "be bold," "think outside the box," and so on. Much harder, however, is to maintain that support when people demonstrate initiative and then stumble. They quickly see that it is important to do things that look like they are taking risks, but to ensure that it is not truly bold or risky. The complexities of this dance are endless, so long as blame is tied to an identified problem.

Disconnect 12: I've Cut This Board Twice and It's Still Not Long Enough

With this disconnect, learning initiatives are not working as planned and the response from the governance system is to push to stay on schedule or even to do more of what isn't working. For example, if team training is not leading to expected results with an initial pilot group, then exhort people to "do better" and run more people through the same program. The only suggestions for change might be that if a short lecture isn't getting the message across, try a longer lecture.

Instead of changing the learning activity that isn't working, the response is to push harder on the same model. This may stem from a lack of creativity or a limited scope of capability on the part of the people designing and delivering learning activities or it may derive from an unwillingness of leaders to take risks with new formats or constraints in funding for redevelopment or other factors. The reality, however, is that pushing harder on a flawed model assures limited results and further fuels cynicism and mistrust.

A closely related situation can be termed, "rearranging the deck chairs on the Titanic." In this case, the learning activities are not working as planned and instead of a fundamental redesign, the strategic level dictates that cosmetic changes be made and presented as significant improvements. This may look better than pushing harder on the same model, but at a fundamental level it is no different.

Disconnect 13: Flavor of the Month

An alternative approach to learning that is not working is to completely abandon one approach (for example, one pilot program) and substitute an alternative without any analysis of what is and is not actually taking place. Essentially, the baby is thrown out with the bath water and a new baby and bath is put in its place—with a similar unfortunate fate being likely in its future. There are many related terms for this disconnect. For example, in one large manufacturing organization they use the initials, "AFP." This stands for "Another Fine Program."

What are the dynamics that drive this disconnect? One of the most visible, centers on leadership turnover. Where managers rotate frequently for career advancement, there is a tendency to disregard the initiatives of your predecessor and to advance new initiatives that will have your stamp on them. But there is more here than just leadership turnover. The process of designing and launching an initiative, while challenging, is much easier than the process of implementing and sustaining an initiative. Moreover, the rewards generally go to the designers of new initiatives rather than the sustainers of these initiatives. Further, the risks of angry stakeholders, administrative problems, and worse, will all increase over time—absent a robust set of support systems. People may shake their heads in dismay as each new flavor of the month is announced, but can much else even be expected given the way most organizations operate?

A variation on "flavor of the month" involves what are termed "islands of success." These are pilot experiments—initiatives bounded by time or by a particular location—that are meant to be a safe way to try out new ideas. Unfortunately, there is a long history of what we call "successful failures"— experiments that were successful, but that failed to win wide support or acceptance. In fact, too often, it is the very success of these experiments that invites a combination of jealousy, fear, and other negative reactions that lead people to actively undermine the experiment.

If any of these disconnects were just an isolated problem they would not be so worrisome. Typically, however, they repeat over time and multiple disconnects may be present at the same time. The result is often a self-reinforcing downward spiral where learning is undercut and the capability for future learning deteriorates.

How can we break the downward cycle? The first step involves treating disconnects as data—without blame. The next step involves the organization and analysis of the data—to create knowledge. Only then is action, based on the data, appropriate.

INCIDENT, COINCIDENT, PATTERN

The first time a disconnect occurs, it is an isolated incident. The second time, it is a coincidence that may or may not have deeper implications. The third time, however, it is part of an emerging pattern that calls for analysis.[18]

Where the disconnect is an isolated event, an open, nonblaming investigation will often be sufficient to guide an effective response. These cases are what Dr. Deming refers to as "special causes"—where the problem is an independent, one-time occurrence or where a group of disconnects has a unique root cause.[19]

More often, however, disconnects are not isolated events but the product of multiple causal factors that will generate multiple gaps between aims and realities over time. These are what Deming refers to as "common causes." Trying to "solve" a common-cause problem with a one-time fix (as though it was a special-cause problem) is likely to make things worse, rather than better. Peter Senge echoed this same theme with his observation that "For every complex problem there is a simple solution, and it is wrong."[20]

The way that "data" cumulate to form patterns has long been the subject of study. This concept is central to the whole field of statistics and the analysis of variation. In order to systematically analyze variation, one has to first measure it in a reliable way and then to classify the data in a meaningful way. The process of measuring and classifying data allows trends to be examined over time and interpretations to be made as to what they mean for the organization. The shared knowledge from these interpretations of the data can then be used to do more root-cause analysis to drive effective action. This is the source for Deming's concepts of special and common causes. Table 4.1 lists a number of ways to classify disconnects, each of which is addressed following the table.

Level   First, disconnects can form patterns that cluster by *level*. There can be a clustering at the strategic level, at the level of governance and decision-making, or at the level of daily operations. It can even involve clusters around the linkages across levels.

TABLE 4.1. Classification of Patterns of Disconnects

Variables	Range of Ways to Classify Disconnects		
Level	Strategic level	Governance and decision-making level	Front-line operations level
Learning process	Data	Knowledge	Action
Content	Technical skills	Interpersonal skills	Process skills
Time	Increasing variability over time	Consistent variability over time	Decreasing variability over time
	Entrained cycles	Independent cycles	Disconnected or interfering cycles
Location	Work area Community	Facility/division Region	Organization Country
Intensity	Low intensity	Moderate intensity	High intensity

Disconnects at the strategic level typically involve top-level leaders. At this level, leaders struggle over how to frame and drive issues related to continuous learning. This includes whether or not to pursue continuous learning, how to set the stage for subsequent activities, and how to sustain progress. Here we find disconnects such as,

If it ain't broke, don't fix it
Do as I say, not as I do
Ready, fire, aim
The emperor's new clothes
Flavor of the month

Disconnects around governance and decision making involve people at all levels of an organization. While strategy frames the issues, the systems for governance and decision making move into the substance or content of the issues. A plan must be made to operationalize or make real what an organizational-learning orientation will "look like" in this particular organization. This operational strategy must consider choices such as what coordinating structures must be developed, what new policies and procedures are needed, what types of training need to be offered, and what support systems need to be created to sustain continuous learning.[21] Underlying issues of governance and decision-making are challenging, value-based concerns about who is legitimately part of the learning process. Here we find disconnects such as,

The train has left the station
Dropping the baton
The left hand doesn't care what the right hand is doing
I've cut this board twice and it's still not long enough

Disconnects at the daily operations level are perhaps the most visible indicators of the struggles to become a learning organization. It is usually readily apparent when an experimental pilot program is not given the resources it needs to be successful, or when training sessions are badly designed, or when training participants are unable to apply what they have learned to the job, or when challenges to the new organizational-learning initiative are met with silence rather than with dialogue. These types of disconnects can occur even where the strategy and principles are well articulated and key governance decisions have been directly addressed. Here we find disconnects such as,

> *A mile wide and an inch deep*
> *All dressed up and no place to go*
> *You can't get there from here*
> *It doesn't take a weatherman to know which way the wind is blowing*

Disconnects do not just occur at different levels within a system but cascade across levels. Once they start sprouting up across levels, people begin to run for cover. The issue here is feedback across levels. The strategic level needs feedback as to how the policies, procedures, and coordinating efforts at the governance level are matched with the goals and strategies that have been espoused by leaders. The governance system needs feedback as to how well the policies and governance structures are being diffused at the daily operations level. The people at the daily operations level need feedback as to whether the specific projects and training programs are supported by and consistent with the strategic direction. Thus, another way to categorize disconnects involves breakdowns across levels.

There can be Bold Visions about learning at each level and a series of disconnects will add up to Harsh Reality within a particular level or across levels. Identifying and examining how the patterns are relevant to a particular level can then lead to questions as to why those patterns are occurring at one level but not at another level.

Learning Process   In chapter 1, we presented the Bold Vision learning cycle involving data, knowledge, and action. Another way of classifying disconnects involves considering where they cluster along this cycle. Figure 4.1 illustrates the different stages where disconnects might occur. Of course, there can also be disconnects in how the whole cycle operates together. If we take disconnects that have been classified by level, we can further analyze them by the location on the learning cycle that is most relevant to the disconnect, which is presented in table 4.2—with the learning disconnects listed to highlight the two states in the cycle where the breakdown occurs. This type of interpretative analysis can focus any efforts to address the observable patterns.

Content   Disconnects can also form patterns based on the *content* of the learning involved. Learning activities in organizations can be broadly categorized as building technical capability, interpersonal/teamwork capability, and systems- or process-improvement capability. Each is associated with var-

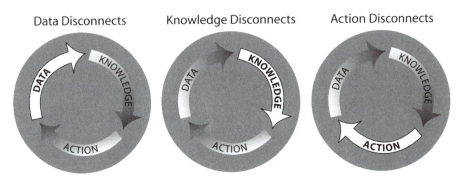

Figure 4.1 Potential for learning disconnects

ious intentional learning processes and each has its own range of predictable disconnects.

Technical capability involves learning about how to do a particular job. Such training might include an understanding of the mix of products and their features, the use of statistical quality-control principles, blueprint reading, computer-aided design/computer-aided manufacturing (CAD/CAM), safety practices, customer sales skills, apprenticeships, and countless other technical skills. These are all skills that are directly associated with doing a given task—whether in a store, office, or factory.

TABLE 4.2. Disconnects Classified by Level and Location on the Learning Cycle

Disconnects by Level	*Disconnects in the Learning Process*
Strategic Level	
If it ain't broke, don't fix it	Data → Knowledge
The emperor's new clothes	Data → Knowledge
Ready, fire, aim	Knowledge → Action
Do as I say, not as I do	Action → Data
Flavor of the month	Action → Data
Governance and Decision-Making Level	
The train has left the station	Data → Knowledge
Dropping the baton	Knowledge → Action
The left hand doesn't care what the right hand is doing	Knowledge → Action
I've cut this board twice and it's still not long enough	Knowledge → Action
Daily Operations Level	
It doesn't take a weatherman to know which way the wind is blowing	Data → Knowledge
A mile wide and an inch deep	Knowledge → Action
All dressed up and no place to go	Knowledge → Action
You can't get there from here	Action → Data

Common technical training disconnects involve providing technical training that is either too narrow or too broad in focus; building technical skills without sufficient opportunities to apply lessons learned; and failing to keep technical skills current. Here we also find disconnects such as a "mile deep and an inch wide." When there are breakdowns in these technical skills, the patterns show up as differences in project delays, machine breakdowns, and other gaps that depend on these skills being current and accessible.

Interpersonal capability taps into the social context and learning how to be effective with others in the organization. This can include public-speaking skills, listening skills, leadership skills, group-meeting skills, conflict-resolution skills, and other interpersonal or developmental skills. These skills are increasingly being woven in with work tasks—such as when work is done in teams—so the distinction between technical and interpersonal capability is one that is blurring.

Common interpersonal learning disconnects include leaders who insist on training in these skills, but who don't practice the behaviors themselves. This indicates a discounting of the interpersonal skills as "soft" and therefore not important, and a failure to focus the interpersonal-skills training around the specific workplace context. Here there are also disconnects such as not "walking the talk." These patterns accumulate and are manifest in a divergence of commitment, communications, and other interactive outcomes.

Systems- or process-improvement skills focus on how effective an individual or group is in seeing the bigger picture in the organization. This includes training in how to contribute to improving systems and processes within the organization, such as through the use of problem-solving models, process-improvement tools, and similar skills. Again, this set of skills is increasingly woven in with the work task, rather than being seen as an add-on activity.

Common systems- or process-improvement disconnects include training only some of the key stakeholders relevant to a given process-improvement tool (such as training work groups, but not midlevel managers), a lack of disciplined use and support for the process-improvement tools, and misuse of the process-improvement tools in service of political or power agendas. Here the problem centers around overall system capability or the failure to sustain a continuous improvement trajectory.

Time Disconnects will often form patterns that revolve around issues of *time*. A pattern of increasing disconnects, for example, can introduce instability in an organization, with many negative consequences. For example, a recent study of a sample of 196 U.S. aerospace facilities compared those reporting higher levels of budget or funding instability (a serious disconnect) with those reporting comparatively lower levels of instability. The facilities reporting higher levels of instability were also nearly twice as likely to report the loss of people with critical skills (43% of those reporting budget or funding instability versus 25% of those reporting less instability). The number of facilities reporting a loss of people with critical skills was also almost twice as high for facilities reporting another, related disconnect—instability due to technological change. Of those reporting higher levels of instability due to technological change, 48% reported a greater loss of people with critical skills in comparison to 26% reporting such loss among those with less instability from technological change.[22]

Therefore, patterns where aims do not meet reality are frequently best seen when visually displayed over time. That is the value of "run" charts used in statistical process control—where the incidence of defects is plotted across time and in relation to "acceptable" upward and lower boundaries on quality. In a study of skill retention, air force trainees were followed for four, eight, and twelve months on the job after training in a career field. The researchers found different patterns in how much breadth and depth of experiences or opportunities trainees were given to practice and improve upon the skills trained. The different patterns had implications for skill retention and improvement that could not be discussed until data was gathered, classified, and understood.[23]

Disconnects can vary by cycle time as well. There are many cycles in an organization—from multiyear product development cycles, to the cycle associated with learning new skills, to the sixty-second cycle on an auto assembly line. Research has highlighted the way these cycles can be entrained or functioning in sync with one another, as well as the ways things can get out of cycle.[24] Delays in product development cycles, for example, may result in the launch of a product that still has "bugs" to be worked out, which then undercuts the much shorter cycle times associated with product assembly.

Location   Disconnects can also form patterns that cluster by *location*. These patterns can be concentrated in a particular facility, corporation, region, or country—with the divergence similarly concentrated. Or, they can span multiple facilities, corporations, regions, or countries—with a broader scope for divergence. For example, in the early 1980s and again in the early 1990s, many companies and unions negotiated what are termed "two-tier" wage schemes as part of their adjustments to economic downturns. Under these agreements, wages for existing workers were maintained at current levels, but new workers were to be hired in at much lower starting wages. Over time, however, patterns of disconnects began to be evident as the highly paid, older workers were reluctant to share skills and knowledge with the lower-paid, new workers, while the growing numbers of workers being paid at the reduced wage were nonetheless developing skills and doing work that was comparable to the workers at the higher wage. Eventually, the tipping point came—as soon as there were a majority of lower-tier workers, the union leadership was voted out of office and new leaders were voted in with a mandate to reconcile the pay scales.[25] The associated divisive dynamics often far exceeded any short-term savings in wage costs that the employer may have enjoyed. This particular pattern of disconnects and subsequent af-

fect on morale would be limited, of course, to unionized locations that negotiated a two-tier wage scale. Many other such geographic or location-
specific patterns can be found.[26]

Intensity Finally, disconnects can form patterns that reflect differences in
intensity. For example, in the early 1980s scholars Thomas Kochan, Harry
Katz, and Robert McKersie observed a growing number of corporate vice
presidents for labor relations reporting reduced power and influence. As the
pattern began to take shape, it became clear that this was a high-stakes shift
in the profession toward what became known as the human resources model.
Their resulting research on this issue led to an award-winning book on *The
Transformation of American Industrial Relations*.[27] Not all patterns point to a
transformation in social institutions, but the range of intensity can certainly
reach this far. Disconnects that arise among systems for strategy typically
involve top-level leaders who struggle with challenges around how to frame
issues related to continuous learning. This includes whether or not to pursue continuous learning, how to set the stage for subsequent activities, and
how to sustain progress.

A SYSTEMS APPROACH TO LEARNING DISCONNECTS

Classifying disconnects in different ways reveals an underlying assumption
of our book—that the disconnects are connected. This may sound odd, but
it is the understanding of the patterns that help to point the way toward appropriate responses—rather than dealing with them in a piecemeal way. In
this sense, we are advocating taking a systemic or systems approach to
disconnects.

The concept of "systems thinking" pervades the theory and practice of
organizational learning.[28] It involves the assumption that all parts of an organization are connected, related, and interdependent. There are many types
of systems—natural systems, engineering systems, metaphorical systems,
and so on. Our focus here is on what can be termed the organizational-
learning system. An organizational-learning system, like all systems involves
processes of input, transformation, output, and feedback. Each process in-
fluences the others. Some consequences of viewing organizations from this
perspective are as follows: (1) issues, events, and incidents cannot be viewed
as isolated phenomena (they must be seen in relation to other issues, events,
and incidents); (2) behind every event is the potential for multiple rather
than single causation; and (3) one can not change any part of the system
without influencing other parts.[29]

The first stage in a systemic approach involves classification. In this chapter we have classified disconnects in many ways, including by level, location in the learning cycle, and others. A systems perspective recognizes that
there is unique information available at different levels of the organization
and that sharing this information is essential to planning and implementing

an organizational learning approach. The Bold Vision of sharing information and building capability must be considered in light of disconnects that will occur.[30]

It is the systemic nature of disconnects that makes them predictable. Organizations go through periods of slow evolution and more rapid revolutionary stages.[31] Individuals within the organization have experienced these shifts over time. So, when a new initiative like organizational learning is touted, organization members have a history of experiences to fall back on, to make sense of what is likely to occur as the new initiative unfolds.[32] In fact, as noted at the beginning of this chapter, we have found that organizational members are quite eager to discuss future changes that the organization will experience, what challenges the organization will face with those changes, and what disconnects are likely to surface between the aims of a new initiative and the realities of the organization. Experienced organization members are remarkably skilled at predicting the likely disconnects of each new initiative. This capacity hints at the deeper learning that is possible once patterns in the disconnects are valued. How valuable the patterns are to an organization will be seen to the extent that efforts are placed in gathering data, classifying the disconnects, and analyzing the patterns, to help drive action.

CONCLUDING COMMENTS

A wide range of disconnects have been identified and labeled in this chapter. These are readily identified and predictable. The issue in most cases is not whether the disconnect will occur, but how often and with what kind of intensity or implications. While some of the labels may be humorous or lighthearted, this reflects a deliberate use of humor when dealing with difficult thoughts and feelings. In fact, the many disconnects and how they are addressed are very serious business. Most serious is the way the disconnects cumulate.

Each individual disconnect widens the gap between the aim of an organizational-learning system and the reality that people experience. By accumulating over time, they set in motion downward, self-reinforcing cycles where learning becomes progressively more difficult for leaders, supervisors, employees, and training professionals and others.

The problem is not that aims and realities do not always meet—though they are, by nature, troubling; the real problem is that when disconnects are not expected, when they are not adequately addressed, or when they are ignored once recognized, the organizational-learning orientation is compromised.

Notes

1. Senge talks about the structural tension that can arise when the gap between vision and reality leads to people taking steps to achieve the vision. He contends

that closing the gap between vision and reality is the essence of the creative arts. He also notes how this tension can lead to someone being uncomfortable, which can lead to reducing the scope of the vision or to misrepresenting the state of the current reality. This dual perspective to gaps is similar to our perspective on disconnects. See Peter Senge, "Creating Desired Futures in a Global Economy," *Reflections The SoL Journal*, 5 (2004): 1–12.

2. Learning disconnects are particularly important. Learning is central to success in so many aspects of an organization's operations. Disconnects in learning systems undermine the success of the learning systems themselves and these disconnects undermine other parts of the organization that depend on skills, knowledge, and capability.

3. There is a long history in the organizational change literature focusing on what has been termed "resistance" to change. One of the first studies of resistance issues was by Lester Coch and John R. P. French, "Overcoming Resistance to Change," *Human Relations*, 1 (1948): 512–532. In addition, there is a literature that attempts to capture why change efforts fail, including work by John P. Kotter, "Leading Change: Why Transformational Efforts Fail," *Harvard Business Review*, 73 (1995): 59–67. For a conceptual treatment of power and politics, see Garth Morgan, *Images of Organizations* (Thousand Oaks, CA: Sage, 1997), chapter 6.

4. The tensions in the system can lead to a renewed emphasis on controlling the workplace or can lead to continued dialogue and actions to facilitate learning. See S. Sitkin, K. Sutcliffe, and R. Schroeder, "Distinguishing Control from Learning in Total Quality Management," *Academy of Management Review*, 19 (1994): 537–564, for a discussion of these issues.

5. Like the characters in the movie by this name, each disconnect has great value when it is properly harnessed.

6. The popular success of the Dilbert cartoon and the skewering of actions taken by management is an example of how events in organizations can be interpreted by those affected by the changes taking place in organizations. See www.dilbert.com for some comic examples.

7. See W. Edwards Deming, *Out of the Crisis* (Cambridge, MA: MIT Center for Advanced Engineering Study, 1986) for a discussion of fueling fear in organizational systems.

8. Thanks to Roger Komer for linking together this common sequence of disconnects.

9. The classic text by Victor Harold Vroom and Phillip W. Yetten, *Leadership and Decision-making* (Pittsburgh: University Pittsburgh Press), presents a decision-making model that distinguishes among autocratic, consultative, and group decision-making processes based on these three dimensions—expertise, timeliness, and acceptance. Based on this model, most governance decisions on organizational learning are conceptualized as a group decision making process but often end up as a consultative process, where top management can veto suggestions or planned efforts at the governance level.

10. See Peter Scholtes, *The Team Handbook* (Madison, WI: Joiner Associates, 1988), for a discussion of problems that can arise in project team settings and strategies for minimizing these problems of team organization and team initiation.

11. For a discussion of forcing and fostering strategies during negotiations between group members see Richard Walton, Joel Cutcher-Gershenfeld, and Robert McKersie, *Strategic Negotiations: A Theory of Change in Labor-Management Relation* (Boston: Harvard Business School Press, 1994).

12. See Jay Forrester, *Principles of Systems,* 2nd ed. (Cambridge, MA: Productivity Press, 1968), for a discussion of the role of feedback loops and systems dynamics.

13. See Robert S. Kaplan and David P. Norton, *The Balanced Scorecard—Translating Strategy into Action,* (Boston: Harvard Business School Press, 1996) for a discussion of measurement systems that are desirable to senior executives that balance both financial and operational measures and is consistent with continuous-improvement strategies.

14. Thanks to Roger Komer for this formulation of a common disconnect.

15. See Irwin L. Goldstein and J. Kevin Ford, *Training in Organizations,* 4th ed. (Belmont, CA: Wadsworth, 2002), for a discussion of the importance of training needs assessment for targeted training design and delivery.

16. See a recent study by George M. Alliger, Scott I. Tannenbaum, Winston Bennett, Holly Traver, and Allison Shotland, "A Meta-Analysis of the Relations among Training Criteria," *Personnel Psychology*, 50 (1997): 341–358 in which they found trainee reactions of how much they enjoyed training were not correlated to how much they had learned in the program or whether they changed their behavior once on the job.

17. These issues are part of the "transfer of training" literature. For reviews of the research literature on transfer see Timothy P. Baldwin and J. Kevin Ford, "Transfer of Training: A Review and Directions for Future Research," *Personnel Psychology*, 41 (1988): 63–105; and J. Kevin Ford and Daniel Weissbein, "Transfer of Training: An Updated Review and Analysis," *Performance Improvement Quarterly*, 10 (1997): 22–41.

18. Thanks to Roger Komer for this simple phrase describing a constructive approach to disconnects.

19. In these cases, the Bold Vision model is set in motion—treating the disconnect as data from which knowledge must be generated and action taken—a process developed in more detail in chapter 7.

20. Peter Senge, *The Fifth Discipline: The Art and Practice of the Learning Organization* (New York: Doubleday, 1990).

21. Examples of choices made at the country level regarding learning strategies can be seen in the book by Robert E. Cole, *Strategies for Learning: Small Group Activities in American, Japanese, and Swedish Industry* (Berkeley: University of California Press, 1989).

22. Joel Cutcher-Gershenfeld, Betty Barrett, Eric Rebintisch, Thomas Kochan, and Robert Scott, "Developing a 21st Century Aerospace Workforce" (Policy White Paper, submitted to Human Capital/Workforce Task Force, the U.S. Commission on the Future of the Aerospace Industry, 2001).

23. J. Kevin Ford, Miguel Quiñones, Douglas Sego, and Joann Sorra, "Factors Affecting the Opportunity to Perform Trained Tasks on the Job," *Personnel Psychology*, 45 (1992): 511–527. Also see Timothy P. Baldwin and J. Kevin Ford, "Transfer of Training: A Review and Directions for Future Research. *Personnel Psychology*, 41 (1988): 63–105 for a discussion of skill retention curves.

24. Joseph E. McGrath and Nancy Rotchford, "Time and Behavior in Organizations," *Research in Organizational Behavior*, 5 (1983): 57–101; Joseph E. McGrath and J. R. Kelley, "Time and Human Interactions: Towards a Social Psychology of Time," (New York: Guilford Press (1986); and Deborah G. Ancona and Chee Leong Chong, "Cycles and Synchrony: The Temporal Role of Context in Team Behavior," (Working paper Sloan School of Management, WP 4066-99, 1999).

25. W. Chan Kim and Renee Mauborgne ("Tipping point leadership," April 2003, *Harvard Business Review* 81: 60–68) discuss tipping-point leadership relevant to effective policing where "once the beliefs and energies of a critical mass of people are engaged, conversion to a new idea will spread like an epidemic."

26. See, for example, Daniel J. B. Mitchell, "Shifting Norms in Wage Determination," *Brookings Papers on Economic Activity*, 2 (1985): 575–608.

27. Kochan, Thomas, Harry Katz, and Robert McKersie, *The Transformation of American Industrial Relations* (New York: Basic Books, 1984).

28. This linkage of systems thinking and organizational learning has been articulated by Peter Senge. See also Joel Cutcher-Gershenfeld, et al., *Knowledge-Driven Work: Unexpected Lessons from Japanese and U.S. Work Practices* (New York: Oxford University Press, 1998); and J. Kevin Ford, The Fifth Discipline."Organizational Change and Development: Fundamental Principles, Core Dilemmas, and Leadership Challenges in the Move to Community Policing Strategy," In *The Move to Community Policing: Making Change Happen*, ed. M. Morash and J. Kevin Ford (Thousand Oaks, CA: Sage, 2002), 251–258.

29. For a discussion of characteristics of systems thinking in management, see J. Gharadjedaghi, *Systems Thinking: Managing Chaos and Complexity* (Boston, MA: Butterworth-Heinemann, 1999). For a discussion of systems thinking in organizational change see J. Kevin Ford, "Organizational Development," in *Intervention Resource Guide*, ed. D. G. Langdon, K. S. Whiteside, and M. M. McKenna (San Francisco, CA: Jossey-Bass, 1999), 251–258.

30. The use of the words "systems" and "levels" is deliberately mixed here. There are systems for strategy, governance, and daily operations if we define a system as containing four inter-dependent elements: inputs, processes, outputs, and feedback. Yet, there are also workplace systems for learning, communications, rewards, information, and so on—all of which involve language around systems within systems. Strategy, governance, and daily operations can also be thought of as levels, which is a cleaner terminology. The concept of levels also has connotations of strata that are not interconnected. In fact, this is precisely the type of disconnect that concerns us. It is also, however, descriptive of reality in most organizations. We will, therefore, continue to use both concepts—systems and levels—when discussing issues of strategy, governance, or daily operations, with the choice of terms reflecting the connotation that we most want to suggest. For a classic text on organizations as systems see Daniel Katz and Robert L. Kahn, *The Social Psychology of Organizations*, 2nd ed. (New York: John Wiley, 1978).

31. A number of researchers have examined the changes organizations undergo over time including Connie J. Gersick, "Revolutionary Change Theories: A Multivariate Exploration of the Punctuated Equilibrium Paradigm," *Academy of Management Review*, 16 (1991): 10–36; Danny Miller and Peter H. Friesen, *Organizations: A quantum view.* (Englewood Cliffs, NJ: Prentice Hall, 1984) and L. E. Greiner, "Evolution and Revolution as Organizations Grow," *Harvard Business Review* (August 1972). See also a book by J. A. C. Baum and J. V. Singh, *The Evolutionary Dynamics of Organizations* (New York: Oxford University Press, 1994), which explores organizational change and pattern using the analogy of organic evolution from the biological sciences.

32. This sensemaking aspect of organizational members engaged in an organizational change initiative has been discussed by Rhonda K. Reger, Loren T. Gustafson, Samuel M. DeMarie, and John V. Mullane, "Reframing the Organization: Why Im-

plementing Total Quality Is Easier Said Than Done," *Academy of Management Review*, 19 (1994): 565–584; Karl E. Weick and Robert E. Quinn, "Organizational Change and Development," in *Annual Review of Psychology*, eds. J. T. Spence, J. M. Darley and D. J. Foss, 50 (Palo Alto, CA: Annual Reviews, 1990): 361–386. For a more general treatment of issues of sensemaking, see Karl E. Weick, *Sensemaking in Organizations* (Thousand Oaks, CA: Sage, 1995).

5

Enduring Dilemmas

N ew learning initiatives will, invariably, surface a flurry of disconnects. These are predicable and they are confusing. It is tempting to treat each disconnect as a special event—a fire to be fought—while continuing to push for the Bold Vision. Yet, the disconnects are persistent. They are not isolated special events. Indeed, because they have underlying common causes, they are inevitable and predicable.

The ongoing struggle between the Bold Vision and Harsh Realities can leave any leader feeling battered and bewildered. What is more, there remains pressure in the system for enhanced knowledge and skill capabilities. This is key to sustainable competitive advantage and enhanced individual opportunity.

In chapter 4, we made the case that individual disconnects are surface-level symptoms that have only limited value for understanding the core issues which drive an effective learning system. We urged a focus not on the disconnects, but on the patterns of disconnects. The patterns can be classified by a number of factors such as level, time, or intensity. These patterns have more value in pointing to issues at a deeper level, building an appreciation for the learning that is possible from the Harsh Realities.

Seeing the patterns in the disconnects is necessary, but not sufficient to ensure effective organizational-learning systems. Underlying an analysis of the patterns is a deeper level of understanding of what are often termed organizational dilemmas.[1] The underlying dilemmas help us to see root causes—the central insights or knowledge most needed to guide action.[2]

Identifying or "naming" the dilemma doesn't make it any less of a challenge. It does, however, mean that you are seeing the learning challenge for what it is. There is generally a sense of relief and recognition that comes with naming the dilemma, as well as a sense of intimidation and fear for knowing that hard choices are unavoidable.

For example, a disconnect may surface in the form of people stating "if it ain't broke, don't fix it." This looks like direct resistance to the learning intervention—an unwillingness by some individuals to accept or embrace change. But what is the appropriate response? Is this a situation where no change is needed—where it really is better to leave things alone? Should there be efforts to assemble data confirming that things really are "broke," which would then presumably warrant action? Should we better identify the benefits that will come from "fixing" things? Or, should action be taken to directly challenge the mindset that is unwilling to abandon the status quo? The appropriate responses will vary based on various circumstances.

Staying with the example, determining the appropriate response really involves finding where people are "stuck" in their thinking or action. If people will acknowledge that some things are "broke" and that "fixing" them may bring some benefits, then continued resistance to change may suggest a deeper dilemma. The underlying dilemma may, for example, have to do with the time it takes to build learning capability as compared to the time it takes to implement a given business strategy. Later in the chapter, we refer to this as the "Short-Term/Long-Term Dilemma." If individuals and groups are accountable for successful strategy implementation and, if learning capability takes longer or draws resources away from short-term success, they may say "it ain't broke," when they really mean "I don't want to know about how badly things are broke because what I learn will pull me away from immediate task accomplishment." Surfacing the underlying dilemmas around the cycle times for strategy implementation and learning capability doesn't make the dilemma any less problematic, but at least it is visible.[3] At least the right issue is on the table for discussion.

As we will see, there are both effective and ineffective ways to deal with dilemmas. But even before considering how they are addressed, the key point is that they can't be ignored. If the dilemmas are not surfaced or incompletely addressed, the likelihood is that disconnects will continue to emerge in various patterns and that learning systems will deteriorate.

DILEMMAS DEFINED

Encountering dilemmas is inherent in the movement toward becoming a learning organization. A dilemma consists of a choice where each alternative has both advantages and disadvantages. We formally define a dilemma as having four elements:

1. no one alternative is clearly superior;
2. each option involves significant trade-offs;
3. any choice will have irreversible consequences; and
4. action is required.

Although dilemmas are often described in the management literature and by practitioners, they are rarely explicitly defined.[4] We have formulated this definition because it is helpful in recognizing a dilemma and provides insights into how to then address it.

The first part of the definition is that a dilemma involves choices where no one alternative is clearly superior. If there is a clear choice, then there is no dilemma. Sometimes, a choice seems clear to some, but not to others. The situation will only be experienced as a dilemma by people who are torn by what they see as alternative choices. Thus, dilemmas are not always readily apparent and they can be experienced at the individual, group, or organizational level—depending on the degree to which there is shared awareness and understanding of the situation.

For example, a supervisor who fails to rotate workers once they have been cross-trained may not see this as a dilemma—daily work pressures may be intense and the supervisor knows that rotating workers may not be an acceptable reason for lower quality or reduced productivity. At a higher level, however, the implications of not doing the rotation may be a loss of flexibility and a limit on other activities that depend on this additional front-line capability. If there is also an awareness of the daily quality and productivity pressures at this higher level, then the dilemma will be experienced here. If the broader importance of flexibility is communicated to the front-line supervisors, then the dilemma can become shared at that level as well. The problem is no less challenging, but at least it is visible, as both levels and choices made will be informed by this reality—there is less risk of the supervisor concealing the problem or of the executives blindly insisting on forced job rotation. Naming a dilemma makes it visible, so that one can understand choices must be made—that there is no single, correct, best choice.

Second, a dilemma is characterized by significant trade-offs. Trade-offs involve situations where making one choice will limit or constrain alternative choices—these are cases where it is not possible to, as they say, have your cake and eat it too. Again, if one alternative does not have any associated trade-offs or drawbacks then it is not a dilemma. This does not mean that trade-offs or drawbacks might not be discovered at a later date—bringing the realization that there was actually a dilemma being faced. In the absence of this awareness, however, it will not be experienced as a dilemma. Also, there may not be consensus in a group or organization that trade-offs need to be made or there may be wide differences of opinion regarding how to value the alternative choices. In these cases some people will experience more of a dilemma and others less so. Sometimes, it can take a series of disconnects before all parties become aware that they are making trade-offs and hence facing underlying dilemmas.

Third, dilemmas involve irreversible consequences. If subsequent events and decisions would proceed unaffected regardless of the decisions made, then there is no dilemma. That is, there are some decisions that involve alternatives in which no one choice is superior and where the choices involve trade-offs, but there is no dilemma because the consequences are minor or easily reversible. Consequences are significant either because they have a very deep effect on some or many people or because they have a broad effect on many people. Consequences are irreversible where a subsequent change in the decision is either not possible or very complicated. Often, some people will experience a situation as involving what they perceive as significant, irreversible decisions, while others will perceive it as having only a minor impact. In time, however, if it was a dilemma, the significance and the irreversibility will become evident.[5]

The final part of the definition is that action is required. If no action is required, then it is not a dilemma. Thus, all dilemmas have a measure of urgency about them. If they are ignored, they don't go away and they often become more accute.

Underlying all four elements of a dilemma is a combined reality that is filled with both uncertainty and opportunity. There is uncertainty about what to do and what will happen subsequently. There is opportunity in that some choices can truly open up new possibilities.

This way of defining a dilemma focuses on what might be called dilemmas in action—the utilization of learning from dilemmas to drive improvement efforts or to guide learning and action. There is a long history of seeing dilemmas in this way. For example, the ancient Greek tragedies each have a dilemma at the core of the play, a dilemma designed to prompt reflection and deepen understanding. In a field such as medical ethics, the dialogue is premised on a number of challenging dilemmas, such as how to value two lives when only one can be saved. Indeed, the entire discipline of philosophy concerns itself with a wide range of moral dilemmas. In the business field, nearly all of the teaching cases developed by the Harvard Business School are centered on a core dilemma facing a business executive.[6]

In the case of movement toward becoming a learning organization, the four elements of a dilemma become evident as a series of choice points or pivotal events.[7] These events are pivotal in that the future course of the learning initiative is, in effect, on the table. The way the four elements of the dilemmas are addressed is critical since the particular choices have implications for subsequent efforts. Even failing to act relevant to one of the elements of a dilemma represents a "choice" with consequences. Many times in the case discussed in chapter 3, the top leadership had opportunities to take actions relevant to a dilemma but failed to do so, leading the organization further down the slippery slope. Thus, dilemmas are important because they involve choices among alternatives, which involve tradeoffs, and these choices are both important and irreversible. While it is important to anticipate dilemmas, organizational learning begins by taking the time to reflect and surface lessons from past events and choices.

LINKING DILEMMAS TO DISCONNECTS

A given dilemma will often be associated with many disconnects. Typically organizations experience these events on a piecemeal basis. As we noted earlier, organization leaders and training experts may come to experience a continual sequence of "fires" to be fought. As a result, movement toward organizational learning is often hectic, fragmented, and fraught with frustration. Individual careers and organizational fortunes are often at stake in this complex and confusing process, increasing the stakes and often constraining a willingness to take risks. In the absence of a coherent framework for understanding the many disconnects, each becomes a factor driving organizations to adopt piecemeal solutions. These may be criticized as "flavor of the month" programs, but they make perfect sense when the focus is only on aggressively addressing the gaps between the vision and the reality.

An extended example of the interplay between disconnects and underlying dilemmas might be helpful to distinguish the concepts. Many organizations are experiencing pressure to establish team-based manufacturing or service-delivery teams in their existing operations. The complex issues associated with movement toward teams are a source of tension for many stakeholders within an organization. Line managers will experience tension over maintaining production or service while increasing training hours for work groups. Controllers will experience tensions over the need to fund such time-intensive learning activities. In unionized settings, union leaders will experience tensions over the selection of workers to be trained and the way seniority-based contractual rights for job movement can undermine team stability. First-line supervisors will experience tension over the overall political implications of the initiative, which they will interpret as a threat to their job security. These are just some of the tensions that a team-training initiative will surface for these and other stakeholder groups.

In this example, many potential disconnects are predictable given these tensions. These include problems of releasing workers from their jobs for training, of training requirements that exceed available funds, and of conflict between elected union stewards and elected union team leaders over the relative priority given to seniority versus team stability. They also include problems of the fear and paralysis that keeps supervisors from becoming effective team coaches and teams that learn more about running their part of the operation but aren't given responsibility and authority commensurate to their new capability. This emerging pattern of disconnects risks increased cynicism and divergence in the way the team model operates.

Underlying the tensions and disconnects is a core dilemma that any organization exploring team training in an existing factory or office must face. This is a dilemma involving a choice between a focus on current operations versus future development, which we refer to as the "Learning Accomplishment/Task Accomplishment Dilemma." This is a dilemma because no one option is clearly superior. Certainly, immediate production or service tasks can not be ignored—this provides the cash flow or task accomplishments necessary to sustain the organization. At the same time, a focus on learning accomplishments represents the future viability of the organization.

The team training case is a genuine dilemma. First, there are real choices to be made, such as who is trained, at what time, and with what degree of intensity. Second, there are tradeoffs among the options. Training large numbers of workers quickly has the advantage of enabling organizational development, while training fewer employees over a longer period of time is less disruptive of operations. Third, any choices about these issues will be significant and irreversible in some important ways. For example, the impetus and initial enthusiasm for team training may dissipate if the training process takes a long time to be completed throughout the organization. This can lead to skepticism about the viability of other large-scale training initiatives. On the other hand, if the training is intensive and critical deadlines are missed, the viability of the operations will be called into question when future training initiatives are contemplated.

Understanding that there is an underlying dilemma doesn't make the choices any easier. In fact, fully surfacing the dilemma may make the decision-making process more complicated and more difficult. On the other hand, we believe making dilemmas visible to key stakeholder groups in the organization can lead to more honest and creative thinking around the dilemma. In this way, options beyond the simple knee-jerk reaction of picking one alternative over the other, may be discovered and acted upon.

An illustrative example of making dilemmas visible so that more effective decisions can be made comes from the work of Charles Hampden-Turner.[8] He poses a classic dilemma of whether to centralize or decentralize functions (in fact this is one of the dilemmas we highlight in our list of learning dilemmas below). As seen in figure 5.1, Turner places the two alternatives or "horns of the dilemma" onto two axes to make a 90-degree angle. The space between the two axes shows the potential for alternative perspectives rather than for simply choosing one alternative (for example, centralization) over the other (for example, decentralization). Instead the two

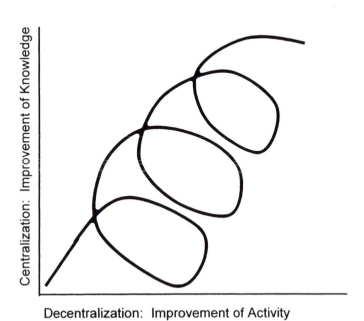

Figure 5.1 Charting the centralization and decentralization dilemma (Source: Trompenaars and Hampden-Turner, 2002)

alternatives are seen as inevitably linked together. The helical progression shown in figure 5.1 illustrates Turner's view, which is that well-led organizations will come to see that activities can become more and more decentralized and at the same time become better monitored or centralized. The key breakthrough is the shared understanding that can emerge by reframing the issue to one of centralized information on decentralized activities. In this way, over time, the organization can expand its activities (decentralization) and at the same time build systems to improve organizational knowledge of those activities, so as to build in feedback loops for continual learning and organizational improvement. We contend that this shift in "mindset" regarding organizational dilemmas that Turner discusses is a critical one when considering the learning dilemmas we identify and discuss below.

DILEMMAS ACROSS LEVELS

Just as disconnects can be found across levels, different dilemmas are also particularly salient at different levels. Our focus here is on three levels: (1) Strategy, (2) Governance/Decision Making, and (3) Workplace Operations. In each case, the dilemmas are manifest as disconnects, which are usually visible through pivotal events. We have selected two key dilemmas for each level, which are presented in table 5.1. All of these dilemmas should be quite familiar—they are commonly found at the root of many disconnects in learning systems.[9]

When discussing dilemmas in levels, we must also remember that they arise in context. As we noted in chapter 4, disconnects are embedded within organizational systems, with every system thought of as having four elements: inputs, processes, outputs, and feedback. Consequently, dilemmas also arise or must be considered in relation to organizational systems. For example, an irreversible and significant choice might arise around the inputs of a training program—with a dilemma over whether to "cream" applicants to ensure program success or accept all applicants and reach more people. Dilemmas can also arise across subsystems, such as the dilemma between long-term investment, which involves systems at the strategic level, and maintaining daily production or delivery of services, which involves systems at the daily workplace-operations level.

STRATEGIC DILEMMAS

The first set of dilemmas organizations face involves the development of an organizational culture or philosophy centered on learning and the linkage or alignment with business or organizational strategy. Training and learning strategy and philosophy can be defined as the stated and unstated purpose and aims for training and learning in the organization, as well as the principles guiding these activities. Similarly, the business strategy can be de-

TABLE **5.1** Selected Enduring Dilemmas, by Level

Strategy Level

Short-Term/Long-Term Dilemma: The cycle time and activities associated with building a learning culture typically exceed the cycle time for formulating and implementing business strategies, creating constant dilemmas around integrating learning capability and business strategy.

Tangible/Intangible Dilemma: Investment in "human capital" is essential for learning strategies, but such investments involve intangibles, so it is impossible to fully calculate the return on the investment. This encourages a bias toward more tangible investments where returns can be calculated, yet the tangibles are interdependent and essential for success.

Governance/Decision-Making Level

Centralization/Decentralization Dilemma: Whenever decision-making is highly centralized the lack of innovation/adaptation can create pressure to decentralize; whenever it is highly decentralized, the increasing variation can create pressure to centralize; whenever it is partly centralized and partly decentralized there can be tension around the mix.

Direction/Empowerment Dilemma: Unilateral and other more directive modes of decision-making provide clear guidance and directly utilize leadership knowledge, but without full benefit of front-line and middle-level input or commitment; participative, consensus, and other more inclusive modes of decision-making provide for increased input and ownership, but may be cumbersome, time consuming, and suboptimal.

Workplace Operations Level

Learning Achievement/Task Accomplishment Dilemma: When you are accomplishing a task, there are limits on your learning; when you are learning there are limits on your task accomplishment. Both are important and there is a tension between the operating pressures and learning opportunities.

Competition/Cooperation Dilemma: Fostering internal competition energizes individuals and groups, but may lead to suboptimization; fostering internal cooperation emphasizes common interests but may lead to complacency or incomplete attention to conflicting interests.

---

fined as the source of competitive advantage and desired outcomes that guide choices around investment, growth, and adjustment. We use the word "culture" here along the lines developed by Ed Schein, which emphasizes not just the visible "artifacts" or even the written mission statements and other policies and principles, but also the underlying operation "assumptions." These underlying assumptions are not always visible, but they are what guide behavior and are uniquely characteristic of the culture.[10] The two key dilemmas relevant to the strategy level are presented as choice points, which are often visible as pivotal events that can be planned or that can emerge in the face of disconnects.

The Short-Term/Long-Term Dilemma

The first set of choice points centers on the alignment of learning activities relative to business or organizational strategies. The dilemma has to do in part with the relative clarity, specificity, and time horizon for the business strategy and in part with the scale, scope, and time horizon of the culture change. Too often, the business time horizon is much shorter than the culture-change time horizon. This creates great tension.

The cycle time for implementing business strategy is usually measured in months and quarters, while the cycle time for building learning capability often extends over multiple annual reviews. Although the two are intimately interrelated, there are aspects of the business strategy that will come to fruition more quickly, which puts the learning initiative at risk. Most business strategies incorporate long-term planning horizons, such as a five-year plan, but the primary focus is on the achievement of quarterly targets. Indeed, business strategies can be reinforced or undercut based on monthly performance results. By contrast, the time horizon for changing an organization's culture to one centered on learning is at least five years and can extend quite a bit longer. The dilemma arises over which planning horizon should have primacy.

A short-term planning horizon will lead to constant disconnects and compromises in the learning initiatives. A long-term planning horizon will allow for a short-term fall off in performance while capability is being built, but the penalties associated with missed performance objectives may include the abandonment of the long-term plan. Again, this is a classic dilemma for which there is no easy solution.

The tension is mitigated to some degree, when the business strategy is clear and specific or when there is a life cycle orientation.[11] At least then it will be easier to see where the strategy is aligned with some learning activities and problematic for others. Where the business strategy is less specific or clear, then there is room for a broader view of learning, but it is harder to link to the business strategy. Similarly, where the objectives for changing the learning culture have a clearly defined scale and scope, and a realistic time horizon, it is easier to trace lines with the business strategy. At the heart of this dilemma is the reality that alignment between learning initiatives and business strategies represent an increased focus in some directions, but also create vulnerabilities due to the lack of focus in other directions.

For example, the newly created auto components company, Visteon (formerly the component parts plants of the Ford Motor Company), has articulated a clear strategy based on delivering integrated component systems, such as integrated vehicle interiors, with innovative features, such as voice-activated controls. Based on this strategy, learning how to combine components and sell integrated systems will be highly valued. Learning how to optimize efficiency within a single component plant will receive lip service but not enthusiastic support. If the market for cars and trucks remains strong, this focus on increased responsibility for product design and innovation holds great promise. If, however, there is a drop in demand, the focus may shift in favor of individual component costs and the reduced learning on this dimension will then compromise the basic business strategy.

If the strategy were less specific, such as a focus on being the best automotive components producer in the world, it would be more likely that many types of learning would be valued. At the same time, however, it would be harder to demonstrate which were best serving the business strategy. Under this second scenario, the learning that is linked to the strongest champion is more likely to prevail, which may or may not be optimal.

This dilemma can also be found in the public sector, where the annual budget cycle and various election cycles impose time horizons that are again shorter than those associated with learning initiatives. Recognizing these dilemmas doesn't make resolution any easier, but it at least clarifies the nature of the challenge.

The Tangible/Intangible Dilemma

Investment in intellectual capital is not the same as investment in capital equipment. Intellectual capital, which includes the established knowledge, skills, and capabilities of the people associated with a given organization, is simultaneously more fragile and more robust than physical capital. It is more fragile in that it depends on voluntary effort and even commitment—intangibles. It is more robust in that it is not necessarily geographically or functionally bound—it can be more adaptable.

Intellectual capital behaves differently than physical capital in other ways as well. For example, such investments can appreciate as well as depreciate—depending on the pattern of continued investment. In some cases, new capabilities in different parts of the organization can be complementary and create value that significantly multiplies the initial investment. In other cases, of course, a fall off in capability is also possible without continued reinforcement and use.

For example, this dilemma was a source of great tension at Activision, one of the largest independent producers of computer software games.[12] This company had pioneered a powerful learning methodology centered on "postmortems" once a new software title was complete. Under this methodology, none of the members of a development team were allowed to be reassigned to new projects until they had completed a month-long capture of lessons learned.

The early postmortem notebooks were full of valuable insights that allowed the company to dramatically improve the software development process. These notebooks recorded key structural lessons, such as insisting that front-line group leaders sign off on completion-timing plans, rather than midlevel managers. They also recorded more idiosyncratic lessons, such as which programmers responded well to pizza late at night. Unfortunately, this is a company that produces an average of over a dozen new titles a year and that faces strong quarterly pressure to meet all scheduled release dates. In this climate, the dedication to the more intangible learning associated with the postmortems directly conflicted with the need to channel all available talent toward the more tangible quarterly performance objectives. Over time, the time investment in the postmortems declined, which reduced the value of the lessons captured, which further reduced the commitment to the postmortems, and ultimately led to the practice being abandoned. In this case, the dilemma was not effectively addressed and a key element of the learning strategy suffered.

As the "knowledge economy" grows in importance, financial analysts are placing greater value on intangibles, such as the inventive capabilities of a company or the vibrancy of its culture. There have been periodic moves to adjust accounting standards to better take into account these and other intangibles, though the results have been limited to date. While such efforts will never eliminate this dilemma, they do serve to make the tradeoffs more visible and hence mitigate some of the harshest realities associated with it.

GOVERNANCE DILEMMAS

The second set of dilemmas concerns issues of governance. We use the term governance to refer to the formal and informal patterns of interaction among relevant stakeholders that guide and constrain decision-making about learning. Governance decisions include: (1) what learning activities to offer; (2) where training will take place, who will attend, who will provide the training, how it will be funded, and how it will be evaluated; (3) what mechanisms exist for decisions on overall direction and guidance to continuous learning efforts; and (4) how the many interests of the relevant stakeholder groups are or are not integrated into the continuous learning efforts.

Among the key stakeholders associated with organizational-learning efforts are top management leaders, middle managers and first-line supervisors, production/service employees, elected and appointed officials in unions (in unionized settings), the training function in the organization, outside-training providers, and government officials at various levels (local, state, regional, national). The patterns of interaction among these stakeholders can include cooperation, confrontation, and information sharing. For example, contention between the training and production leaders over the size of the training budget is a classic governance issue. Similarly, the decision to create a joint union–management steering committee for driving a continuous learning approach in a unionized setting raises key questions of what decisions remain managerial prerogatives and what decisions are now subject to joint oversight.

Inevitably, when multiple stakeholders are brought together to make decisions, core issues will arise regarding the structure for decision-making, the process for decision-making, and the outcomes of decision-making. Often there are complicated issues of fairness and justice that parties will face.

Centralization/Decentralization Dilemma
Perhaps the most familiar governance dilemma (discussed earlier in this chapter) involves the structural issues around centralization and decentralization of training and learning decisions. Centralized decisions have the advantage of consistency and coordination with parallel initiatives, but often lack the flexibility to adapt to local circumstances. Decentralized decisions will be more closely aligned with local needs, but are likely to introduce variation and inconsistency across settings. For example, many companies have decentralized training

by setting up train-the-trainer systems where a number of incumbents are trained to provide training to others in the organization. While increasing participation across incumbents in the training process, the decentralization can lead to wide variations in the quality of training. Consequently, there is never a "correct" choice, but rather a perpetual process of achieving an effective balance between the two. Thus, while governance dilemmas around centralization and decentralization will arise early in a training effort, they continue to resurface as issues of service delivery and evaluation arise over time.

The trade-off between centralization and decentralization can also be expressed in terms of a trade-off between autonomy and interdependence. Where individuals and groups have substantial autonomy in making decisions about creating learning systems, it will come at the expense of attention to the interdependence that these individuals and groups have with others.

Direction/Empowerment Dilemma
A second set of issues involves process choices regarding direct, representative, or limited participation by various stakeholders in decisions, which is overlaid by choices regarding the use of expert, consultative, or consensus decision-making procedures. This dilemma involves constant trade-offs between expediency versus quality and shared ownership of decisions. Increased advance participation by relevant stakeholders and application of consensus procedures will generally lead to higher-quality decisions with greater ownership in implementation. However, high levels of participation and consensus procedures can also substantially extend the time it takes to reach a decision and even sidetrack the entire process as other relationship issues also join the agenda.

In the absence of pressure for visible progress in learning efforts, this would not be a dilemma—the choice of quality and ownership through increased involvement would be clear. But the pressure for results and the sheer complexity of high levels of participation inevitably leads to individuals or groups who are not fully involved or are even excluded from decisions—with high subsequent costs imposed on the process as a result of their not having been involved earlier.

This dilemma is vividly illustrated in the many activities that are lumped together under the rubric of "empowerment." The dilemma is manifest when groups are delegated to accomplish a task, but are not given proper authority to drive the change—or are given an overly ambiguous mandate—or are given an overly restrictive mandate—or are not provided proper training or other tools to accomplish the mandate—or are undercut since the project is not the top priority for any member—or are overridden by contradictory recommendations coming from higher power/status sources. In short, this dilemma is the typical experience of most task forces and project teams.

We have highlighted two governance dilemmas, but there are many others. For example, a third dilemma involves both issues of procedural justice and issues of distributive justice. Issues of procedural justice include whether training decisions are consistent, based on unbiased information, and accessible to people who will be affected by the decision.[13] Issues of distributive justice include access to training and rewards for training. For example, should everyone be entitled to a given form of training (equal treatment) or should decisions be based on certain criteria such as need or seniority (equitable standards)? Similarly, is it more fair to treat everyone the same or is it more fair to recognize individual or group differences? Should pay recognize newly acquired skills and does that mean seniority is given proportionally less weight? If people are making extra efforts as part of the learning process should that extra effort be rewarded even if it is not directly tied to specific skill acquisition?

The core issue is that standards for procedural justice and distributive justice are inherently contradictory, not usually well defined, vary across cultural groups, and change over time. For example, there are inherent trade-offs between when pay should be linked to skill acquisition. Also, people do not often think systematically about the contrast between equity and equality. Similarly, in some cultures, such as Japanese or Korean, case-by-case handling of disputes will be valued over the consistent application of rules, which will be more highly valued in other cultures, such as German or American.[14] Also, use of seniority for decision-making in a unionized team setting may be in tension with the importance of team needs. Thus, where there are scarce training dollars, limits on available training time, joint ventures, and multicultural work forces, or new work systems, dilemmas will arise in the administration of training.

On a given issue of fairness it is often the case that there is no one choice that is clearly superior. Moreover, there are typically costs associated with any choice. For example, if a choice is made to tie rewards to the acquisition of skills, there will be costs associated with the dissatisfaction of people who are less aggressive in acquiring skills or talented in ways not covered by the pay system. On the other hand, if pay is not linked to skill acquisition then there will be costs associated with the people who are acquiring skills, but being rewarded the same as others who are not making such efforts. Importantly, when issues of fairness arise, the choices often have enduring consequences—both in terms of actual outcomes and in terms of attitudes and perceptions.

WORKPLACE DILEMMAS

Operations problems are quite familiar to training personnel. They involve the delivery and evaluation of training activities. Typically, we think of delivery of training issues as consisting of what method of instruction is used (lecture, group discussion, simulation, role-playing) and the quality of the instruction given. Training delivery, though, also involves the intrusion of training activities into the ongoing operations of the organization. Many disconnects can arise when attempting to link training for continuous learning with the ongoing operations of the company. Two key linkages are between training efforts and on-line production efforts and between training efforts and existing human resource policies and procedures.

Movement toward a learning organization has major implications for day-to-day operations at the production or service-delivery level. It requires a large increase in the amount of training conducted (i.e., number of hours trained and the percentage of employees trained each year), the diversity of training (i.e., the breadth or variety of courses offered), and the diffusion of training within and across hierarchical levels in the organization (i.e., the degree of participation in training from the shop floor to managers and across functional groups within the company). Individuals at the shop floor are given both technical training on how to operate equipment, and cross-training on multiple jobs, to allow for more flexibility in the system; they are also often asked to obtain additional technical expertise not normally required as part of their job duties, such as blueprint reading and statistical process control. This pressure leads to a number of core enduring dilemmas.

Learning Achievement/Task Accomplishment Dilemma

Learning and development activities are expected to pay off by providing the tools needed for individuals to continuously improve methods, systems, and processes relevant to their job. In addition, the movement toward team-based work systems has typically led to a greater emphasis on developing interpersonal or team skills, problem-analysis skills, and decision-making skills. The core dilemma associated with the many operating-level issues involves the challenge of doing all of this, while still maintaining ongoing business operations. Here the dilemma is between the accomplishment of learning goals and the accomplishment of business or organizational tasks. It is the daily operations equivalent of the short-term/long-term dilemma at the strategic level.

The nature of a dilemma includes the notion that there is no one best resolution to the problem, there are trade-offs among the possible forms of resolution, and any choice is likely to have significant irreversible consequences. Clearly, in balancing out the demands of learning against the demands of daily production or service delivery there is no best resolution. This is illustrated in a series of operational choice points, such as the choice between building internal training capability versus using external talent, or the choice between training many people at once in a large time block versus training people in smaller modules spread out over a longer time, or the choice between training in-tact groups together versus training sprinklings of people drawn from across the organization. In each of these cases, the second option is less intrusive on production or service delivery—bringing in external talent, spreading out the training, and drawing people from across the organization. Yet each of these options has the potential of compromising long-term capability in the organization. Thus, there is a core trade-off between short-term operating requirements and long-term capability and investment.

Cooperation/Competition Dilemma

Cooperation/Competition Dilemma This dilemma is woven so deeply into the operating assumptions of most organizations that it is very hard to surface. The setting of budgets, the individual performance-appraisal process, the negotiation of contracts with suppliers, and countless other aspects of operations involve competitions where individuals, groups, or organizations are pitted against one another. There is an underlying assumption that competition will drive excellence.

By contrast, there are countless cases where individuals, groups, and organizations are expected to cooperate with one another. This includes the expectation that teams will work jointly to improve operations, the expectation that functions (such as sales and product development) will integrate their efforts, and even the expectation of cooperation among members of the executive leadership team. Here the underlying assumption is that cooperation will optimize the whole.

The tension between cooperation and competition is hard to observe because each is embedded into the operations. Yet the dilemma (and related tensions between "integration" and "differentiation") will surface more and more frequently as learning is emphasized. For example, the aerospace industry is increasingly being pressured by competition and customers to operate with greater flexibility, less waste, and more value. Given the great complexity of many aerospace products, any improvement effort requires coordination with hundreds and sometimes thousands of suppliers. This has led to an increasing prevalence of long-term supplier agreements—emphasizing cooperative relations. Concurrently, the cost pressures facing the industry drive executives to launch successive waves of cost-cutting initiatives, including the review of existing supplier contracts—threatening the very relations emphasized in the long-term agreements.

This tension is also evident at the individual level. Many organizations operate with individual performance-appraisal systems that pit individuals against one another. Dissatisfied with the effectiveness of such systems, two opposite responses are triggered—sometimes at the same time in the same organization. One response is to intensify the link between pay and performance—with stretch goals, increased use of stock options, and even forced distributions (with usually 10–15% of people in a high-performance category, 70–80% in a middle category, and the force ranking of 10–15% of people in a low-performance category). This is premised, of course, on the competitive assumption. The second response is to intensify the use of teams, participative processes, collaborative forums, and continuous improvement initiatives. These responses are premised on cooperative assumptions. Needless to say, the concurrent pursuit of initiatives that are premised on both assumptions drives many disconnects, with this dilemma as the root cause.

There are, of course, many other dilemmas at the operations level as well. For example, a third dilemma at the operating level concerns the alignment between the systems for the delivery of training and other organizational systems. If the training function looks too much like the rest of the organization in terms of how decisions are made, how customers and stakehold-ers are treated, and so on, then it is hard for trainers to champion change—they are easily disregarded. The response is, "if this is so important, why isn't it reflected in what you do?" The image here is of a training function that is bureaucratic and seen as a "dumping ground" where those who "can't do, teach." Alternately, if the training function looks too different from the rest of the organization in terms of how it operates then it is also hard for trainers to champion change—they are also easily disregarded. The response is, "you are so different, nothing that you say will apply to us." The image here is of a training function that is seen as overly "touchy-feely" and just "too far out." Hence the dilemma for training operations involves manag-ing the creative tension of not looking too familiar or too different. There is no one right answer, there are clear trade-offs with any choice, and what-ever choice is made will be irreversible in important ways (especially around the reputation of the function).

One special aspect of this dilemma involves the alignment of the training function and other aspects of the human resources system. Often, it will be the trainers of new ideas and concepts who then become the lighting rods for perceived inconsistencies between these new ideas and other personnel or labor relations practices. For example, trainers may be delivering train-ing in continuous quality-improvement principles only to encounter legiti-mate, but hard-to-answer questions about how these principles relate to the existing performance-appraisal process.

Training of team leaders and managers is also often extensive. The train-ing can be focused on technical skills but is more likely to be oriented to-ward issues of leadership. A key component of the move toward continu-ous learning is the transition from a "command and control" authority structure toward one in which leaders focus on removing barriers that limit the effectiveness of their people. This requires a recalibration of roles within the organization. Training programs may focus on issues such as team build-ing, developing a vision/strategy for a group or department, communica-tion skills, problem solving skills, and mentoring skills in order to transition from a leader within a "command and control" authority structure to a leader who serves as coach and facilitator.

DILEMMAS AND TIME

The dilemmas we have identified and described do not happen all at once. They arise over time—in an iterative series of choice points or pivotal events. Sometimes the events can be widely spaced in time. It is also possible for them to follow closely after each other or even occur simultaneously.

Regardless, it is clear that time is inherently scarce and immutable. We attempt to manage time by prioritizing and sequencing activities. Yet, we do not often reflect on or challenge our own conceptions of time and how they may differ across an organization. As well, we don't give sufficient attention to the way in which time is the ultimate constraint on all organizational activity. As Joseph McGrath and Nancy Rotchford observed:

> We each have, ceteris paribus, about two billion seconds. We spend about a half-a-billion of them growing up and another half-a-billion in adult sleep. That leaves each of us only one billion seconds, give or take, in which to live, love, work, achieve, earn, relate, recreate, enjoy, believe, hope, pray, and remember. (p. 58)[15]

Organizations can thus be understood by examining the time frame within which goals and priorities are set and the dilemmas that can arise from these time issues. In particular, organizations have to resolve three critical, time-related problems: uncertainty, conflicts of interest, and scarcity.[16] The solutions to these problems involve the need for scheduling actions, synchronizing or coordinating actions, and allocating time in an efficient and rational manner.[17] These issues of time highlight the importance of scheduling, coordination, and the allocation of efforts to the tasks to be performed.

Two of the dilemmas—one at the strategic level and one at the operating level—directly involve issues centering on the cycle time needed to build learning capability. At the strategic level, the cycle time for learning is set against the cycle time for strategy implementation. At the operations level, the cycle time for learning is set against the short-term operating pressures.

As these two dilemmas suggest, the issues of scheduling, coordination, and other time-dependent activities differ across levels and functions in an organization. In fact, the scholars Paul Lawrence and Jay Lorsch[18] highlight time orientation as a key factor that differentiates departments within an organization. One way to consider time is the span or interval required for receiving definitive feedback about the results of work efforts and behavior. For example, sales and production personnel deal with problems that provide rapid feedback about results from other employees, supervisors, and customers. Consequently, people in these types of jobs tend to focus their attention on short-term matters. By contrast, strategy and research and design personnel have longer-range concerns, since tangible feedback on their work is often a long-delayed result. These differences in time orientation are visible by examining the differences in scheduling, coordination, and allocation decisions across departments and levels. These differences in time orientation can lead to conflicts between departments or functions within the organization.

Similarly, Eliott Jaques has identified a strong and consistent correlation between time horizon and level in a hierarchy.[19] At the lowest levels of many organizations, the time horizon for most tasks may be a matter of minutes, days, or weeks. At the highest levels of an organization, decisions and actions may have a time horizon of three to five years or even longer. His analysis suggests that any changes in an organizational structure must anticipate and attend to the requisite adjustments in time horizon.

Learning disconnects often arise because of the different ways that time unfolds at different levels and in different functions. Without seeing the underlying time dynamics, the disconnects create pressure to "do something." These time pressures can lead to short-term solutions that fail to deal with underlying dilemmas.

Dilemmas and time are therefore intricately linked. Choices must be made within a small window of opportunity, which often means that not all people affected by a decision can participate in the decision process. There can only be a limited search of the possible alternatives. Thus the extensiveness of "rational" decisions are bounded. The consequences of the choices can not be easily predicted but will unfold or emerge over time.

As McGrath and Rotchford point out,[20] time in our culture is seen as: (1) homogeneous (each second is like every other) rather than epochal (this day is somehow different from all other days), (2) divisible (tiny units strung together) rather than continuous (wholistic and not easily separated), (3) linear (time marches forward) rather than cyclical (recurrent), and (4) objective and concrete (something external to people and quantifiable) rather than internal to people or subjective (something perceptual and abstract). Other cultures can differ on any of these dimensions.

What is of particular interest here is the way such assumptions can support or undermine organizational learning. Consider, for example, the way one former Toyota manager characterized the approach toward time in that organization. He stated that time is seen as the ultimate constraint against which to organize all activity. Instead of seeking to increase the number of parts produced, for example, a system of "level" production is used where the goal is to save seconds in cycle time. The reclaimed seconds are not used to increase output, but to focus on preventative maintenance, continuous improvement, and other ways to add value. In this sense, the organization has reframed time from being a barrier to being the basis to guide improvement.

In a recent popular book entitled *Einstein's Dreams* by Alan Lightman[21] we see a playful treatment of many different conceptions of time. In the book there are brief sketches of possible dream worlds where time is uneven, flows backwards, starts and stops, as well as numerous other possibilities. The book is important in the way that it encourages thinking of time in new ways. Although our analysis is more prosaic in format, we hope it can trigger additional new perspectives on time as a root cause of many dilemmas.

DILEMMAS AND LEARNING

Learning is seriously constrained if an underlying dilemma is not recognized. In the context of our learning model, failure to surface the dilemmas means that data—such as observable disconnects—cannot be fully interpreted. At the same time, just recognizing or labeling a dilemma does not guarantee learning. Even if the data is interpreted, it also has to be applied through action.

Consider our examples of dilemmas from other domains. In the case of a Greek play, it becomes a tragedy when the protagonist sees the dilemma but is not able to reframe or avoid his or her inevitable demise. To state this using the terminology of our learning model, data is interpreted and knowledge is generated, but action is constrained.

The same kind of constraint can happen in the use of a Harvard Business School case in teaching. As Chris Argyris has argued, there is a risk of teaching the case with predetermined answers in mind—leading only to what he calls "single-loop" learning. In this case there is again the interpretation of data to generate knowledge, but a limited range of action that is possible because the knowledge isn't paired with the kind of self-awareness associated with "double-loop" learning. The second loop involves the integration of experience and reflection on the part of students as well as teachers—as well as shared awareness of the way that learning is shaped by the learning process itself.[22]

Our use of examples as diverse as Greek tragedies and Harvard Business School cases reflects the notion that dilemmas are enduring. Thus, dilemmas are inevitable even if the particular form or manifestation is not totally predicable. Regardless of the source or kind of dilemma, they can be ignored at some peril or identified and aggressively examined. If, in this examination, an understanding of the dilemma is reached, it can serve as a guide to action.

Dilemmas are inherent in the process, and we contend that a number of dilemmas have an enduring quality. Based on our experiences, we have identified six of these enduring dilemmas faced by organizations moving toward cultures of organizational learning. These were listed earlier in the discussion of levels. They are enduring in that organizations will face these dilemmas repeatedly, whether they want to or not, and they do not go away simply because we would like them to disappear. Thus, working on dilemmas is hard and may or may not lead to success in addressing their core issues. Additionally, different dilemmas arise over time, with new dilemmas sometimes even arising as a result of the choices made in the face of a prior dilemma. The dilemmas are also enduring in the sense that they are embedded in the various levels of the organization and addressing them can have ramifications across organizational systems.

In addressing dilemmas, we have highlighted three key characteristics that affect how one can understand and act upon them as they arise in an organization. First, different dilemmas will arise across the strategic, governance, and workplace levels that require choice, the pursuit of alternatives, and the subsequent monitoring of the consequences of actions. Second, dilemmas also must be understood within context. We have described this context as a system of inputs, throughputs, outcomes, and feedback embedded in and across the three levels. Finally, dilemmas arise over time within an organization, especially since conceptions of time can differ across people, departments or functions, and levels within an organization.

CONCLUSION

In this chapter we have focused on six dilemmas. Although different aspects of each dilemma have been talked about in the organizational behavior literature, our goal here is to link them together as an integrated set of dilemmas to guide reflection and action.

Each of the dilemmas highlighted in this chapter will become more or less salient at different stages in the movement toward becoming a learning organization. The dilemmas associated with strategy, for example, first arise at the outset of a learning initiative. If they are ignored, the issues will continue to resurface as roadblocks to subsequent efforts. If they are effectively addressed, they help drive subsequent activity.

Subsequent learning activity encounters additional dilemmas around decision-making and governance. Again, these dilemmas can serve either as building blocks or roadblocks depending on their resolution. Finally, the dilemmas around daily operations come back full circle to raise difficult questions about the long-term viability and direction in strategy.

Although each dilemma is well-grounded in research and field experience, we do not see this as a complete or final list of dilemmas. It is important to modify these formulations and to add new dilemmas as they match the realities encountered in different learning journeys. In fact, it is truly not possible to specify in advance which dilemmas will be the root causes for a given set of disconnects. This suggests one very complicated aspect of a dilemma, which is that the full scope and nature of a dilemma can only be fully appreciated in retrospect.

In defining a dilemma, we have highlighted four dimensions—alternative choices, trade-offs, irreversibility, and action. Each of these dimensions maps onto one of the three parts of our learning cycle.

First, the recognition of alternative choices inevitably points toward the first stage of our learning cycle—data collection. This can be formal or informal data collection. Either way, the data helps to define the problem, clarify the choices, and gauge consensus around the extent to which the dilemma is shared.

Second, the issues around trade-offs relate to the second stage of the learning cycle—the interpretation of data to generate knowledge. Recognizing trade-offs depends not just on the development of individual knowledge, but also on the development of shared knowledge about the issues.

Third, wrestling with the trade-offs links to the third stage of our learning model—action, based on data and knowledge. It is in taking action (or not taking action) that a decision becomes irreversible.

Fourth, there is never a "right" answer to the dilemmas, nor are the dilemmas ever completely resolved once action is taken. At best, the dilemmas are addressed with creativity, constancy of purpose, and in ways that anticipate the future dilemmas. The difficulty of moving toward being a learning organization is clear.

Even when dilemmas are faced head on, what the learning initiative will look like is changing and emerging. Within the organization itself, some parts may be experimenting with new processes and procedures that closely represent the ideal behind the continuous learning vision. Other parts of the organization may be struggling to maintain current operations and have much difficulty embracing the continuous learning ideas as they are continuously putting out fires. Still other parts of the organization may be in active rebellion against the new initiative as it is seen as counterproductive to overall effectiveness.

Thus, even while disconnects and dilemmas are being faced, the learning that is going on in the organization can be viewed as differentiated. The differentiation of learning is a natural by-product of dilemmas that hit different parts of the organization in different ways. Indeed, as we will see in the next chapter, the combination of disconnects and dilemmas underpin many different forms of learning in organizations—this combination may complement each other, unfold independently, or undercut one another.

Notes

1. This notion that learning has multiple levels is consistent with work by Chris Argyris and his colleagues on single, double-loop, and deutero-learning. For example, see Chris Argyris, *On Organizational Learning,* 2nd ed. (Malden, MA: Blackwell, 1999); and Chris Argyris and Donald A. Schön, *Organizational Learning* (Reading, MA: Addison-Wesley, 1996).

2. Consistent with this perspective to dilemmas is the work of Fons Trompenaars and Charles Hampden-Turner, *21 Leaders for the 21st Century* (San Francisco: McGraw Hill, 2002). They note that leaders who reconcile value dilemmas are more successful than leaders who do not. They contend that effective leaders see the horns of the dilemma as a stimulus for creative thinking and action (called the virtuous cycle), while less effective leaders see a dilemma as a threat leading to pushing harder on existing rules and procedures (called the vicious cycle). We want to thank Peter Senge for pointing out the work of Hampden-Turner in his review of an earlier draft of our manuscript.

3. In Charles Hampden-Turner's *Charting the Corporate Mind* (New York: The Free Press, 1990), he notes that leaders often see a dilemma as requiring a choice between two sets of alternatives similar to where a choice has to be made to take one path or the other. Similar to our perspective, Hampden-Turner suggests that it is an error to think that one must choose one set of alternatives in preference to another. As he notes "value creation lies in the capacity of acknowledging those dilemmas which arise from competing and contrasting claims and of combining both horns of these dilemmas in a resolution which enhances all values in contention" (page 3). He suggests that rather than leaders generating solutions, they facilitate resolutions.

4. Discussions about dilemmas have a long history in philosophy. Discussions include moral dilemmas (where only two courses of action are available and each requires performing a morally problematic action) and social dilemmas (the good of the individual and good of the community) (see the *Stanford Encyclopedia of Philosophy* for some examples). In addition, the "prisoner's dilemma" has been discussed

as part of game theory of cooperation and competition. See Robert Axelrod, *The Evolution of Cooperation* (New York: Basic Books, 1984) or Keith Murnighan, *Bargaining Games* (New York: William Morrow and Company, 1992).

5. This suggests a complicated aspect of a dilemma, which is that it may only be fully evident in retrospect.

6. Dilemmas have been talked about in the organizational literature in a variety of ways. See work such as Beryl Hesketh, "Dilemmas in Training for Transfer and Retention," *Applied Psychology: An International Review*, 46 (1997): 317–386 who discusses the dilemmas in making decisions about appropriate methods of training to cope with rapidly changing job requirements. A book framed around dilemmas was written by Robert McLaren, *Organizational Dilemmas* (New York: Wiley, 1982). Robert Moorman and Lynn Harland, talk about the dilemma faced by companies using contingent workers between the need to employ a flexible workforce and the need to employ a workforce providing performance above and beyond the call of duty "Temporary employees as good citizens: Factors influencing their organizational citizenship performance," *Journal of Business and Psychology*, vol. 17 (2002): 171–187. Louise P. White and Kevin C. Wooten talk about the ethical dilemmas in various stages of organizational development in "Ethical dilemmas in various stages of organizational development," *Academy of Management Review*, vol. 8 (1983): 690–697.

7. A sequence of pivotal events figures prominently in the case *Tracing a Transformation in Industrial Relations: A Case Study of Xerox and ACTWU*, written by Joel Cutcher-Gershenfeld (Washington, D.C.: U.S. Department of Labor, 1988).

8. For this illustrative example of centralization and decentralization, see Fons Trompenaars and Charles Hampden-Turner, *21 Leaders for the 21st Century* (San Franciso: McGraw Hill, 2003). Additional examples of graphing dilemmas can be found in Charles Hampden-Turner, *Charting the Corporate Mind* (New York: Free Press, 1990); and Charles Hampden-Turner and Fons Trompenaars, *Building Cross-Cultural Competence* (New Haven: Yale University Press, 2000).

9. We provide a list and description of dilemmas that we feel are particularly relevant to the Bold Vision and Harsh Realities of organizational learning systems. Charles Hampden-Turner in his book on *Charting the Corporate Mind* offers eight key organizational dilemmas: (1) the extent to which the departments of the organization have divided labors and where functions can also be coordinated; (2) the extent to which registering rather than buffering the turbulence of the environment can enable an organization to respond fast; (3) the extent to which economies of scale are compatible with economies of flexibility; (4) the extent to which one can aim rationally for a large mass market and still discover market or defined particular niches; (5) the extent to which the subsidiary to a parent company be both a means to making a profit for that parent and an end in itself; (6) the extent to which the necessary introduction of new technology can be combined with the effective reoganization of working relations around that technology; (7) the extent to which workers, while adapting their demands to exigencies of the market, still feel themselves to be justly treated and consulted; and (8) the extent to which suppliers can create sufficient value for retailers, so that the latter do not resort to discounting at the supplier's expense. These are broad organizational dilemmas in which one (or more) dilemma will be seen as more pivotal to an organization at any given time.

10. Edgar H. Schein, *Organizational Culture and Leadership* (San Francisco: Jossey-Bass, 1985).

11. Arnaldo Hax and Nicolás Majluf, "The Life-Cycle Approach to Strategic Planning," (working paper, Sloan School of Management, 1983): 1–36.

12. Data from Activision based on site visit (1999) and extended dialogue with former vice-president of creative affairs, Alan Gershenfeld.

13. A review of justice research can be found in a recent study by Jason Colquitt, Michael Wesson, Christopher Porter, and K. Yee Na, "Justice at the Millennium: A Meta-Analytic Review of 25 Years of Organizational Justice Research," *Journal of Applied Psychology*, 86 (2001): 425–445; and Stephen Gilliland and B. Beckstein, "Procedural and Distributive Justice in the Editorial Review Processs," *Personnel Psychology*, 49 (1996): 669–691.

14. Joel Cutcher-Gershenfeld, et al., *Knowledge-Driven Work: Unexpected Lessons from Japanese and U.S. Work Practices* (New York: Oxford University Press, 1998).

15. Joseph E. McGrath and Nancy Rotchford, "Time and Behavior in Organizations," *Research in Organizational Behavior*, 5 (1983): 57–101.

16. See Joseph E. McGrath and J. R. Kelley, *Time and Human Interactions: Towards a Social Psychology of Time* (New York: Guilford Press, 1986); and Joseph E. McGrath and Franziska Tschan, *Temporal Matters in Social Psychology: Examining the Role of Time in the Lives of Groups and Individuals.* (Washington DC: American Psychological Association, 2004).

17. McGrath and Rotchford, "Time Behavior in Organizations."

18. Paul R. Lawrence and Jay W. Lorsch, "Differentiation and integration in complex organizations," *Administrative Science Quarterly*, 12 (1967): 1–47.

19. Eliott Jaques, *Requisite Organization: A Total System for Effective Managerial Organization and Managerial Leadership for the 21st Century* (New York: Gower, 1997).

20. McGrath and Rotchford, "Time Behavior in Organizations."

21. Alan Lightman, *Einstein's Dreams* (New York: Warner Books, 1993).

22. See Chris Argyris, *Strategy, Change and Defensive Routines* (Boston: Pitman, 1985); and Chris Argyris, *Overcoming Organizational Defenses: Facilitating Organizational Learning* (Boston: Allyn and Bacon, 1990).

6

Divergent Learning

W hen it comes to knowledge and learning, two things are always happening in organizations—convergence and divergence. The learning cycle for Bold Visions repeats in countless ways, with people examining data, generating knowledge and taking action. This cycle is designed to enable convergence around Bold Visions for organizational learning.

But not all learning is the same and not all learning results in convergence. There are intended and unintended forms of learning taking place at the same time in work organizations. Some forms of learning have more to do with Harsh Realities than with Bold Visions. Here the Harsh Reality of learning systems is primarily characterized by divergence, not convergence.

The visible indicators of Harsh Realities are countless disconnects. They are predictable and, for the most part, unwelcome. In each case, the Harsh Reality intrudes into what was a Bold Vision. Each is an unfortunate event, and they combine over time. This is what drives the divergence.

UNDERSTANDING DIVERGENCE

The concept of divergence has a fairly precise, technical meaning. Divergence is a phenomenon that takes place over time and involves deviation from an established pattern or a given point of departure. Divergence can happen slowly or quickly. It can occur in a direct, linear way that is easily observable or it can occur with great variation and a great deal of "noise" that makes it hard to see.

In statistics, there are a variety of ways to measure the dispersion from a mean, the degrees of variance over time, the amount of "scatter" on a plot, and other such measures—all of which are ways of quantifying divergence.[1] For example, measuring parts produced per hour will allow one to calculate the mean and standard deviation around that mean. Such data collected over time provide a window into understanding what is currently happening, how current performance compares to past performance, and allows trends to be examined.[2]

Organizations have become more comfortable with the notion that variation is inherent in all processes and that measuring the variation is the critical first step in gaining some control over the variation. Without greater understanding and control, the difficult problem of system improvement can't be initiated. A leader in extending these concepts to organizational operations, Dr. W. Edwards Deming, highlighted the difference between what are termed "common causes" of variation and "special causes" of variation. Knowing if variation was the result of a one-time event or factor (a "special cause") has very different implications compared to variation that has an underlying, ongoing driver (a "common cause"). There are certainly many quantitative indicators in learning systems (numbers of individuals trained, response rates on feedback forms, changes in training budgets over time, and so on) and the variance in these numbers is often at least as important as the base levels of the numbers.

Divergence, though, is not a purely quantitative phenomenon. Attitudes, values, goals, understanding, and many other intangible factors can also diverge over time. These "below-the-surface" issues are often shaped by the styles and values of organizational leaders as well as the culture that has developed over time in an organization. The implications for leadership are clear. Leaders, not just front-line workers, must understand the concept of variation and deviation in order to manage effectively. As noted by Peter Scholtes, an author and expert in systems change, leaders who do not understand variation are prone to (1) see trends that do not exist, (2) miss trends where there are trends, and (3) not understand their systems and how to improve them.[3]

Some divergence in organizations is clearly functional. As organizations grow and mature, for example, scholars have observed that they must differentiate functions and create new organizational levels.[4] But divergence can also be associated with separation and even deterioration in organizations.

Recently, one of us was working with a pair of entrepreneurial companies, each experiencing rapid growth and development.[5] One company was a start-up e-learning company, while the other was a start-up natural health food company. In both cases, the entrepreneurial companies were launched with only a few people all of whom were focused on the same goals and directions. For example, in the newly developed e-learning company, each person was a "jack of all trades," including computer programmer, software developer, designer, salesperson, marketer, and administrator. Over time as the organizations grew and developed, the roles and responsibilities of the expanding employee base became differentiated into specific areas, such as marketing or software development, with a staff and supervisors. In two years, for example, the food company had moved from a five-person operation to a forty-person operation with plans to continue to double in size within a year.

With the differentiation came contrasting priorities and emerging subcultures. There were also increased tensions over how to integrate functions and levels that previously relied on personal contact and friendships. With expansion came the predictable disconnects—in learning systems and in other parts of the operation. In both cases, a key dilemma revolved around delegation (or lack thereof) by the founding partners (the centralization/ decentralization dilemma). People had differentiated responsibilities, but not the independent authority needed for these distinct roles. Leaders spoke often about the need for employees to be empowered, with statements such as: "They need to pick up the ball. We can not do everything here." But often the actions of these leaders indicated just how uncomfortable they were in giving up control of the organization. The leaders when questioned on this would point to the need to minimize mistakes and their concerns that the employees did not have the knowledge, skills, and experience to handle the autonomy that leaders "wanted" the employees to have.

A closer look at the two cases reveals that the employees did not experience the issues of empowerment in the same way. For example, in one of the entrepreneurial companies, the sales and marketing department had a highly participative, supportive leader while another department had a leader who favored a more centralized, high pressure, authoritarian management style. The climate, norms, and learning that developed in these two areas were quite different, which then affected what individuals were or were not learning. Employees with the authoritarian leader, learned which strategic directions were to be valued or followed closely. They were also learning what actions to avoid doing, so as not to draw attention from their leader or top management. Employees with the participative leader learned that their leader would shield them from the seemingly arbitrary changes coming from the top leadership and that the workgroup would reframe how the strategic plans were enacted at their level.[6] Regardless, it became clear that the top leaders were not interested in understanding the divergence in their own organization, why it existed, or what opportunities and threats this type of divergence posed for the future viability of their operation. They were more likely to blame the problem on personality conflicts among their managers and thus placed even more emphasis on pushing their own agenda harder in order to overcome those personality problems. Not surprisingly, they were forever wondering why things were not working out as "planned."

As we see in these cases, combinations of disconnects formed patterns. These patterns diverged from the Bold Visions. But why is that? A close look at the patterns in the disconnects revealed underlying dilemmas. As we saw in chapter 5, each dilemma involves hard choices—such as the choice between centralization and decentralization or the choice between investment in tangibles and investment in intangibles. Over time, these dilemmas will be resolved in different ways, sending different signals, adding a deeper set of drivers to the divergence. The result will be many concurrent forms of learning in an organization.

DIVERGENT TYPES OF ORGANIZATIONAL LEARNING

There is a special moment when a learning connection happens. It has been sometimes portrayed as a lightbulb going on. Indeed, there is an almost palpable "click" that we observe within ourselves and in others when a connection is made.[7] The connection can happen when data is interpreted to create knowledge or when knowledge is processed to drive action or when action is examined to generate data (starting the cycle over again). At any point in the cycle the connections represent genuine learning. Over time, a series of related connections is manifest as increasing expertise—for individuals and organizations. Such expertise is critical for effective performance and for continuous improvement. This is at the heart of the Bold Vision and it is assumed to be manifest in increased convergence for the organization.

The phrase "organizational learning" conjures up images of people working together effectively, people and technology becoming more integrated so that production or service runs more smoothly, internal customer-supplier networks becoming more coordinated, and human resources leveraging to adapt to new challenges. This is the Bold Vision. In fact, vast resources have been devoted to seminars, training, and interventions aimed at fostering this vision. In most cases, the participants report satisfaction and even enthusiasm as a result of the dialogues, problem-solving activities, and new ideas triggered.

At the same time, organizations have proven unexpectedly resistant to these new ways of thinking and interacting—they are not easily woven into daily operations. This is despite the best intentions of leaders and employees at many levels. Part of the problem is that organizational learning is not one single thing—it is not a unitary phenomenon. There are different types of learning, each integrated into operations in different ways.

As we noted in chapter 2, organizational learning varies depending on the type of expertise involved. Developing expertise in the technical, interpersonal, and process skill domains is certainly important in an organization's learning environment. Nevertheless, not all expertise is the same. Some expertise centers on the handling of routine challenges in each of these domains, while some expertise centers on responding to unexpected challenges in each domain. This distinction between "routine" and "adaptive" capabilities or expertise has been an area of special focus for instructional and applied psychology.[8]

Organizational learning that is routine in nature might occur around skills training, safety practices, policies and procedures, quality processes, and other matters that involve the acquisition of already-identified knowledge, skills, and abilities. This contrasts with more adaptive forms of organizational learning, such as might occur around handling a crisis, generating a process-improvement suggestion, providing coaching on career planning, or understanding a change in competitive realities.

Equally important, organizational learning varies depending on the relations among the key stakeholders involved. Learning is very different when all of the stakeholders involved are (1) in relationships that are interdependent and oriented in the same direction, which we refer to as *aligned* relationships; (2) more fragmented and independent, which we refer to as *loosely coupled* relationships;[9] or (3) in what we term *opposed* relationships.[10]

In classifying different types of relationships, we are making an underlying assumption that may seem obvious, but should be noted. We assume that virtually all organizational learning situations involve multiple stakeholders. These may be separate organizations—such as suppliers and customers; these may be distinct functions—such as finance, purchasing, human resources, and so on; these may be separate levels—such as senior management, middle management, and front-line supervision; these may be separate subcultures or communities of practice—such as new hires, high-seniority workers, Latinos, women, engineers; these may be separate institutional relations, such as a union and an employer; or it may be any number of other groupings. In all cases, there are clusters of people who have both common and competing interests—manifest in patterns of aligned, loosely coupled, or opposed relations.[11]

The classification of forms of learning based on relationships is not strictly causal. That is, loosely coupled or aligned relationships don't necessarily cause one form of training or another. Instead, the relationships act as a baseline or ceiling, accounting for what types of learning are possible. Thus, some types of learning that are possible with aligned relations may not be possible with loosely coupled or opposed relations. Of course, such patterns of relations can change over time—with significant implications for what organizational learning does and does not take place among the stakeholders.

When combined together, these two dimensions—Expertise and Stakeholder Relations—form a 2×3 matrix, which is presented as table 6.1. The six cells in this matrix represent six very different forms of organizational learning, as is illustrated below.

Each of these six types of organizational learning involves its own unique (and divergent) patterns of data, knowledge, and action cycles. We examine each in turn, including the very different traditions that are associated with each form of learning. We will begin with the more familiar forms of learning and save the discussion of "Entrenched" and "Revolutionary" learning for last, since these are the least often discussed in the training and learning literatures. Then, we consider how these forms of learning converge and diverge from one another and otherwise interact. This will include a deeper look at the dynamics associated with the two defining dimensions—Stake-

TABLE **6.1** Types of Organizational Learning

EXPERTISE	ORGANIZATIONAL STAKEHOLDER RELATIONS		
	Loosely Coupled	*Aligned*	*Opposed*
Routine	*Incremental* Learning	*Continuous* Learning	*Entrenched* Learning
Adaptive	*Experimental* Learning	*Synergistic* Learning	*Revolutionary* Learning

holder Relationships and Expertise—and similar scholarship by others on different types of organizational learning.

Incremental Learning
When incremental learning takes place at the organizational level we are referring to the process by which groups of people in an organization extend their existing capabilities in ways that build on (but do not significantly change) already existing routines or operations. These modifications have little impact beyond the group and the process is essentially linear and time bound.

In terms of the Bold Visions, the cycle of data, knowledge and action is employed in a relatively modest way. A restricted set of data is involved, which is very similar to data seen in the past. The new knowledge involves relatively modest extensions of existing knowledge and is not necessarily intended to be cumulative. The actions in this case are very similar to past actions taken in response to previous data. We use the term "incremental learning," since it involves incremental changes that occur as people make choices around how to address circumstances that vary only in small measure from existing policies, procedures, or guidelines.

This kind of "learning" has its roots in many of the classic texts in the organizational behavior literature. For example, Herbert Simon, James March, and others have highlighted what can be thought of as cognitive processes.[12] These writings are important for having built the historical foundation for the learning metaphor. At the same time, this form of incremental learning is highly mechanistic and may seem far removed from the realities facing many of today's organizations.

In our analysis, we build on this early work with respect to the form of organizational learning that takes place in a bureaucratic or structured context. Relations in this case need only be loosely coupled. The expertise developed is routine. Examples of this form of learning include formal training activities, such as apprenticeships or technical skills training. It also includes other forms of incremental learning, such as the micro adjustments to managerial routines based on cost, quality, schedule, and other performance data.

In their enthusiasm around organizational learning, people sometimes discount the importance of this form of learning. In fact, incremental learning is not only pervasive, it is also essential to organizational success. Disconnects in incremental learning will result in skill shortages, gaps in succession plans, and managerial decisions that are not rooted in data. The dilemmas here are initially faced by individuals on a piecemeal basis, though the consequences can be far-reaching in their impact.

Continuous Learning
While incremental learning can be identified in terms of specific tasks or skills mastered by groups of people, there is a very different process that occurs when a group seeks mastery over a broader type of capability, such as advancing quality or becoming more entrepreneurial. These types of learning objects do not just involve more incremental gains, but the launch of a long-term learning process. A long-term learn-

ing process requires relationships among key stakeholders to be aligned and relatively stable. We will use the term "continuous learning" to refer to this sort of organizational learning.

In terms of the learning cycle associated with the Bold Vision, a much broader range of data is involved, though it is generally still prescribed in advance. The knowledge generated is also much broader and intended to build on past knowledge to form an ever-broadening base of knowledge— knowledge that is shared among a team or group. Similarly, the actions are intended to have a cumulative impact within the team with potential impacts outside the team as systems are improved.

This sort of learning is often highlighted in the training and development field. Here many authors have highlighted the continuous learning ideal.[13] Toward that ideal, they urge greater investment in training and development. For the most part, the reference is still to formal training, which primarily involves routine expertise. This literature is important for elevating the training function in an organization to a strategic level. It is a training model that depends on a relatively high degree of alignment among stakeholders. The continuous learning approach is continuous in that there is a constant flow of new training experiences designed to build ever-increasing capability in the organization.

A common example of continuous learning occurs when an entire workforce is trained in statistical process control skills and then are empowered to apply what they have learned. Another would be when a leadership team receives training in strategic planning principles and then seeks to incorporate these principles into organizational routines. In each case, the Bold Vision is broader in scope because the learning is intended to build on an aligned set of stakeholders.

With the bolder vision, also comes the potential for increased disconnects and deeper dilemmas. A disconnect, such as being "all dressed up with no place to go," is magnified when it is a large portion of the workforce that has received a given type of training, but is unable to apply what they learned. An underlying dilemma, such as the trade-off between task accomplishment and capability development is felt more acutely since the choice involves large groups of people who are either accomplishing tasks or building capabilities.

Experimental Learning   Both incremental and continuous learning are linear in nature, with the difference being along the dimension of time (incremental is time-bound and continuous is not) as well as stakeholder alignment (loosely coupled or aligned). Some organizational learning may be time bound, but not necessarily linear. These are cases where the learning is based on an interactive process of inquiry by a group of people. Something new is tried, the outcome is unknown in advance, and the implications of the results must be collectively interpreted. These efforts are occurring within stakeholder relationships that are loosely coupled or not well aligned. We will refer to this as "experimental learning."

In this case, the Bold Vision is concentrated into the experiment. The data is uniquely tied to the particular experiment. The knowledge involves assessments of the success, failure, and other lessons learned. Subsequent action generally involves judgments around how to extend, diffuse, adapt, or otherwise apply lessons learned from the experiment across the fragmented stakeholder groups so they can become more aligned.

There are parts of the organizational development literature, the quality literature, and the literature on the diffusion of innovation that highlight an experimental kind of learning.[14] This includes pilot experiments, the technique known as "design of experiments," and the general notion of emergent examples of innovation or best practice. Each experiment is bound in ways that only require loosely coupled relations among stakeholders. Indeed, that is often the point—keeping a boundary around the experiment so as to minimize risk and disruption. On the other hand, such experiments involve an adaptive form of expertise—both in the design or setting up of the experiments and in the interpretation of the results.

An example of experimental learning involves an individual or small group of workers who set up their work area in a new way and then compare the results before and after the change. A large-scale version of this experimental learning occurs when an organization sets up an entire new facility, often termed a "greenfield" plant, to experiment with a new production system or another new way of operating. In a service organization, the experiment may involve a new line of service or a new service delivery model that is implemented within a defined geographic location or a defined period of time.

The intentional use of experimental learning is often motivated by a direct concern about disconnects. By utilizing a bounded experiment, there is the often explicit acknowledgement that failures—or at least mixed results—are possible. This approach to learning may be designed to directly mitigate the risk of a "mile-wide and inch deep" disconnect, but presents the results of an integrated, successful experiment that has both breadth and depth in this targeted application.

Of course, not all experimental learning is intentional. Sometimes, it is only after the fact that contrasting approaches to a situation are revealed as "naturally occurring experiments." Learning occurs when these instances are recognized—with the data interpreted to become knowledge that then drives action.

Even though experimental learning is most likely to contemplate disconnects in advance, there are still many unanticipated disconnects that can arise which serve to blur or undermine the experiment, not just mitigate its impact. As we noted in chapter 4, a variation on "flavor of the month" disconnects involves "islands of success." Here, it is the very success of the experiment that proves threatening to others and prompts people to discredit the efforts and prevent diffusion.

Synergistic Learning   A second form of nonlinear learning occurs when we remove the bounds of time and place. Instead of the learning that is as-

sociated with a single or time-bound experiment or a specific location, there is a different form of learning that comes from observing and interpreting ongoing interactions. Typically, this kind of learning involves linking seemingly separate activities, processes, and stakeholders. The metaphor of a system is often helpful in organizing thinking during this kind of learning.

The Bold Vision for learning is perhaps most compelling and engaging in this case. Widely varied forms of data are valued in order to better see complex interdependencies. "Out of the box" thinking is encouraged to produce new knowledge involving deep insights. Actions can be highly varied, with implications at all levels of the organization.

This is a form of learning described in the work of Peter Senge and others building from a systems theory,[15] which highlights the highly adaptive process of understanding complex interdependencies. Some of this type of thinking can also be found in the work of an emerging group of scholars who study what are termed "communities of practice." This literature is especially noteworthy for pointing to gaps between what people know, what they do, and what is supposed to be done.[16] These scholars are often building from ethnographic research methods and attempting to make sense of some very complicated organizational realities.

Given the systematic, but often counterintuitive ways that change happens in organizations, these system specialists emphasize a dynamic learning process as essential to achieve the necessary mastery in order to provide organizational leadership. There is often an implicit assumption that stakeholder interests are aligned or at least that the shared-learning process will produce such alignment.

Examples of synergistic learning are found when groups of people gather for what is termed a "learning dialogue," where there is a free-ranging open discussion that emphasizes deep listening to others. This sort of learning commonly occurs during off-site events or strategic retreats, where there is a formal effort to step back from the day-to-day routines and alignment is sought among a given stakeholder mix.[17] This sort of learning is, of course, one of the primary attractions of work and study at a university, though many of us in universities are distressed by the relative infrequency of synergistic learning even in this setting.

Disconnects around synergistic learning arise in direct proportion to the Bold Visions that have been articulated. If expectations are high, great things are possible, but the range of possible disconnects also increases. The likelihood of disconnects such as "do as I say, not as I do" and "the Emperor's new clothes" increase dramatically with bold public pronouncements of visions that contemplate synergistic learning.

Entrenched Learning Some time-bound and linear learning at the organizational level is noteworthy because it involves learning in the context of opposition and disagreement. For example, a group of workers may learn to all work at the same pace and thus protect themselves from managerial pressure to work at the pace of the strongest or most capable worker. There is learning taking place here at a level greater than that of the individual, but it is learning centered on opposition between one group (workers) and another (first-line supervision). The same dynamic can take place between departments or across other subgroupings in an organization. We refer to this as "entrenched learning" to reflect the notion of relatively static opposition.[18]

Using the term "Bold Vision" may seem to be a misnomer in this case, but there is certainly an intentional, if limited, learning process going on that is associated with a vision on the part of some stakeholders. It is a vision of success against or in spite of established leaders or procedures in the organization. The data here is relatively standard, but it is data that has strong negative connotations attached. For example, it might be data about new, seemingly unrealistic levels of performance that are imposed. Consequently, the knowledge generated is not just about the data, but also about people associated with the data. The actions may center on the data, but they are as much actions around the negative associations.

For example, recently a state government adopted an information system for human resources that failed to live up to its initial promises. Instead, human resource professionals have come to see this as a flawed system that can never meet the objectives. New data about the system is now labeled very quickly by these negative associations as another piece of evidence that the system has to go while the financial and budgetary officials who pushed for the system remain steadfast in their belief that problems are just a necessary part of the move to a new and better system.

There is very little in the traditional literature on organizational learning that addresses oppositional learning, though there is scholarship in the Marxist and sociological literatures along these lines. For example, a classic reinterpretation of the Hawthorne studies points to evidence of a constant theme in which the workers acted collectively in response to various pressures from management and the experimenters.[19] The point here is that learning is routine, but indelibly shaped by the oppositional relations among the stakeholders.

This sort of learning is often disregarded as merely another disconnect—an example of things not happening as planned. This may be true from the point of view of proponents of a given change initiative. From the perspective of opponents to the change, however, a great deal of effort and even pride is concentrated in a distinct oppositional learning process. Indeed, one of the primary tactics used by opponents involves the fostering of disconnects, whether through intentional action or inaction. The failure to appreciate the potency of this sort of entrenched learning was, for example, a key lesson highlighted in the analysis of the downed Black Hawk helicopter in Mogadishu, Somalia.[20] Similar learning in embattled organizations is less visible, but can be just as intensive. It would be a great oversight to only concentrate on disconnects and miss the intense, concealed learning that is taking place as well. Simply put, this is a necessary and too often overlooked part of the learning landscape.

Revolutionary Learning While oppositional relations and the associated learning can be entrenched and relatively static, it can also be quite dynamic. The recent push for reengineering in organizations can be thought of as involving a dynamic, even revolutionary kind of learning by one group—senior management—that is threatening to the perceived self-interest of many others. Indeed, given the many reengineering initiatives that are accompanied by the elimination of jobs and the movement of work to new locations, such opposition is not at all surprising.

We use the term "revolutionary" with caution. In some cases, such as what are referred to as scientific revolutions,[21] the shift may take many years or decades and the change is enduring. In other cases, such as with some ostensible political revolutions, the change may be concentrated in a very short time frame and the results relatively superficial—with many institutional patterns unchanged. In all of these cases, however, stakeholders have opposed interests, a fundamental change in regimes is at least on the table, and unique types of learning are possible.

When revolutionary learning is taking place, many types of data are relevant. The key here is that the data is examined in fundamentally new ways. Consequently, dramatically new and different actions are suggested. Here Bold Visions are often articulated and there are typically more than one competing Bold Vision around learning.

The term revolutionary can have both constructive and pejorative connotations. In a review of the organizational theory literature, Gibson Burell and Gareth Morgan[22] identify the notion of radical approaches to change that are either "subjective" or "objective"—reflecting different assumptions around the degree to which the approach is presumed to be universally true. Kuhn's classic analysis of the history of science fueled treatment of paradigm shifts as a revolutionary type of change.[23] Note Kuhn's observation that many revolutionary ideas in science were seen negatively at the time and only later appreciated for the new insights derived. When revolutionary learning is taking place, the opposition is between those focused on preserving the status quo and those advocating change—with adaptive learning occurring among all parties.

DIVERGENCE WITHIN THE SIX TYPES OF ORGANIZATIONAL LEARNING

Each of the above six types of organizational learning can drive divergence in two basic ways—more divergence within that type of learning and divergence across combinations of the six types.

Incremental learning, for example, will diverge as a result of many classic disconnects. As we have noted, one example would be incremental learning that takes place in varying amounts of time prior to when the skills are needed, with variation in the degree to which the capability is there when it is needed. Here the same incremental learning might be taking place in all training sessions, but there would be a divergence in how useful it is depending on the delay in use. One or two disconnects like this does not constitute divergence—it is a combination of many of these disconnects and the variance over time that results in successful or unsuccessful incremental learning in an organization.

Continuous learning often diverges around the mechanisms for dialogue and sharing of information. Different patterns of cancelled meetings, access to performance data, support for root-cause analysis, and other such variation will produce divergence in continuous learning processes. Here the most prevalent divergence is around the degree to which the learning cumulates over time. Again, one or two disconnects does not result in much divergence, but many of these disconnects shape the way that learning is or is not continuous—in different parts of the organization and over time.

Experimental learning tends to diverge when there are isolated islands of success. Pilot experiments are supposed to be diffused to other parts of the organization, but this may be undercut due to indifference by others (what some have termed the "not invented here" syndrome) or even active (oppositional) resistance (undercutting the careers of managers associated with the pilot or starving it for resources). Whatever the causes, divergence will be fueled by a growing mix of pilot experiments each of which is disconnected in important ways and hence not driving a diffusion and transformation process.

Synergistic learning will diverge depending on the defined boundaries of the system within which learning is to occur. If, for example, the synergistic learning is centered on a particular facility, then its performance as a system may be optimized at the expense of other facilities or the organization as a whole. Even optimizing the performance of an entire enterprise through synergistic learning may occur at the expense of an industry or sector. Take the General Electric Corporation. The GE strategy of only retaining businesses that are the top three in their sector may have the effect of elevating the overall level of performance of an entire sector or it may result in the "dumping" of spent organizations that leaves the overall sector worse off. We don't have sufficient data to know one way or another. The point is that synergistic learning involves systems thinking and divergence is likely at the boundaries of the system.

Entrenched and revolutionary learning seem, on their face, to be inherently divergent in nature. For example, the entrenched learning in a group around informal, peer-driven work standards would represent a divergence from the point of view of a supervisor. Note, however, that this same observable disconnect might also involve powerful connections from the point of view of the workers around habitual forms of behavior. Indeed, from the worker's perspective, intervention by the supervisor would be a disconnect in their entrenched learning dynamic. The same is true for proponents and opponents of revolutionary learning.

DIVERGENCE ACROSS AND AMONG THE TYPES OF ORGANIZATIONAL LEARNING

The six different types of organizational learning can also diverge in relation to one another. For example, incremental learning of technical skills can become connected so as to generate continuous learning. When this does not occur, however, the mix of incremental learning activities and unsuccessful attempts to foster continuous learning would drive increased divergence. The rhetoric of continuous learning will ring hollow for participants in incremental learning activities, fueling cynicism and mistrust.

Similarly, continuous or experimental learning both have the potential to complement synergistic learning. If the two are disconnected, however, then the attempts to foster synergistic learning will represent further divergence and cynicism in the organization. In fact, if synergistic learning is not grounded in incremental learning of technical skills there will be divergence there as well. Too often, Bold Visions of organizational learning are not well linked to the messy details of building routine levels of expertise. Advocates of synergistic learning either have little to do with these more mundane activities or, worse yet, have disdain for the incremental training events and activities. Yet we are suggesting here that the lack of this link represents a disconnect that will drive divergence over time in the organization.

Revolutionary learning may only occur for a brief period of time, such as when a hostile takeover is occurring in an organization. If the hostility persists, the cycles of data, knowledge and action may center on the mode of entrenched learning—with opposed relations still being the operative context, but the learning being more routine in nature. Alternatively, if stakeholders reach a new accommodation, many other forms of learning will be possible.

Therefore, learning is integrally wrapped up with the level of expertise and the stakeholder relations that are fostered and rewarded in the organization. When stakeholder relations are aligned, we have highlighted two forms of organizational learning that are possible—continuous learning and synergistic learning. Having relations that are aligned does not mean that the interests of all stakeholders are identical. It does mean, however, that they are working toward a set of shared goals that are more important to each other than any separate or competing goal. For example, when customers and suppliers are engaged in continuous learning about the Six Sigma quality principles, the common goals of overall product quality dominate potentially competing goals of supplier contract costs or proprietary information. Similarly, when unions and employers are aligned in their interest to explore the principles of interest-based bargaining through joint training, synergistic learning about how to transform the bargaining process can occur. When only one party attends such training or even when they each attend separate training on the subject, additional alignment is needed before synergistic learning can take place.

In any given organization, a subset of stakeholders will be substantially aligned and it is these parties who will be engaged in these two forms of learning. Other stakeholders will not have these same experiences—creating a divergence that may increase over time. The parties involved in continuous and synergistic learning become more aligned with each other, while others become even further removed. The result can then be "in groups" and "out groups" when it comes to these forms of organizational learning.

Loosely coupled relations involve stakeholders who may be fragmented, linked in highly flexibile ways, or not closely related to one another.[24] The loose coupling may stem from organizational structure, geography, functional boundaries, resource constraints, historic patterns of interaction, or other factors. Incremental and experimental learning is possible in these cases, while the ability to foster continuous and synergistic learning will be constrained. Further, incremental and experimental learning have the potential to increase the divergence over time.

Opposed relations are rarely discussed in the organizational learning literature, yet these are common. In this case, there are again multiple stakeholders, but the focus of the learning for one or more of them centers on points of conflict or difference. The same customers and suppliers that were engaged in interdependent thinking with respect to Six Sigma principles might also stumble as they learn what can happen to a supplier that is not capable of supporting this level of quality. Suddenly their shared interest in quality will be less salient and their competing interests over supplier selection may dominate.

We should also note that a given set of stakeholder relations can involve relatively few stakeholders or very many stakeholders. In the aerospace field, for example, companies have systematically cut back on the number of people being sent into skilled trade apprenticeships—a form of incremental learning.[25] The resulting gap in the pipeline represents a potentially serious disconnect for the particular business operations that depend on these skills, for the workers who didn't have these opportunities to develop their capabilities, and for government or educational institutions involved in apprenticeship training. This is a serious pattern of disconnects, but one that directly involves a limited number of stakeholders. This means that it will be hard to generate concern from other stakeholders for this set of disconnects, though it also means that an agreement to address the situation among those directly involved can produce rapid action.

At the same time, a broad cross-section of engineers, production workers, and technicians in the aerospace industry is approaching retirement age. Given that there was a long period of time during the 1990s when there was comparatively little hiring, it is estimated that between one-fifth and one-quarter of the workforce will be eligible for retirement in the next five years.[26] Here it is both incremental and continuous learning that is at risk. The problem is similar to the skilled trades apprenticeship issue—a gap in knowledge and skills—but the number of stakeholders is substantially broader. As a result, coordination and even alignment will be more difficult to sustain, though the sense of urgency may be greater.

IMPLICATIONS OF DIVERGENT FORMS OF ORGANIZATIONAL LEARNING

We have identified six distinct types of organizational learning, various combinations of which are taking place at any given time in an organization. Divergence can occur within each type of learning and among them. The result challenges any unitary conception of organizational learning. Learning, in this respect, is "a many splendored thing."

In fact, viewing learning as a many splendored thing can lead to more complex thinking about the change process. In essence, an underlying "learning dilemma" is that multiple patterns are forming around different types of learning whenever the organization is attempting to make change happen. For example, creating the conditions favorable for synergistic learning will also create the conditions favorable for oppositional learning patterns to emerge.[27] Rather than being frustrated that "resistance" is occurring, leaders can anticipate that this dilemma is inevitable. The key is for leaders to focus on habitual ways of thinking and behaving, recognizing that these oppositional learning strategies have deep roots that must be "coaxed downstairs one step at a time."[28] Pushing harder on the Bold Vision and relegating the resistance to the background will not make the dilemma go away. Instead, accepting the ambiguity and using it to draw the various stakeholders into a dialogue about options given the Harsh Realities can lead to creative thoughts and actions.

Our model attempts to provide some clarity in understanding the range of connections and disconnects that had previously been lumped together under this one label. Discussions about transformational change to a learning organization must include an understanding of the variation in the organization and the inevitable divergence in learning that is occurring presently and will occur with the transformational change. Rather than seeing the variation as "out of control," leaders need to recognize variation as opportunities for sustaining a change initiative.[29]

It is of note that another scholar also conducting research on disconnects has identified a spectrum of different types of organizational learning. In studying the learning process associated with accidents in nuclear reactors, John Carroll and colleagues distinguish among what they termed a Local Stage in learning, a Control Stage in learning, an Open Stage in learning, and Deep Learning.[30]

This model builds on the concepts of "Single Loop Learning" and "Double Loop Learning" from Argyris and Schön[31]—adding to it the concepts of "Improvised Learning" and "Structured Learning"—forming a 2 × 2 matrix with the various stages occupying the cells in the matrix—as is illustrated in table 6.2.

TABLE 6.2 A Framework Presenting Four Stages of
Organizational Learning Derived from Analysis of Disconnects

	IMPROVISED		STRUCTURED
SINGLE LOOP	Local Stage	⇒	Control Stage
	Action Focus		Component Focus
	Expertise		Behavior Compliance
	Resilience	⇐	Anticipation
DOUBLE LOOP	Open Stage		Deep Learning Stage
	Multicomponent Focus		System Focus
	Emotions	⇒	Mental Models
	Sharing		Integration

Carroll's "Improvised" and "Structured" dimensions of learning correspond closely to our "Adaptive" and "Routine" dimensions of learning. As a result, Carroll's "Control Stage" of learning corresponds to our "Incremental Learning." Similarly, Carroll's "Deep Learning" corresponds to our "Synergistic Learning" or "Revolutionary Learning." Interestingly, the improvised "Local Stage" in Carroll's model may also correspond to our "Synergistic, Experimental, or Revolutionary Learning."

The correspondence across the frameworks is interesting—both make clear that there is no one form of learning that takes place in organizations. Both models distinguish different forms of expertise. Carroll links expertise with single- and double-loop learning, while we link expertise with different types of stakeholder relationships. Interestingly, both approaches point to the different kinds of skill sets and mindsets needed across different types of learning (an issue addressed in part III of the book).

CONCLUSION

There are many different types of organizational learning including, Incremental, Continuous, Synergistic, Experimental, Entrenched, and Revolutionary. Each form of learning is associated with different change dynamics, different potential disconnects, and different underlying dilemmas. As well, the combination of multiple concurrent forms of organizational learning adds a further overlay of possible disconnects and dilemmas. The resulting picture conveys both the rich meaning that is embedded in the term organizational learning and the great challenge associated with establishing a learning organization.

As we saw in chapter 4, these disconnects, can vary along many dimensions, including organizational levels, learning content, time, location for learning, and intensity of what is at stake. If the disconnects are only addressed on a piecemeal basis, as independent, isolated events, the patterns of divergence will be hard to see. The result will likely be piecemeal responses that may make things worse rather than better. By contrast, an affirmative, nonblaming look at the patterns of disconnects can reveal deep insights that will better guide action.

Moreover, there are cases where the patterns of disconnects confirm that there is what is termed a "common cause" problem—typically linked to an underlying dilemma. As we saw in chapter 5, the underlying dilemmas do not resolve disconnects, but they do facilitate the treatment of disconnects as data. Indeed, the dilemmas represent what Dr. W. Edwards Deming terms "profound knowledge" about the data.

Finally, here in chapter 6, we see that disconnects and dilemmas do not converge into Bold Visions for organizational learning. Instead, they accumulate into a Harsh Reality that consists of multiple types of divergence. There is divergence within each of the six forms of learning highlighted here, and there is divergence as they interact with one another.

In the process, we see that the cycle associated with the Bold Visions—involving data, knowledge and action—directly corresponds to the cycle associated with the Harsh Realities involving the 3Ds—disconnects, dilemmas and divergence. In part III of this book, we will explore the many ways to address skills sets and mindsets, attentive to the interdependence between Bold Visions and Harsh Realities.

Notes

1. See, for example, W. Edwards Deming, *Out of the Crisis* (Cambridge, MA: MIT Center for Advanced Engineering Study, 1986); Margaret J. Wheatley, *Leadership and the New Science: Learning about Organization from and Orderly Universe* (San Francisco: Berrett-Koehler, 1992); Donald J. Wheeler, *Understanding Variation: The Key to Managing Chaos* (Knoxville, TN: SPC Press, 1993).

2. There are many books on issues of controlling quality that are relevant to this discussion. For example, see James R. Thompson and Jacek Koronacki, Statistical process control for quality improvement (New York: Chapman & Hall, 1993).

3. Peter R. Scholtes, *The Leader's Handbook* (New York: McGraw-Hill, 1998).

4. See, for example, see P. R. Lawrence and J. W. Lorsch, "Differentiation and Integration in Complex Organizations," *Administrative Science Quarterly*, 12 (1967): 1–47.

5. The vignettes presented here are based on formal and informal technical assistance provided to these organizations.

6. Learning across organizational subunits also diverges due to differences in time orientation. Time orientation focuses on the time frames within which goals and priorities are set, the work is produced, and feedback regarding the appropriateness of the work produced is available to the workers. Time of course is an inherently scarce and immutable resource. Researchers have shown how subcultures within organizations develop dominant conceptions of time and these time orientations create temporal problems for organizations seeking to be as effective as possible. A production system may be used to a very compressed time schedule as parts or assemblies are being produced on a minute-by-minute or hour-by-hour basis. This places a premium on the need to schedule actions, the need for synchronizing or coordinating actions, and the need for allocating time in an efficient and rational way

to maximize organizational goals. Engineering specialists may focus more on providing long-term support for production with a time frame of diagramming new parts and developing new blueprints or redesigning machines to produce different outputs—all of which might be projects that take days or even months to complete. In addition, it might take months of study to determine if the redesign of the machine is meeting cost and benefit expectations. From this perspective, the time orientations of the production and engineering groups are quite different. Thus, what individuals come to understand "lean manufacturing" to mean may differ by subunit due to how the new initiative fits within their time orientation. Paul R. Lawrence and Jay W. Lorsch discuss these issues of time orientation in their book *Organization and Environment: Managing Differentiation and Integration* (Boston: Harvard Business School Press, 1986).

7. Indeed, a recent study sponsored by the Lemelson–MIT Program and the National Science Foundation summarized extensive research on the biological and social dynamics associated with such "clicks" in the process of invention. Note that this was paired with an appreciation for the "long-slog," which is also instrumental in the invention process. See "Invention: Enhancing Inventiveness for Quality of Life, Competitiveness, and Sustainability," (Report of the Committee for the Study of Invention, Merton C. Flemings, Chair, 2004).

8. Expertise is typically defined as the achievement of consistent, superior performance through the development of specialized mental processes acquired through experience and training. Successful performance is a necessary but not sufficient condition for defining expertise. Expertise involves the possession of a well-organized, task-specific knowledge base. More specifically, the key principles differentiating novice and experts include (1) the proceduralization of knowledge and skills; (2) the development of highly integrated mental models of situations and actions; and (3) the creation of highly developed meta-cognitive or self-regulatory processes. In other words, experts have established ways of doing things, an understanding of why or when different skills or approaches are needed, and ways to figure out if things are going as planned. For a discussion of issues of expertise, see K. J. Holyoak, "Symbolic Connectionism: Toward Third Generation Theories of Expertise," in *Toward a General Theory of Expertise: Prospects and Limits*, ed. K. A. Ericson and J. Smith (Cambridge: Cambridge Press, 1991); and Giyoo Hatano and K. Inagaki, "Two Courses of Expertise," in eds. Harold W. Stevenson, Hiroshi Azuma, and Kenji Hakuta. *Child development and education in Japan* (San Francisco: Freeman, 1986).

9. This term, which was coined for use in the organizational context by Karl Weick, appropriately conveys the notion that stakeholders are neither highly aligned nor deeply opposed. This can have a slightly negative connotation, such as when relations are fragmented, or a slightly positive connotation, such as when relations are flexible. We intend the term to span this spectrum. See Karl Weick, "Educational Organizations as Loosely Coupled Systems," *Administrative Science Quarterly*, 21 (1976): 1–19; and Karl Weick, *Making Sense of the Organization* (Malden, Mass: Blackwell Business, 2001).

10. These concepts come from the literatures on negotiations, industrial relations, and organizational development. Again, we will have more to say about these three different types of stakeholder relationships shortly.

11. The relationship dimension of this analysis has its roots in the negotiation literature, which begins with what is termed a "mixed-motive assumption"—assuming that parties or stakeholders in a negotiation have a mixture of common and competing interests. See, for example, Richard Walton, Joel Cutcher-

Gershenfeld, and Robert McKersie, *Strategic Negotiations: A Theory of Change in Labor-Management Relations* (Boston: Harvard Business School Press, 1994).

12. See Herbert A. Simon, *Adminstrative Behavior: A Study of Decision-Making Processes in Administrative Organizations* (New York: Free Press, 1997); and James G. March and Herbert A. Simon, *Organizations* (Cambridge, Mass: Blackwell, 1993).

13. See Anthony Carnevale and Leila Gainer, *The Learning Enterprise* (Alexandria, VA: American Society of Training and Development, 1989); also, M. Dierkes, A. Antal, J. Child, and I. Nonaka, *The Handbook of Organizational Learning and Knowledge* (Oxford, England: Oxford University Press, 2001).

14. William R. Shadish, Thomas D. Cook, and Donald T. Campbell, *Experimental and Quasi-Experimetnal Designs for Generalized Causal Inference* (Boston: Houghton Mifflin, 2002).

15. See Kenneth E. Boulding, *The World as a Total System* (Newbury Park, CA: Sage, 1985); and Peter Senge, *The Fifth Discipline* (New York: Doubleday, 1990); Peter Senge, Art Kleiner, Charlotte Roberts, Richard Ross, George Roth, and Bryan Smith, *The Dance of Change: The Challenges to Sustaining Momentum in Learning Organization* (New York: Doubleday, 1999).

16. See J. E. Orr, "Sharing knowledge, celebrating identify: Community memory in a service culture." In *Collective Remembering*, ed. David Middleton and Derek Edwards (Newbury Park, CA: SAGE, 1990): 169–180; and Etienne Wenger, *Communities of Practice: Learning, Meaning, and Identity* (Cambridge, UK: Cambridge University Press, 1998).

17. The emerging literature on developing learning histories is consistent with this perspective. See Philip Mirvis, Karen Ayas, and George Roth, *To the Desert and Back* (San Francisco: Jossey-Bass, 2003); and George Roth and Art Kleiner, *Car Launch: The Human Side of Managing Change* (Oxford, England: Oxford University Press, 2000).

18. Peter Senge, Otto Scharmer, Joseph Jaworski, and Bettery Sue Flowers note that in a state of fear or anxiety, people's actions often revert to habitual forms of behavior. They cite this limited type of learning of reacting to circumstances as reactive learning where people discount interpretations and options for action that are different from those they know and trust and so they act to defend their interests. This notion of reactive learning is similar to our concept of entrenched learning. See *Presence: Human Purpose and the Field of the Future* (Cambridge, MA: The Society for Organizational Learning, 2004).

19. See Dana Bramel and Ronald Friend, "Hawthorne: The Myth of the Docile Worker and Class Bias in Psychology," *American Psychologist*, 36 (1981): 867–878.

20. Mark Bowden, *Blackhawk Down: A Story of Modern War* (New York: Atlantic Monthly Press, 1999).

21. See Thomas Kuhn, *The Structure of Scientific Revolutions*, 3rd ed. (1962; Chicago IL: University of Chicago Press, 1996).

22. See Gibson Burell and Gareth Morgan, *Sociological Paradigms and Organizational Analysis* (London: Heinemann Educational Books, 1979); and Dennis Gioia and Ellen Pitre, "Multiparadigm Perspective to Theory Building," *Academy of Management Review*, 15 (1990): 584–602.

23. Kuhn, *Structure of Scientific Revolutions*.

24. See Karl E. Weick, *Sensemaking in Organizations* (Thousand Oaks, CA: Sage, 1995); Karl E. Weick and Robert E. Quinn, "Organizational Change and Development," *Annual Review of Psychology*, 50 (1999): 361–386.

25. Joel Cutcher-Gershenfeld, Betty Barrett, Eric Rebintisch, Thomas Kochan, and Robert Scott, *Developing a 21st Century Aerospace Workforce* (Policy White Paper

submitted to Human Capital/Workforce Task Force, The U.S. Commission on the Future of the Aerospace Industry, 2001).

26. Ibid.

27. Thanks to Peter Senge for suggesting this dilemma as one way of talking about the different pathways or patterns that can emerge when thinking about multiple learning types.

28. The quote "Habit is habit, and not to be flung out of the window by any man, but coaxed downstairs a step at a time" is attributed to Mark Twain.

29. Some advocates of transformation change efforts have focused on the power of positive thinking such as through Appreciative Inquiry. A key principle of Appreciative Inquiry is that building and sustaining the momentum of change requires large amounts of positive outlook and bonding around things like hope, inspiration, and a sense of urgent purpose in creating something meaningful together. See Peggy Holman and Tome Deane, *The Change Handbook* (San Francisco: Berrett Koehler, 1999), for a chapter on Appreciative Inquiry and other positive-oriented change strategies such as Preferred Futuring. We do not deny the power of a positive perspective for sustaining high participation and enthusiasm for a change process. What we are advocating is seeing the power in addressing the positive aspects of the Bold Vision *and* the power of learning from the Harsh Realities of organizational life.

30. John S. Carroll, Jenny W. Randolph, and Sachi Hatakenaka, "Learning from Organizational Experience," MIT Engineering Systems Internal Symposium (May 29–30, 2002). See also: John S. Carroll "Organizational Learning Activities in High-Hazard Industries: The Logics Underlying Self Analysis," *Journal of Management Studies*, 35 (1998): 699–717.

31. Chris Argyris and Don Schön, *Organizational Learning II: Theory, Method, and Practice* (Reading, MA: Addison-Wesley, 1996).

7

Changing Skill Sets

In most organizations, increasing skills and capabilities is simultaneously a top strategic priority and a constant source of disconnects. What is to be done when Bold Visions and good intentions are undercut? Is it best to resort to blame or knee-jerk reactions or increased cynicism? These are certainly the typical responses and none is very functional—indeed, as we saw in part II, each risk creates additional disconnects.

Instead, we have urged that disconnects be treated as data—in a constructive, nonblaming way. Doing this well, requires two very different types of capability that we term "skill sets" and "mindsets." Skill sets are the tools and techniques associated with analyzing and working with disconnects, divergence, and dilemmas. These issues are the focus of this chapter. Mindsets are new ways of thinking about the value of divergence, the importance of fostering relationships, and the integration of the Bold Vision and Harsh Reality learning cycles. These are the focus of the next chapter.

BUILDING CORE SKILLS

One approach to skill-building involves decomposing complex challenges into discrete skills. An alternative, and complementary, approach involves reassembling the skills in order to accomplish a given task. We will do both here.

First, the two learning cycles can be decomposed into six discrete skills. Each skill is simple to state, but they can take years and even decades to master.[1] There are three core skills for the Bold Vision:

1. *Gathering Relevant Data.* Collect appropriate data about any issue, challenge, problem, or opportunity—data that can be organized, analyzed, and interpreted in ways that will be compelling to others.

2. *Building Shared Knowledge.* Develop shared knowledge across stakeholders based on data that has been organized and interpreted.

3. *Taking Appropriate Action.* Take informed action that is based on shared knowledge and is guided by data.

Building capability on each of these dimensions is woven throughout the Bold Visions of any learning system. We have found that this formulation—centered on data, knowledge, and action—is particularly effective and accessible. Such Bold Visions drive efforts to collect data associated with work processes, empower individuals and teams to develop shared knowledge based on the data, and take action guided by that knowledge. Less attention has been placed on the skills associated with appreciating the Harsh Realities.

The skills rooted in the Bold Vision will minimize, but not prevent disconnects. Hence, the need for three additional core skills rooted in the Harsh Realities of organizational learning—what we have termed the 3Ds:

1. *Valuing Disconnects.* Take a nonblaming, constructive approach in order to learn from the disconnects.

2. *Surfacing Underlying Dilemmas.* Name the underlying dilemmas—make wise choices based on a full appreciation of the options and alternatives.

3. *Managing Divergent Learning Dynamics.* Appreciate the value of divergent forms of organizational learning—plan for the opportunities and tensions.

Like the first set of skills, the skills rooted in Harsh Realities are easy to state but can take years and even decades to master.

Valuing disconnects involves a stance toward learning and knowledge that is comparable to the stance of a judo master facing an attack. The attacker represents harm, but the attacker also brings kinetic energy that can be used to great advantage by the judo master. Disconnects are like the attacker. They can do harm, but they can also open up a window into the organization. Valuing disconnects means making a commitment to avoid knee-jerk reactions and finger-pointing when confronted with disconnects. Instead, it is a behavioral commitment to probe further—to understand why a disconnect has happened, to contain immediate harm, and where appropriate and feasible, to prevent recurrence. It is a commitment to identify implications for the overall learning system and the larger organization.

CORRESPONDENCE BETWEEN BOLD VISIONS AND HARSH REALITIES

These two sets of skills are not separate from one another. In each case, there is a correspondence between the cycle associated with the Bold Vision and the cycle associated with the Harsh Realities. The first correspondence involves treating disconnects as data. The second correspondence involves appreciating dilemmas as knowledge. The third correspondence connects divergence to action. This overall correspondence between the two cycles is illustrated in figure 7.1.

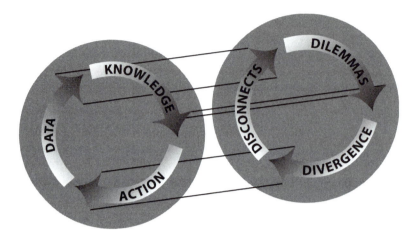

Figure 7.1 Connecting cycles associated with Bold Visions and Harsh Realities

Most organizations do have a clear sense of their current capabilities with respect to these three corresponding sets of skills. This not only requires an understanding of the resident skills associated with the Bold Visions (for example, capability for problem solving, root cause analysis, evaluation techniques, team-facilitation skills), but also involves an assessment of the resident skills associated with uncovering disconnects, developing shared knowledge about dilemmas, and taking action around complex forms of divergence. None of this is necessarily difficult, but it does take sustained effort.

To appreciate the need for new skill sets, consider the experience of one of the authors on a church strategic task force that was looking to translate a new vision for the church into a more operational plan. The process began with a vision that was comprised of seven statements, which had been created from a large number of focus groups using techniques such as brainstorming, nominal group techniques, and prioritization. The data from these focus groups and the new vision had been given to this planning and implementation team.

Leaders exhorted the group to work hard as the efforts would be rewarded by real change occurring in the church. The leaders stated that they only agreed to champion this team after assurances from the senior most church leaders that the implementation plans would be carried out. The task force was imbued with the Bold Vision and worked explicitly from this learning cycle, taking the data from the focus groups and the shared knowledge that had been codified as the seven vision statements, and translating it into actionable steps.

Despite the energy within this dedicated group, there was also some skepticism as to whether anything would come of the effort. Previous attempts were pointed to as examples of how these types of efforts often do not go very far in actually changing the church—often revealing a divergence between various stakeholders. Despite the potential for such disconnects, the task force attempted to move along and meet its stated goal. Individuals on the team had been well-trained in problem-solving techniques and many of them actually helped conduct the focus groups that provided the key data to drive the new vision statements. So the skill sets associated with learning were well-developed.

Still, there has been discomfort over whether the team members have the skill sets to make disconnects, dilemmas, and divergence real or visible—so they can be discussed and dealt with in a more productive way (rather than coming up as side comments in different meetings). It was particularly challenging to find ways to discuss the Harsh Reality learning cycle when the press is to work hard toward the stated goals.

SKILLS FOR TREATING DISCONNECTS AS DATA

Treating disconnects as data represent a particularly high-risk situation in the context of learning systems. Generally, disconnects cast the efforts of some individuals in a negative light. Also, as we have noted, there is often a history of blame associated with disconnects when they are made visible. This is all particularly ironic, since the whole point of a learning system is to foster constructive, nonblaming learning. But this is most certainly the reality in many cases.

A simple, but powerful mechanism to avoid such difficulties was noted earlier in the book. This mechanism involves listing potential disconnects that might be encountered in advance of the launch of a learning or knowledge-based initiative. Usually, such launches are marked by great fanfare and bold announcements. Focusing on likely disconnects may seem almost defeatist. In fact, we hold that this is a form of prevention or what is sometimes termed "error proofing" for the initiative. It also has the advantage of diffusing personal risk at a later date, since the potential for the disconnect has already been acknowledged.

A similar approach to disconnects can be found in how "errors" are treated during training. The traditional approach to training and learning activities is to minimize incorrect responses, to avoid errors at all costs, and to focus on modeling only effective behaviors. Recent efforts have shown the advantages of designing errors into training and learning experiences. The error-filled experiences allow learners to develop more complex models of the behaviors that are expected of them.[2] In this sense, the errors represent a form of disconnect.

The research suggests that incorporating errors can increase a learner's attention because they signal unexpected events. Errors also alert individuals to incorrect assumptions that they may be making about situations and behaviors. For example, individuals on a radar-tracking task can be given a list of potential errors that may occur and can be instructed to intentionally make some of the errors to see what happens. Error-based experiences such as these have been found to lead to greater exploration during learning and to a greater number of skills transferring into new settings and situations.[3] Thus, errors are encouraged and supported as a way of learning more about the task and about situational effects.

Once new initiatives are launched, brainstorming disconnects in advance and error encouragement are valuable tools for use in focus groups, skip-level sessions, and other gatherings aimed at constructively surfacing disconnects and patterns of disconnects, as well as the underlying divergence that may be key to addressing the disconnects. Again, the focus is on incorporating disconnects into a routine, rather than having them stand out as exceptions requiring special attention.

For example, a process-improvement team was launched in a state agency to revamp the recruitment and selection systems. One of the authors led the group through a discussion that involved classifying a very simple kind of data—their personal definitions of the sort of change that they were aiming for. The exercise included defining change-oriented terms such as modification, substitution, mutation, and transformation. After defining these terms and applying them to their project, it became clear to the team members that there was not agreement on what type of change the group was actually trying to accomplish. This was a revelation to some members that there could be divergence in the team on such a seemingly simple issue—some members thought of the change mandate as a call for a simple modification of the existing systems, while others saw the change as truly transformational. By raising these issues of divergence across individuals, the team could then have a dialog about the reasons for the differences in perspective and probably avoid major disconnects later, such as some members fighting to limit the initiative while others try to expand it. In this case, making what was hidden visible came to be seen as an aid to the Bold Vision, rather than as a barrier to it.

Beyond the listing of disconnects, there are also a variety of charting and mapping tools for organizing data on disconnects. A matrix is a valuable tracking tool in this regard, recording locations or individual names along one side of the matrix and training/learning accomplishments along the other. The result is both a clear picture of accomplishments and a visual indicator of gaps or disconnects, as is suggested by table 7.1.[4]

One approach for classifying disconnects is to organize them by level, as we did in chapter 4. There, we distinguish three categories of disconnects: strategic, governance, and daily operations. If most of the disconnects reside at a given level, then the dilemmas and divergence are likely to be characteristic of that level. This provides orientation in dealing with reality. Where the disconnects have implications that span more than one level, which is often the case, then this too is important information—potentially preventing too narrow a response.

Charts of disconnects over time can be quite valuable. For example, a plant may chart the successful implementation of workgroup-improvement

TABLE 7.1 Sample Skills Tracking Matrix

	COMPLETED MODULES			EXPERT, ABLE TO TRAIN OTHERS		
Names	Mod 1	Mod 2	Mod 3	Mod 1	Mod 2	Mod 3
J. Brown	✓					
W. Smith	✓	✓	✓	✓	✓	
I. Lopez		✓			✓	
S. Wonder	✓	✓	✓	✓	✓	✓
D. Ross						

suggestions, along with open issues pending resolution. Table 7.2 is a sample of issues within a tracking matrix. What is important about such a matrix is not its specific columns and rows, but the way it is used. For example, we have seen plants where such matrices were only maintained by workgroups and, too often, the failure to follow through on individual items became more visible, but the improvements were only a small gain over what would have happened had they not used the matrix. In other locations, the matrix is entered into a central database for the organization, so that it is visible on a broader basis. Indeed, some locations even have items move off of the workgroup matrix and onto an area or plant steering–committee agenda after sixty or ninety days. These last two concepts—making the matrix more visible and having a time-bound automatic escalation—can be powerful motivators for resolution at the workgroup level.

But there is a delicate balance—disconnects that are made visible at higher levels still have to be addressed in a problem-solving, nonblaming way. The assumption is that good faith effort was being made and it couldn't be resolved within the time period or at that level. If, in fact, it could have been resolved closer to the source or more quickly, that message will be quickly

TABLE 7.2 Sample Issues Tracking Matrix[5]

Item #	Initial Date	Issue	Action Needed	Responsible	Due Date	Status
1						
2						
3						
4						
5						

communicated. If not, then the increased visibility ensures resolution at the appropriate level. The value of the matrix is both as a record of accomplishment and an indicator of gaps or disconnects to be addressed.

Another useful tool in classifying data associated with learning and knowledge initiatives is a "stakeholder map," which can be constructed with a form such as is presented in table 7.3. This involves a listing of key stakeholders associated with the change initiative. Once listed, analysis quickly reveals stakeholders who are or are not constructively engaged in the initiative—pointing out disconnects that have a high potential to deteriorate into active opposition. A more colloquial version of the boxes in column three might be "can make the journey," "can make the journey with help," "can't or won't make the journey."

More complex than a stakeholder map is what is termed a "value stream map." This involves a mapping of the flow of a product or service through a facility or organization—highlighting points where value is added.[6] Among disconnects that can be revealed by a value stream map are a classification of what are termed the "seven wastes." They are: overproduction, waiting, transportation, inventory, processing, motion, and defects. As well, such maps can reveal "bottlenecks" or "constraints" in an operation, which is a way of classifying disconnects into those that have high leverage for improving a work system and those that are less central to the operation.

TABLE 7.3 Stakeholder Map

Key Stakeholders (individuals or groups)	Primary Interests or Concerns Regarding Change Initiative	Assessment and Implications
_____	• • •	☐ Committed and capable ☐ Needs skills and support ☐ Divided or opposed Comments:
_____	• • •	☐ Committed and capable ☐ Needs skills and support ☐ Divided or opposed Comments:
_____	• • •	☐ Committed and capable ☐ Needs skills and support ☐ Divided or opposed Comments:
_____	• • •	☐ Committed and capable ☐ Needs skills and support ☐ Divided or opposed Comments:
_____	• • •	☐ Committed and capable ☐ Needs skills and support ☐ Divided or opposed Comments:

Importantly, value stream mapping is not usually undertaken as a part of a learning system that deals with both the Bold Vision and Harsh Realities. It is primarily utilized as part of a "lean" or quality initiative with the focus of the efforts on meeting the vision of "lean." Our point, however, is that it is not a static activity—it is meant to foster learning through the use of data, knowledge, and action. It is also not a neutral activity—it reveals disconnects, dilemmas, and divergence as much as it documents the flow of products and services to a customer.

A classic form of data classification and analysis involving disconnects comes from survey data. Consider the continuous quality-improvement initiative highlighted as being on a slippery slope in chapter 3. A survey was conducted after briefings for the employees in this state agency. Over eight hundred employees were surveyed at a series of approximately forty orientation sessions. In response, approximately 9 percent of the employees indicated having enthusiasm about the change effort, 37 percent were interested in learning more about the change effort, 48 percent were skeptical about the potential of the change effort to really make a difference, and 5 percent had decided that it would be a waste of time. This divergence in reactions is typical in any change effort and serves as a baseline. The key question concerns just how to interpret the data.

One interpretation of the data is that 53 percent of the employees are skeptical or see the new initiative as a waste of time—a majority that might be seen as "against" the change effort. From this perspective, the resistance to change appears daunting. Another way of examining this data is to consider that 85% of the employees are expressing reactions that are more to the neutral position (somewhat positive or somewhat negative), rather than the two extremes. With demonstrated early successes, the skeptics might be won over and a strong majority could swing into support for the initiative. Needless to say, both interpretations are plausible and the "correct" interpretation depends on unfolding subsequent events. In this case, the data illustrates underlying divergence. The real question concerns whether subsequent events will exacerbate or moderate the splits.

In addition to survey data, there are also case examples that are instructive as data. For example, Sandra Goins, a former Boeing employee, recently presented testimony to the National Commission on the Future of the U.S. Aerospace Industry regarding her four-year apprenticeship training. She completed the training just after the September 11th, 2001, tragedies. The cruel irony of the situation is that she received her pink slip on the same day that she received her apprenticeship diploma certifying 8,000 hours of in-class, on-the-job, and off-hour studies in cutter-grinder skills.[7]

The training she received was invested in by herself, the company, and the union and included 680 hours of in-class training on how to read blueprints and use numerically controlled machines, 1760 hours of drill-grinder training, 2520 hours of tool-grinding training, 1720 hours of carbide-tool-grinding training, 1360 hours of machine-shop time, as well as 640 hours of math, physics, and trigonometry at Seattle Community College. Ms. Goins said the training was challenging and succeeding at it felt good but getting laid off forced her to change her career plans—seeking employment outside of the aerospace industry.

The disconnect could be dismissed as an unfortunate, isolated event—the fall-out from a massive shock to the economy and this company. But that would be an incomplete analysis of the data. Embedded in this case example are deeper questions, such as the level of company awareness of skills lost and skills at risk if there are further downsizing efforts, as well as the stories just like this that are unfolding at other aerospace companies. With such data, knowledge might be generated around ways to use temporary assignments with other area firms or other mechanisms to ensure a better return on the investment for all parties.

As we will discuss further in the chapter on mindsets, data on disconnects can be seen as opportunities or as threats. However, not collecting and classifying data on learning and knowledge disconnects merely increases the likelihood that disconnects will continue and the learning and knowledge efforts will deteriorate.

SKILLS FOR CONVERTING DILEMMAS INTO KNOWLEDGE

Generating knowledge is a different skill than classifying data. Classification involves collecting as much data as possible and then organizing it into categories. It is in the analysis of the data that knowledge is generated. When it comes to generating knowledge about disconnects, some of the most important knowledge concerns the underlying drivers or root causes, which frequently can be summarized in the form of underlying dilemmas.

Generating knowledge involves issues of time and resources. The first issue is time. Some actions are more immediate, while others are long-term. For example, the eight-step problem-solving process followed by the Ford Motor Company and the United Automobile Workers (UAW) union includes both a step for "containment" and a step for a more enduring solution.

The second issue involves resources. Many actions may be suggested, but not all are feasible. Certain actions may require people or funds that simply are not available. At the same time, action options shouldn't be summarily rejected on this basis. Sometimes, key stakeholders may see sufficient value in the effort to take action on a given disconnect that new resources will be brought in. This could be as simple as people who continue to puzzle over an issue on their own time, or as substantial as the identification of public training funds, or as dramatic as the enthusiasm of a stock market that increases a firm's valuation because of its perceived adaptability. The later situation, for example, accounts for a great deal of the value that the stock market has placed on the General Electric Corporation. It is a value placed not on its mix of businesses at any given point of time, but on its ability to act in response to challenges that emerge with any given business.[8]

Sometimes the generation of knowledge is more organic. This often occurs during what Peter Senge terms a "Learning Dialogue." Groups of stakeholders will sit in a circle with precise ground rules—only one person talks at a time, others all have to listen in a deep and focused way, and silence is okay. Such dialogues will often reveal organic connections among disparate disconnects, prompting "light bulbs" to go off as the connections are made.[9] Making the time available for such dialogue seems difficult in advance. Once connections are made between various disconnects and deep learning takes place, the time involved seems worth the effort.[10]

In addition to time and resources, individuals must have the skills and commitment to generate knowledge from the data on disconnects. One valuable set of skills in this regard revolves around what is termed "relapse prevention." With this approach, trainees are asked after training to consider the types of situations that will arise once back on the job which will hinder the application of the skill sets gained in training. Once those situations are identified (the disconnects), then the trainee can examine the common elements of those situations (patterns) and develop a proactive response to those situations. The underlying idea of relapse prevention is to anticipate and plan for difficulties in using new learning skills. More specifically, individuals should: (1) identify circumstances or situations posing a high risk for not using the new skills (for example, time pressures); (2) be trained in problem solving in a way that individuals learn to treat potential high-risk situations as challenges to be not only anticipated but negotiated and planned for; (3) have actual practice in how to cope with high-risk situations so as to learn how to avoid disconnects; and (4) be trained in cognitive strategies to cope with feelings of guilt and the sense of failure associated with "slips" or times when individuals revert back to habitual ways of acting rather than ways consistent with the new convergent skills.

Research indicates that people who have been through relapse-prevention interventions are often more likely to actually use the skills in spite of the situational constraints where the press to return to the "normal" way of doing things is high.[11] For example, studies have found that trainees (for example, in a supervisory skills training course) exposed to a relapse-prevention program reported more communications with their managers regarding how to develop their skills, had a greater understanding of how to use and apply the new skills, and reported greater recognition of bad habits that might inhibit skill use in comparison to a group that did not receive the intervention.[12] This approach then attempts to clearly identify situations that are likely to cause disconnects, systematically examines them, and proactively plans for ways to deal with disconnects prior to these situations arising.

Another powerful tool for generating knowledge is strategic planning. In its simplest form, strategic planning involves three steps: (1) identifying a desired future state, (2) describing current state realities, and (3) listing "delta" state milestones that will get from the current state to the desired state.[13] Here the knowledge is converted into an action plan with a clear sequence of milestones aimed at bridging the gap between current reality and the desired future state. The power of strategic planning goes far beyond the set of milestones generated. If this were the only outcome, one individual could produce a plan and leave it at that. More important are the shared insights or knowledge generated as a group contemplates the gap between the current state and the desired state—enabling them to be more prepared even if circumstances dictate that they depart for the sequence of milestones.

Another important way to generate knowledge involves the use of pilot or demonstration experiments. Here there are not sufficient resources or sufficient certainty to apply knowledge across an entire operation, but there are sufficient resources and certainty to support one or more experimental efforts aimed at addressing disconnects or opportunities. As we noted in chapter 6, there are many factors that can limit the ability to diffuse lessons learned from pilot initiatives, but a pilot experiment can be more robust if these limits are surfaced explicitly.

Coaching and mentoring processes are also key knowledge-building mechanisms—specifically oriented around identifying and addressing disconnects. Coaching has frequently been seen as a relatively low-level activity that was nice when it occurred, but not essential for organizational success. Increasingly, however, almost everyone in an organization will have some domain of expertise where they need to coach others. It could be peer-to-peer coaching as part of job rotation, it could be coaching among internal "customers" and "suppliers," it could be coaching by expert employees to novices, or other knowledge and capability transfers.

Mentoring has historically been seen as something reserved for the elite few employees singled out for their high potential by senior leaders. Increasingly, however, organizations are launching broadly based mentoring programs where all new employees are assigned to mentors to help the new employees find their way through the organization. But mentoring can go in the reverse direction as well. For example, the (now retired) director of Worldwide Training and Development for the Ford Motor Company, Ed Sketch, commented that he divided his time as a mentor with half of it devoted to providing career support for the more junior employees for whom he was the assigned mentor; and half asking these junior employees to mentor him in what it is like to be a Generation X member entering this corporation. He was particularly interested in their helping him to better understand the system barriers and other realities with which they have had to cope—in the exact same way that he shares his experience around the system barriers and other realities with which he has had to cope. It is a true, two-way mentoring process that fully values experience and the development of knowledge by all parties.[14]

At the Rockwell Collins avionics operations in Cedar Rapids, Iowa, a mentoring program has recently been set up to help a broad cross-section of employees gain professional skills and insight. Senior managers and workers mutually select one another and meet each week for one to two hours. Currently, 105 mentors are working with a total of 130 employees in 11 out of

12 business units. Of these pairs, approximately 15 to 20 are cross-functional. Beyond the direct learning, these relationships are credited with helping to reduce turnover. There is a 3% attrition rate among those who are mentored as compared to the normal 5–8% rate in this location. Both members of a mentor pair receive skills training to support their work.[15]

In building skill sets around coaching and mentoring, we have adapted our Bold Vision learning cycle to this context. In this adaptation, which is presented in figure 7.2, the particular form of data relevant during coaching and mentoring comes from "Observation," while the knowledge relevant comes from "Discussion," and the action is represented by an "Agreement" on next steps. In the absence of observation and discussion (the first two steps), coaching and mentoring is just the imposition of preconceived views based on unchecked assumptions. In most cases, there is some observation and discussion. Coaching and mentoring initiatives fall apart, however, in the third step, action, which involves agreements based on the discussion. It is in these tangible agreements to apply new knowledge that coaching and mentoring reach their fullest potential. In the absence of such agreements, coaching and mentoring is undercut.

Note that this Coaching and Mentoring Cycle was adapted from the Bold Vision learning cycle in response to a series of disconnects. As we saw in chapter 2, the Lucent Corporation had a fast-track degree program in new finance principles (developed by Babson College), but they found the graduates were underappreciated and underutilized on the job. Instead of casting blame, both the college and the corporation took a closer look at the data on disconnects. They found that the supervisors and managers responsible for these new graduates were, for the most part, not knowledgeable about the new finance principles, nor were they skilled in the area of coaching and mentoring. The response was the development of a training/intervention in which about one-half of the training was in new finance and entrepreneur-

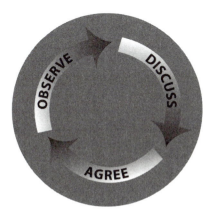

Figure 7.2 Coaching and mentoring cycle. (Adapted from the Bold Vision learning cycle)

ship principles and the balance built on the coaching and mentoring cycle to provide needed interactive skills to be effective in this new role.

SKILLS FOR TRANSLATING DIVERGENCE INTO ACTION

Linking "divergence" with "action" represents the final two areas in which the two cycles correspond. This can be done in a constructive way where divergence is understood as a feedback loop, necessary in order to sustain progress toward a Bold Vision. Most valuable here are various types of feedback and evaluation tools, which are typically underutilized in organizational learning systems.

Traditional approaches to evaluation of training sessions, conferences, seminars, and other learning events can include the following:

A. Pre-session "baseline" assessment of knowledge and skills

B. Immediate postsession assessment of knowledge, skills, and satisfaction

C. Subsequent follow-up assessment on actual application of knowledge and skills

Such assessments can be done with survey forms, individual interviews, focus group interviews, and other means. Of the three, the most common (and perhaps least useful) is "B"—the immediate postsession evaluation survey. While this will reveal some divergence in views that can be instructive, far more valuable is the divergence in baseline skills prior to any intervention and the divergence long afterwards, when people have had a chance to apply what they have learned.

A different form of assessment on action involves the examination of archival performance metrics. These might be metrics on quality, safety, schedule, cost, or other performance indicators. There are many ways to set up such assessments so that they can be run as what are termed "quasi-experimental" designs.[16] For example, an effort to focus team knowledge around quality improvement might also involve the tracking of quality performance data before and after the launch of the initiative. This is illustrated below as "Design 1," where the measurements are taken at each of the five time periods (T1 to T5). The aim is always two-fold: what worked well and what could be improved.

DESIGN 1 : Pre- and Postsession Assessment

T1	T2	T3	T4	T5
Before Launch		Launch	After Launch	

A similar design can be used in comparing the results in three comparable work areas where one serves as the "control" with no intervention and the other two feature staggered launches, as is illustrated in Design 2:

DESIGN 2: Control Work Area and Staggered Launches in Two Other Work Areas

Area 1	T1	T2	T3	T4	T5	T6
	Control					
Area 2	T1	T2	T3	T4	T5	T6
	Before Launch		Launch	After Launch		
Area 3	T1	T2	T3	T4	T5	T6
	Before Launch		Launch	After Launch		

Again, performance measures would be tracked at each time period with the aim of assessing the impact of the learning or knowledge initiative. Many other such designs are possible. The point here is the creative use of archival performance metric data and "naturally occurring" experimental opportunities.

There are always ethical and practical issues in such experimental designs concerning the "withholding" of launch/implementation resources from some areas and not others. There are also selection issues if the launch and implementation is done on a nonrandom basis, such as managers who do or do not volunteer. Even with these and other barriers to reliability or validity of the analysis, examining such data has the great advantage of assessing actual performance outcomes—not just process or throughput measures.

"Postmortem" reviews are a useful assessment tool for project-oriented work. Some organizations will not assign people to new projects until such postmortems are complete. Developing the knowledge-management process that ensures the use of the postmortem data by future project teams is often difficult—a disconnect in its own right. However, properly utilized, this kind of analysis of action can prevent countless future disconnects.

While these traditional evaluation tools are important, the key issue is what is being measured. The traditional approach is to measure progress on the project or task at hand—whether the convergent learning cycle is leading to behavioral and performance changes. Individuals can be trained in skills to help in this type of evaluation process. The less traditional approach involves assessing action relevant to the divergent learning cycle. This approach to evaluation would focus on less tangible but nevertheless critical actions and events that can be made more visible by an evaluation system. For example, one could anticipate that the move to organizational learning will actually lead people to feel more role conflict and ambiguity early on in the process. Here, what has normally been seen as a problem (increasing conflict and ambiguity) is viewed as a positive sign that something is happening in the process of becoming a learning organization—something that needs to be measured.

In addition, one could also expect more discussion of disconnects and underlying divergence that have been hidden. Thus, individuals and teams within the organization need to develop skill sets on what to look for when change processes are in action and how to make the seemingly intangible aspects of change more tangible so that learning can occur to drive the change. This skill set would have to include a greater understanding of the organization, how it is structured and why, what pressures are faced by different functions or departments and how systems within the organization interrelate. Only then can individuals begin to see productive dialogue around disconnects, divergence, and dilemmas.

One example of this need to develop new criteria for success is indicated by a recent case involving survey feedback. A state agency was interested in surveying all personnel on their perceptions of the organizational culture. A critical aspect of this process was to focus attention to how the data would be interpreted prior to even collecting the data from the survey. Leaders and officers needed to be trained on the basic issues of survey methodology and data analysis. In addition to this traditional Bold Vision approach, there was also a need to deal with the Harsh Reality of training leaders around what is data and what is not. Leaders were trained that data is not the same thing as "knowledge" and knowledge at an individual level is not the same thing as shared knowledge throughout the organization. Data not only has to be classified (analysis of the data) but then has to be interpreted by a number of people in the organization to form shared knowledge about what the survey results actually represent. Only with shared knowledge about interpretation across various people in this organization, could action planning for improvement really begin. Leaders were led through an exercise to show how data can be interpreted in multiple ways. This led to a discussion of how to view divergent interpretations of seemingly straightforward data from surveys as opportunities for learning rather than as something to avoid or ignore.

Leadership skills are a final and essential set of skills in the nexus between divergence and action. The Sloan School of Management has highlighted four key skills along these lines, which we have adapted and expanded into the following five skills: visioning, analyzing, relating, inventing, and enabling.[17] Each is a skill that is well-grounded in the literature and essential for action. Each, however, has its own disconnects, dilemmas, and divergence. Visions can be imposed, rather than shared. Analysis can be rooted in unchecked assumptions. Relations can be built, but key stakeholders excluded. Invention can be rejected as "not invented here." Enabling can be undercut by internal competition for scarce resources. Rather than bemoaning the barriers to leadership, however, we urge that it is the very work of leaders to value these disconnects so that they can play appropriate leadership roles with respect to organizational learning systems.

LINKING NEW SKILL SETS TO FORMS OF ORGANIZATIONAL LEARNING

The skills required for classifying disconnects, understanding dilemmas, and addressing divergence span many types of organizational learning. Overall, many of the skills listed above are relatively routine. As a result, when stakeholder relations are fragmented, the skills associated with the Bold Vision learning cycle will result in incremental learning for the organization. Those individuals using the skills associated with learning from disconnects will generate incremental gains for the organization. Where relations among key stakeholders are more aligned, the sustained use of these same skills will set in motion continuous learning dynamics—where the learning and skills represent ever-increasing, self-reinforcing capability. In other words, constructively engaging the disconnects, dilemmas, and divergence can generate different types of learning.

Note, however, that some application and assessment skills are more than just routine. There is adaptive expertise woven throughout some of the skills associated with valuing disconnects. For example, the evaluation models such as quasi-experimental designs can be integral to experimental learning. As well, coaching and mentoring processes and experimental initiatives can often trigger more synergistic learning when there is sufficient alignment among stakeholders for these different perspectives to come together.

On the other hand, entrenched learning and revolutionary learning are not the intended outcome of increasing the skills associated with learning from disconnects. It does mean, however, that these forms of learning will be more readily recognized and understood, rather than just being suppressed.

In many respects, the entire field of organizational development (OD) is centered on the skillful bridging between the Bold Visions and the Harsh Realities. Constructively engaging all six forms of learning is central to the work of OD professionals. While the concept of OD is most often associated with adaptive capability, there are many routine skills on which this is built. As figure 7.3 illustrates, there are relatively routine skills, such as facilitation or training delivery, that can expand into more adaptive skills, such as process expertise or being able to train trainers. Other skills listed on the chart are more adaptive even at the lower level, such as strategic planning or organizational assessment, but even here the spectrum extends to include exceptionally adaptive skills, such as being a strategic visionary or an organizational architect.

The set of skills associated with facilitation and training involves a broad spectrum, as we have noted, but it is mostly centered on incremental and continuous learning. This stands in contrast with the skills associated with strategic planning and systems thinking, which are mostly centered on experimental and synergistic learning. Meanwhile, the skills around mediation and serving as "thermometer" are particularly salient in the context of oppositional and revolutionary learning.

If we only focus on the Bold Visions, it may be possible to see learning systems as separate from organizational development. If we also take into account Harsh Realities, it becomes virtually impossible to disentangle organizational development from organizational learning systems. Organizational development professionals must be skilled in learning systems and

Basic Skills	Competent	Expert	Master

Facilitator . . . . Process Expert

Trainer . . . . Trainer of Trainers

Mediator . . . . Shuttle Diplomat

"Thermometer" . . . . Moral/Ethical Sounding Board

Strategic Planner . . . . Strategic Visionary

Systems Thinker . . . . Systems Designer

Organizational Assessor . . . . Organizational Architect

Figure 7.3 A spectrum of skills associated with distinct OD roles

learning professionals much be skilled in OD. In this respect, the skills sets for success in both domains are identical.

A CASE EXAMPLE: SKILL SETS AS A FOUNDATION FOR ORGANIZATIONAL TRANSFORMATION

Great Lakes Industries (GLI), a small manufacturing company in Michigan, provides an example of a company committed to building both routine and adaptive skills sets from both the Bold Vision and Harsh Reality learning perspectives. A maker of sprockets and gears, GLI recognized in the late 1980s that their survival depended upon developing a more efficient and effective operation—where productivity, quality, and timeliness were the keys to competitive advantage. They moved from a functional, assembly line manufacturing process to a cellular manufacturing process. The cellular manufacturing philosophy involves the development of a team-based work system, where employees are owners of a manufacturing process that leads to a finished product. This required individuals to learn how to operate different types of machines (lathes, drills, broaches, hobs) in order to operate a cell to produce a product. In addition, the organization has focused on improving interactive group-process skills to build its adaptive capabilities.

This transformational effort began with the creation of the overall vision and underlying values that the organization wanted to pursue and create. A team of employees and management generated the vision and values. The vision included the following components:

1. to remain competitive, we must continually improve quality, productivity, and profitability;

2. everyone in the company will have access to business knowledge, will understand the company's financial performance, and will share in the long-term success; and

3. the focus must be on meeting and exceeding customer needs and maintaining long-term relationships with valued customers.

The underlying values by which the vision would be accomplished were identified as:

1. the operative principle is one of teamwork, involvement, empowerment, and responsibility among its members;

2. interactions among members will embody a climate of trust, mutual respect, and open communication; and

3. we will be characterized by continuous learning that integrates problem solving, technical updating, and people skills.

Meeting the vision and values of the company required first a heavy emphasis on developing basic skills and knowledge within the workforce. These basis skills could then be expanded to develop more advanced skills so that the level of expertise in the organization around work processes was enhanced. In addition, the move to develop these critical routine types of expertise—including basic and advanced skills—were created within an emerging framework that supported the development of adaptive expertise.

Building Routine Expertise   There were a number of interventions to move the organization towards its vision and values that had major implications for the need to build routine expertise across all employees rather than relying on specialists or a few highly trained individuals. One intervention was to use group technology to achieve high-quality standards in product design, and planning. Group technology involves grouping like problems to exploit similarities in product and processes in an effort to simplify and control the quality of work. Second, the manufacturing process was reorganized around manufacturing cells that operate as discrete, "focused" factories within the company. All aspects of cell operation, production, and quality are controlled by the teams of people who operate and set them up. Third, the focus was on building and designing quality at the source. The primary responsibility for quality was to lie with the operators and cell team members. To make it right the first time, the operator was given the resources, responsibilities, and the tools to do the job.

The move to group technology, manufacturing cells, and quality at the source was accomplished through the shared efforts of management and line workers. Companywide teams were created to operationalize the vision by developing a prototype for the plant, evaluating its success, and developing procedures for generalizing from the pilot program to the development of other manufacturing cells. Cross-cell teams were formed to develop guidelines for safety procedures, quality, machine maintenance, and tooling. Other teams were formed to develop a standardized set of procedures on how to operate the various machines (hobs, lathes, drills, broaching) in the factory. Within each cell team, weekly meetings are held to review quality and safety concerns and to consider ways to continuously improve cell processes.

Consequently, much effort and resources were devoted to employee training. One of the first steps was to build internal technical expertise to run the cells. This required the standardization of work since individuals performed the same tasks in different ways. Individuals were then assessed and given priorities as to training needs across the various skills (A = immediate need; B = somewhat of a need, and C = low need). A training plan for the entire workforce was developed and implemented. Cooperative educational programs were utilized to improve skills in areas such as statistical-process control, group technology, quality at the source, print reading, gauge usage, and geometric tolerance. Train-the-trainer systems were put into place where technical specialists trained less experienced employees to build technical expertise in running the various machines in a cell.

The second phase of learning activities involved building interpersonal expertise. Employees in the company had been used to coming to work and producing what was expected without much interaction across functions. Interpersonal or team skills included learning how to work effectively with others. These skills also included analyzing internal customer-supplier relationships and considering ways to improve those relationships, as well as developing assertiveness skills, teambuilding skills, and meeting skills. This was also mostly a routine process, but it involved much higher levels of interdependence—a form of continuous learning.

The third phase was the development of process skills. The process skills focused on how the work gets done through other people and included problem solving, process improvement, and continuous learning. At GLI, every operator attended courses on problem identification and problem solving. These skills are put to the test each week as the team meets to discuss problems in the cell and to develop solutions to problems of quantity, quality, safety, maintenance, and housekeeping. A new position of integrator across cells was created. The person in this job attends cell team meetings and helps facilitate the discussion around process-improvement strategies. The person also brings innovations made in other cells to the attention of other teams to help diffuse the innovation. A major duty of the integrator is to ensure that there is consistency across cell teams in terms of running meetings, identifying problems to be addressed, creating action plans, as well as monitoring and following up on projects.

For such a small company, training and learning have become integral to how they do their business. The heavy investment in training and learning is supported by the human resource system. For example, employees can obtain higher hourly salaries by obtaining their two-year college associates degree and for adding new technical skills to their repertoire. The level of routine expertise has risen dramatically across manufacturing, shipping, and engineering groups over the last twelve years.

Building Adaptive Expertise Building adaptive expertise requires a commitment to deal with the realities of the workplace and to use those realities to help transform work.[18] In other words, the challenges of the realities of the workplace (for example, predictable disconnects) should come to be viewed not as barriers but as opportunities to learn and improve. For example, employees and managers at GLI had to become comfortable and skilled in solving problems creatively; in dealing with uncertain and unpredictable work situations; in learning to plan for, participate in, and learn from developmental activities; and in adjusting one's interpersonal style to work with others and achieve a goal.

The transformational effort to build adaptive skills rests on the pillars of systems thinking, employee participation, and learning. Rather than being solely the "transformation" part of the manufacturing process (for example, drilling a hole into a piece of steel all day), each employee and team has become a minisystem within the larger system. Each cell or minisystem is in charge of the inputs (for example, determining what jobs to run), transformation (taking raw material and transforming it into a product), outputs (preparing output for shipping directly to the customer), and feedback (checking own quality). Cell members have become empowered to set up the machines in their cell in whatever way made sense and to calculate their own cycle times for getting the work done. Eventually, cells were able to schedule their own work, to do their own maintenance, to make purchases to improve cell operations, and to improve daily operations.

In addition, an emphasis has been placed on providing workers with extensive information on the company's financial situation. In this way, employees are seeing the "big picture." GLI took this idea of providing information to employees and developed an extensive thirty-hour, fifteen-module training program called GLI Business 101. During the various modules, employees not only learned more about the pressures facing the company, but also gained knowledge and skills typically reserved for managers. Employees were led through information- and skill-building exercises, such that they became "accountants," "sales and marketing representatives," and the "plant manager" for that module or set of modules. For example, employees were led through standard accounting practices and applied that to their company. They calculated the various factory costs of doing business as part of this course (how much it costs to purchase steel, what factors impact cost within the factory) as well as completed exercises on nonfactory expenses, such as sales commissions, interest, federal taxes, and profit sharing. They completed various scenarios, such as what the implications are for profit given different factors (for example, steel prices, required price adjustments demanded by customers, reject rates, set-up times, production rates).

The different scenarios drilled into the employees the complexity the organization faces and the choices that must be made on a regular basis which can impact the shop floor. It also highlighted the choices that employees have to make on the shop floor and their implications for profitability. For example, one person noted that he had not realized how much set-up times affected the bottom line, given other constraints in the system, and the limited profit margins for certain products, given customer demands for reduction in pricing. When jobs hit the floor and when predictable disconnects occur, that person and others are now poised to make more intelligent choices regarding scheduling, downtime, who needs to do which setups, and so on.

From the initial set up of the pilot teams until today, the focus has been on making all individuals in the organization aware of the bigger picture, on encouraging people to stretch their skills, on tolerating mistakes especially early in the application of new ideas, on valuing new ideas, and on minimizing situational constraints to learning and performance.[19] This has led, over time, to a perspective of not hiding disconnects in the system. For example, the scenario-planning process has become embedded in the daily operations of the organization. When new ideas are presented, employees are comfortable talking about likely scenarios (both good and bad) and the impact they might have relevant to the new idea. When new systems are put into place and they do not work out as expected, teams of individuals are formed (like a SWAT team in policing) to delve into the issues and use the disconnects as data to drive learning. Systems and divergence within those systems are examined to determine multiple root causes and potential solutions.

In addition, real-life scenarios have been developed so as to aid learning in other groups in the organization. For example, one team was faced with a customer problem, conducted a problem-solving process, and discovered a number of problems that cut across what marketing/salespeople thought was possible and what engineering people assumed that production people would recognize. They also discovered that a relatively new person had put on a job regarded as fairly routine, when it was not actually routine due to a seemingly minor change in the customer order from previous orders. The systems thinking that went on in that team not only was used to drive new knowledge about disconnects and divergence within the organization but was then shared across teams so that similar problems would not occur.

Recently, employees on one of the first established teams (formed about ten years previously) had a one-day retreat to reflect on their progress. The first hour was focused on developing a historical chart of key events, people, and work issues. It was a lively discussion. Individuals on the team then described their own personal struggles around issues of (1) work pressure and the introduction of new products, and quality; (2) technology and how equipment is maintained; (3) personal development and cross-training, computer skills, and interpersonal skills; (4) workplace support and dealing with other cells, interacting with other departments on the floor (for example, shipping), and working with other areas off the floor (engineering, sales/marketing, management); and (5) cell members and dealing with leadership changes, moving personnel in and out of the cell, maintaining cross-shift relations and introducing new employees. After individual reflection and discussion, the team summarized the key issues surrounding the struggles and discussed lessons learned such as what individuals would do differently if similar situations that caused personal struggles came up in the future. They completed the retreat by applying the lessons to dealing with the predictable future changes or challenges that GLI faces so they can remain adaptable. What was amazing was the level or depth of personal reflection, and a willingness to share what from an outsider perspective would be difficult issues to discuss.

It has taken a number of years for the change effort at GLI to unfold—"top-management supported, long-range effort to improve an organization's problem-solving and renewal process, particularly through a more effective and collaborative diagnosis and management of organizational culture."[20] For example, it took time for members to see that management was actually serious about taking a systems perspective (rather than blaming individuals for problems), empowering others, and developing an organizational learning orientation. In addition, it has taken some time for employees to feel comfortable with uncertain and unpredictable work situations. Through sustained leadership and the efforts of the members to make this happen, the company has moved from the brink of collapse to a company that is profitable, growing, and learning.

CONCLUSION

Changing skill sets so that disconnects can be valued, dilemmas understood, and divergence harnessed is a fundamental challenge for most organizations. The skills involved are relatively standard analytic skills associated with problem solving, quality, employee involvement, and other initiatives. What is new is the use of these skills in a systematic way to examine learning and knowledge disconnects. The building of these skill sets also required a change in mindset among managers and employee groups. The case study has indirectly touched on that issue. Chapter 8 pursues the importance of changing mindsets more directly.

Notes

1. One Japanese executive, commenting on the PDCA cycle from which the Bold Vision cycle is derived, noted that it had taken nearly a decade to develop mastery of "Plan," another decade for mastery of "Do," another decade for mastery of "Check," and another decade for mastery of "Act." We have great respect and appreciation for this sort of learning journey. See Pascal Dennis, *Lean Production Simplified: A Plant Language Guide to the World's Most Powerful Production System* (New York: Productivity Press, 2002), 17.

2. See Karolina Ivancic and Beryl Hesketh, "Making the Best of Errors During Training," *Training Research Journal*, 1 (1996): 103–134; Timothy P. Baldwin, "Effects

of Alternative Modeling Strategies on Outcomes of Interpersonal Skills Training," *Journal of Applied Psychology*, 77 (1992): 147–155; and Doete Heimbeck, Michael Frese, Sabine Sonnetag, and Nina Kieth, "Integrating Errors into the Training Process: The Function of Error Management Instructions and the Role of Goal Orientation," *Personnel Psychology*, 56 (2003), 333–362.

3. See Michael Frese, "Error Management in Training: Conceptual and Empirical Results," In *Organizational Learning and Technological Change*, ed. Cristina Zucchermaglio, Sebastiano Gagnara, and Susan U. Stuchy (New York: Springer-Verlag, 1995), 112–124; Brad Bell, "An Examination of the Instructional, Motivational, and Emotional Elements of Error Training." (Unpublished dissertation, Michigan State University, 2002); and Stan Gully, Stephanie Payne, K. Lee Kohls, and Jon-Andrew Whiteman, "The Impact of Error Training and Individuals Differences on Training Outcomes: An Attribute-Treatment Interaction Perspective," *Journal of Applied Psychology*, 87 (2002): 143–155.

4. List of ideas from brainstorming sessions are often prioritized, but we do not recommend prioritizing disconnects. Any list of disconnects can be prioritized in many different ways. A group that is thinking along different lines will not be aided by a prioritizing process, even if one or two priorities seem to emerge. Are these priorities for immediate attention? Are these priorities in terms of potential long-term impact? Are these priorities as cost-effective or high leverage items? In most cases, disconnects are too far removed from underlying factors to be usefully prioritized.

Converting a list of disconnects into action implications does, however, set the stage for a useful prioritization. Here distinctions can be made among immediate containment actions versus longer-term issues. Similarly, distinctions can be made between low-cost and high-cost actions. However the actions are organized, it is then possible to prioritize the actions within a given category—to surface the most important immediate actions or the actions that require the least amount of new resources or the actions that are likely to have the highest leverage.

5. This matrix is adapted from a model developed by Roger Komer and others in the UAW-Ford system.

6. Mike Rother and John Shook, *Learning to See Version 1.2* (Brookline, MA: Lean Enterprises Institute, Inc., 1999).

7. Testimony to the National Aerospace Commission, cited in Joel Cutcher-Gershenfeld, Betty Barrett, Eric Rebintisch, Thomas Kochan, and Robert Scott, "Developing a 21st Century Aerospace Workforce" (Policy White Paper submitted to Human Capital/Workforce Task Force, The U.S. Commission on the Future of the Aerospace Industry, 2001).

8. We should note, however, that the resources flowing to a company such as General Electric on this basis do reveal a dilemma inherent in the process of taking action. Many actions will involve hard choices that are less advantageous or even directly threatening to the interests of a given set of stakeholders. New resources may be forthcoming to a company such as GE due to its willingness to sell off underperforming businesses, for example. This is more feasible in the case of a diversified conglomerate corporation. It is still possible, but it is much more complicated for a company that is primarily focused on a given industry—such as automobile manufacturing, steel making, or health care. In these cases, new resources from shareholders will depend on other ways of adding value—such as through constant innovation or the pioneering of new business models. Even in these cases, however, hard choices will be involved—stakeholders who are threatened by a given set of actions.

9. See Peter Senge, *The Fifth Discipline: The Art and Practice of the Learning Organization* (New York: Doubleday, 1990).

10. This, in itself, is a dilemma—the allocation of time is only valuable in retrospect.

11. See Robert D. Marx, "Improving Management Development Through Relapse Prevention Strategies," *Journal of Management Development*, 5 (1986): 27–40; Lisa A. Burke, *High Impact Training Solutions* (Westport, Connecticut: Quorum Books, 2001).

12. See Lisa A. Burke and Timothy P. Baldwin, "Workforce Training Transfer: A Study of the Effect of Relapse Prevention Training and Transfer Climate," *Human Resources Management*, 38 (1990): 227–242.

13. Note that these terms (desired state, current state, and delta state) are used by Jeanenne LaMarsh and other change models.

14. Personal conversation with Ed Sketch, 2000.

15. Betty Barrett, *Rockwell Collins and IBEW* (Labor Aerospace Research Agenda case study, 2002). Cambridge, Mass.: MIT Press.

16. See William Shadish, Thomas D. Cook, and Donald T. Campbell, *Experimental and Quasi-Experimental Design for Generalized Inference* (Boston: Houghton Mifflin, and William Shadish, Thomas D. Cook, and Laura Levion, *Foundations of Program Evaluation: Theories of Practice* (Newbury Park, CA: Sage, 1991).

17. We have changed the wording to "analyzing" and we have added the concept of "enabling," based on the observation that leaders do some of their most important work by providing others with needed tools and resources. The original model was developed by Deborah Ancona, Thomas Kochan, John Van Maanen, Maureen Scully, and D. Eleanor Westney in *Managing for the Future: Organizational Behavior & Processes* (Cincinnati, OH: South-Western College Publishing, 1996).

18. See Elaine D. Pulokos, Sharon Arad, Michelle A. Donovan, and Kevin E. Plamondon, "Adaptability in the Workplace: Development of a Taxonomy of Adaptive Performance," (2002), *Journal of Applied Psychology*, 85 (2000): 612–624, for a discussion and definition of adaptability in the workforce.

19. These characteristics have been identified as the hallmark of a continuous learning system. See Scott Tannenbaum, "Enhancing Continuous Learning: Diagnostic Findings from Multiple Companies," *Human Resource Management*, 36 (1997): 437–452.

20. Definition of organizational development by Wendell L. French and Cecil H. Bell, *Organizational Development*, 6th ed. (Englewood Cliffs: Prentice Hall, 1999).

Changing Mindsets

A s human beings we excel in the ability to recognize and interpret patterns. It is the primary way that infants make sense of the world and learn. It lies at the heart of all scholarly disciplines. In this respect, the mindset for appreciating learning-system disconnects should come naturally.

But there is a problem here: Disconnects are around learning and knowledge. How can we harness our natural abilities to recognize and interpret patterns when we are encountering barriers to learning and knowledge? After all, learning and knowledge disconnects are doubly pernicious—they are directly frustrating as disconnects and they undercut the general ability to engage these and other disconnects.

We have seen barriers to engaging disconnects such as "action-oriented" organizational cultures that demand quick, knee-jerk solutions to disconnects, as well as "good news" organizational cultures that respond to disconnects with blame, cover-ups, or attempts to downplay their impact. In these cases, disconnects get narrow, short-term treatment that is more likely to exacerbate the situation than to help it.

A more constructive approach, as we saw in chapter 7, depends on new skill sets. A preponderance of people in the organization need to be able to analyze data, apply knowledge, and take action relevant to both Bold Visions and Harsh Realities. But building new or expanded skill sets alone will not assure success. Equally important, as we explore in this chapter, are the mechanisms for ensuring the mindsets needed to address constructively the learning and knowledge disconnects.

The most successful learning organizations that we have seen are ones in which the first response to a disconnect is to seek understanding rather than to blame individuals or institute a quick fix. This appreciation for disconnects was evident in a statement by a senior executive in one of the world's leading Japanese auto companies. He was meeting with the manager of an engine plant and asked why production had not been shut down due to engine shortages during the three years that he had been plant manager. The plant manager was confused. He stated that shutting down an assembly plant was the one thing he should never do. The executive countered that it was not something that he should do with any frequency, but if it didn't happen at all then it meant the organization was not learning about the full capabilities of the system. In other words, disconnects properly embraced and managed are a tool for pushing at the frontiers of knowledge. A fire burns hottest at its edges.[1]

THE MINDSET FOR LEARNING FROM DISCONNECTS

Many powerful tools and techniques were reviewed in chapter 7 as part of the skill set needed to address disconnects that arise in the context of training, learning, and other knowledge-based initiatives. However, use of these tools and techniques is constrained by the mindsets in many organizations.

There is a growing array of change initiatives that call for new ways of thinking or different mindsets. In the field of organizational learning, there has been great attention to the need to foster "systems thinking."[2] In his book *The Fifth Discipline*, Peter Senge highlights systems thinking and "mental models"—both of which are concerned with changing mindsets—as two of the five key disciplines. In discussions of "lean" principles, there are calls for the importance of "lean thinking."[3] As one leader from Toyota commented "Lean is a way of thinking, not a list of things to do."[4] In the domain of policy deployment initiatives, there is a call for what is termed "A3 thinking," reflecting the need to put on a single page key ideas for policy deployment across an organization (A3 paper is the European size of paper that roughly corresponds to 11×17).[5] Sometimes there are just more general calls for a change in the culture. But these and related shifts in mindset are not easily induced.

In new, entrepreneurial start-ups it is possible to establish a culture that values disconnects from the outset, though this can deteriorate over time. In existing operations, the challenge is even deeper since cultures that undercut new mindsets are already in place. Organizational cultures don't change quickly,[6] so the process of shifting mindsets must be understood as a long-term undertaking.

To fully appreciate the scale and scope of the challenge, return to two cycles, one representing the Bold Visions for organizational learning and the other representing the Harsh Realities. When building new skill sets, we highlighted the correspondence between the two cycles. It was our recommendation that disconnects be treated as data, dilemmas be understood as knowledge, and divergence be linked to action. Shifting mindsets goes further; it involves the integration of each.

One way of thinking about this integration is presented in figure 8.1 with the Bold Vision cycle embedded in the spaces between each of the elements of the Harsh Reality cycle and vice versa. At each stage of the 3Ds—disconnects, dilemmas, and divergence—there is a process of analyzing data to generate knowledge that then guides action. There is also the reverse cycle, where disconnects, dilemmas, and divergence are embedded in the Bold Vision around data, knowledge, and action.

This may not be the only way to represent the integration, but the key point is that every disconnect should be met with a mindset centered on

Figure 8.1   Integration of Bold Visions with Harsh Realities

data, knowledge, and action. The same is true for every dilemma and for all the dynamics around divergence. Conversely, data must always be understood as embodying disconnects, dilemmas, and divergence—which is also true for knowledge and action.

SIMULTANEOUSLY EMBRACING BOLD VISIONS AND APPRECIATING HARSH REALTIES

While we may have a vision of holding these two thoughts in mind at the same time, the reality is that most people find this hard to do. Often the focus is on one cycle or the other. Building such capability is a process, which involves stages comparable to the stages that are associated with any change initiative. To illustrate this process, we draw on a relatively standard representation of the stages associated with a change in mindset.

Presented as a curve, figure 8.2 tracks seven distinct stages or phases that are loosely derived from the stages of loss:[7] (1) shock, (2) denial, (3) awareness, (4) acceptance, (5) experimentation, (6) understanding, and (7) integration. For the interested reader, the appendix to this chapter provides supporting definitions and additional guidance associated with this transition curve. Notice that these stages are mapped against "time" on one axis and "perceived competence"[8] on the other. Note too that perceived competence rises quite high during the "denial" phase which can reinforce resistance to any change initiative. In this framework, the high level of perceived competence doesn't reach that height again until the "integration" phase. This is not a purely linear process—new events can shift some or all stakeholders forward or backward in rapid ways. In particular, the shift backward can skip many steps (such as a shift from "experimentation" back to "shock" when a major cut in funding is announced), while the movement forward does generally proceed step-by-step.

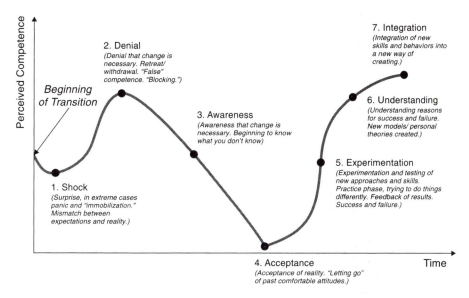

Figure 8.2 Leadership transition curve

Along this curve, the Bold Vision—linking data, knowledge, and action—is only going to be embraced in stages 5, 6, and 7—when experimentation, understanding, and integration is taking place. This is why so many initiatives that just depend on Bold Visions will have limited impact—the model doesn't include mechanisms to help people travel through stages 1 through 4. Any Bold Vision for learning that begins with experimentation is destined to encounter numerous disconnects across departments, levels, and individuals. Simply put, this mindset is rarely a viable point of departure. There has to be a degree of recognition and even legitimacy accorded to the steps of denial, shock, and awareness—which all figure prominently in the domain of the Harsh Realities.

How can leaders at all levels travel the initial distance through stages 1, 2, 3, and 4—from shock and denial through awareness and acceptance? We contend that this is only possible where there is both the skill set and the mindset to constructively deal with the predictable disconnects, underlying dilemmas, and the multiple forms of divergence.

One recent illustration of a way to facilitate the mindset change needed to move across the leadership transition curve occurred in an auto factory where the members of the plant operating committee were each asked to provide three ratings. First, they rated themselves on this curve. Second, they rated where on the transition curve that they felt best represented their operating committee. Third, they rated how people in the organization see "me." The results from this self-assessment process are presented in figure 8.3—plotted on the Leadership Transition Curve itself.

As is evident from this data, each member of the operating committee rated himself/herself higher than he/she rated the overall operating com-

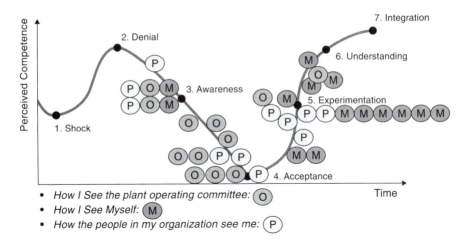

Figure 8.3 Plotting self-assessment data on the leadership transition curve

mittee. The members mostly saw themselves in the process of experimentation, while they saw their peers as somewhere between awareness and
acceptance—not too far from denial!

When presented with the data, the disconnect was immediately apparent
and it prompted extensive dialogue. The leaders realized that each could see
his or her own experimentation, but didn't know as much about the experimentation and learning by others on the operating committee. Further probing revealed that most of the time in their operating committee meetings
was spent reviewing weekly cost data—with little time for calibration or
shared learning. Here they faced a dilemma—focusing on short-term cost
performance versus long-term coordinated planning. Ultimately, the resolution was a restructuring of their weekly schedule to have a shorter-focused
cost meeting and a separate time devoted to dialog on strategic planning
and change management.

This example highlights a growing level of stakeholder alignment around
the changing nature of work—moving toward more of a knowledge-based
organizational model. This is not always the case. Consider the Black-
mer/Dover Resources Company, a pump manufacturing company that was
recently featured in a *Wall Street Journal* article. The article targeted a common disconnect—workers not willing to share specialized knowledge with
coworkers for fear that it would compromise their job security.[9]

Yet, buried in the *Wall Street Journal* article was the note that, for many
years, the assemblers in the plant "built most of a single pump at their workstations." This is a classic craft production model. New management brought
a new system that combined what might be termed the worst features of
lean production and mass production. On the one hand, "the new system
sought to eliminate excess inventory by producing only the type and number of pumps ordered"—which would be consistent with a lean production

model. On the other hand, "assemblers no longer built most of a single pump at their own workstations. Instead, the task was broken up into a series of steps along a short assembly line"—which is a classically Tayloristic approach. Those managers have since been replaced, but the result of their approach was increased delays in customer deliveries, increased costs, and reduced job satisfaction. The root of the problem, as the article points out, "was that former management hadn't given workers any input into the redesign." One of the plant's most seasoned pump builders was quoted as saying "They ignored our experience, because they thought any monkey could build pumps." In this case, the disconnect around not valuing the experience and intelligence of the full workforce would need attention before getting to the disconnects around older workers not sharing their wisdom with newer workers.

By contrast, consider the experience of a large computer and peripheral maintenance company at one of its California facilities.[10] This location provides maintenance services and support to a major customer located nearby. Complaints from this customer began to surface at corporate headquarters, which prompted a visit to the location by a senior corporate official. What he found was an operation where customer problems were well-known to the front-line service technicians and sales staff, but the facility manager consistently behaved in ways that indicated an interest in only hearing good news. Reports of complaints or problems invited rebukes and an insistence that they be "fixed right away."

This facility manager was reassigned to another operation where his strong technical skills could be effectively utilized and then the corporate official set about on the complicated task of changing the mindset among the workforce in this location. He called all staff together and held up a box full of plastic snakes. He turned to the group and asked, "What do you do when you see a snake in your back yard? Do you leave it alone, hoping it will go away and not come back? Or do you kill it if you can so that you know it won't come back?" People were a bit confused, but interested to hear where he was headed. He then held up one of the snakes and said, "Think of this snake as a problem with our customer. Every time one of these appears in our back yard, I want you to let me know and I want you to go after it until it is resolved." He said that he would give a plastic snake to everyone who came to him with a problem and an action plan for how they were going to address the problem. He said that it is not fun to go after a snake. It takes some guts. But failing to do so will not make the snake go away—it could even result in more coming. The corporate official indicated that he would stay around to help get operations back on track and then appoint a new facility manager.

There had been some concerns that this would just prompt frivolous claims of problems, but a vast majority of the issues that people brought forward were genuine problems. Soon the snakes became a badge of honor in the facility—proudly displayed outside offices and cubicles. Enthusiastic feedback began to come from this customer. Long-standing problems were being resolved and new problems were being addressed as soon as they came up.

Of course, the intervention in this case was not just a matter of giving out snakes. What really mattered was the way this executive responded to the problems and action plans that were brought forward. Taking each one seriously, allocating appropriate resources to address the issues—all in a non-blaming, constructive way—was key to the change in mindset at this location. The problem-solving skill sets of management and the workforce at all levels of the organization was necessary, but not sufficient to solve the customer service problems that were being experienced. Equally critical was the mindset that encouraged the constructive use of these skills.

CHANGING MINDSETS BY ANTICIPATING DISCONNECTS

In some respects, group dialogue in disconnects involves discussing what was previously "undiscussable." How can this be done in a constructive, nonblaming way that helps to shift mindsets? Using brainstorming skills to identify disconnects in advance is not just a valuable part of a skill set. It is also a process that impacts on mindsets.

For example, here is a list of disconnects generated from a workshop facilitated by one of the coauthors on the implementation of lean principles and practices in the aerospace industry. The participants included individuals from a wide range of organizations all with lead implementation responsibilities. One break-out group focusing on new roles and responsibilities in a lean work system, highlighted the following predictable disconnects:

- Champion does not "walk the talk"
- Lack of clarity with goals
- "Hollow" authority
- Unclear decision-making process
- Roles and responsibilities unclear
- Lack of a mechanism to build and sustain trust

The same group listed typical knee-jerk or Band Aid solutions to these disconnects. Again, these items were generated very easily, including:

- "Pep talk" mentality
- Leadership by designee
- Executive override of the decision-making process
- Call in the cavalry when things start going south
- Blame it on training
- Bigger banners

There is nothing unusual in the list of disconnects—these might arise with respect to any number of systems-change initiatives in many different sectors of the economy. In itself, there is some value in this list. For example, there are direct action implications that come off of the first list, such as clarifying roles and responsibilities or decision-making procedures.

But a deeper value comes for the growing comfort in talking about disconnects—this is a first step toward a mindset change. The mindset changes further with the experience of listing the second set of likely knee-jerk or "Band Aid" responses. If the response to disconnects involves pep talks, an insistence that middle-level managers just "go do it," or reactions such as "bigger banners," it is easy to see that the result will be more disconnects.

Deeper value comes from analyzing disconnects. This triggers appreciation for underlying dilemmas and various forms of divergence. What, for example, in this case will make it hard to clarify and implement new roles and responsibilities, which was one of the disconnects listed? Here we might encounter the cooperation/competition dilemma or the centralization/ decentralization dilemma in how roles have been defined. First-line supervisors may have been told that their new role is to empower work groups, but that their career advancement depends on performance outcomes. These are not simple issues in that you really do want to hold people accountable for performance outcomes, but you also want to hold them accountable for achieving the outcomes in appropriate, new ways. Although there are no easy solutions to such dilemmas, they at least focus attention on underlying root causes rather than on symptoms. Now the mindset is fully engaged. It becomes clear that the appropriate response to the disconnect is not to dust off old role and responsibility statements or to draft new ones—it is to analyze what factors are driving ambiguity and tension as people enact their roles and responsibilities.

Similarly, consider the analysis of another group at the same aerospace implementation workshop. This group examined the impact on lean implementation of aerospace mergers and consolidations. The following list of predictable disconnects were identified:

- Communication—internal and external
- Transition issues
- Integration—cultural and systems
- Personnel issues—rumor mill, morale, productivity impacts
- Union versus nonunion operations
- Personnel movement (migration)—loss of key talent
- Infrastructure—computer systems, etc.

Again, the list is not unique. Also, it flags many important issues. Still, the full value comes from a deeper look at what is driving the disconnects.

The group identified some typical knee-jerk or "Band Aid" solutions in the case of mergers or acquisitions, including,

- Transfer freeze
- Assurances with no information
- Rumor mill—informal information search
- Distrust

This list could be much longer, of course, but even these items illustrate again how reactions just to disconnects are likely to be superficial. By probing further and, in effect, appreciating the divergent learning cycle, progress is more likely.

With further analysis of both lists of disconnects from the aerospace workshop, we see yet further connections. The first list concerned disconnects about roles and responsibilities, which were mostly disconnects involving the levels of daily operations and governance. For example, a champion who does not "walk the talk" or an organization with unclear goals primarily has an operations issue. An organization that lacks a mechanism to build and sustain trust or has hollow authority primarily has a governance issue.

The second list concerned disconnects about mergers and acquisitions, which spanned all three levels. Many of the personnel issues concern daily operations, such as issues of morale and productivity. Issues of union and nonunion operations have strategic implications, but are most salient with respect to governance since these represent two different structures for representation and decision-making. Personnel movement is an operational issue in one respect, but this loss of talent is also a strategic issue. It is operational in that work areas are literally shorthanded and missing key knowledge. It is strategic in that the valuation of the merger and acquisition typically assumes certain transaction costs, but when these are exceeded by the loss of talent, the entire strategic decision can be undermined. Integration and communication are both linkage issues, with implications across all three levels.

As should be evident, the classification of both lists is useful in itself and it raises deeper questions. It is useful in providing orientation and focus to the analysis. This involves the first two stages of the learning cycle—interpreting data to generate knowledge. Where a preponderance of disconnects reside at one level, responses or action may still occur at more than one level, but the focus is clear. Where disconnects are spread across many levels, it suggests a deeper, more complex challenge—but that too is valuable knowledge. Now notice the mindset change—instead of disconnects being occasions for blame or knee-jerk responses, they have prompted serious and sustained inquiry.

GAPS BETWEEN POLICY AND PRACTICE

A key window into mindsets that are not changing is provided whenever new policies are designed to be beneficial for people, but the use of these policies is limited. This is particularly evident, for example, in the growing number of organizations drafting "work-family" or "work-life" policies. These polices are intended to address the worker as a whole person, complementing strategies that rely on employee commitment rather than on compliance. Beth Boland, a partner in the Boston law firm of Mintz Levin, Cohn, Ferris, Glovsky, and Popeo, P.C., recently led a study of leading Boston area law firms for the state bar association and found that over 90% of these firms now provide a part-time option for associates and partners. Yet she also found that less than 5% of those eligible actually take advantage of the option. Moreover, more than one-third of lawyers reported that they believed doing so would hurt their careers.[11]

Similar low rates of uptake on work-family policies are reported in other studies of these matters. The importance of face-time and full-time commitment appear to still permeate the culture of many organizations and professions, with the dominant mindset of senior executives and even peers still centered on a very traditional conception of work.

Key insights into what it takes to shift these mindsets comes from the scholarship of Lotte Bailyn,[12] who has urged that an analysis of the dilemmas underlying the very nature of the work itself is required if the disconnect is to be properly understood. This has involved, for example, a study of the work of design engineers who complained of frequent work/family conflicts at the end of the day due to late-evening meetings and deadline pressures. A close analysis of the data found that the problems at the end of the day were driven by constant interruptions during the day—with time lost due to these starts and stops in the work. The resolution involved establishing blocks of time in which people could work without interruption and that alone enabled the workday to end at a more reasonable time. The mindset had to shift so that end-of-the-day work/family conflicts were not seen as inevitable but understood as a function of work practices throughout the day.

In the legal community, Beth Boland came to a similar insight. She pointed out that, with a change in mindset, it is actually possible to see that legal work itself is well suited to part-time arrangements. Most lawyers divide their time among many clients. As a result, reduced time arrangements just mean a reduced number of clients, not a reduction of effort in support of any one client—assuming some flexibility in hours on a week-to-week basis. In other words, the constraint here is not the work itself, but the mindset that uses long hours as an indicator of motivation and capability. The shift requires a demonstration of equal motivation and capability, but within a different mix of hours and a reduced number of clients.

COMBINING SKILL SETS AND MINDSETS

Expanded skill sets are useless if the mindsets are not beginning to change. Changing mindsets is not possible without the core skill sets being in place. The two are interdependent—both are needed if the Bold Visions and Harsh Realities are to be integrated.

A practical example of how skill sets and mindsets together is to take a closer look as the "ARRIVE" process improvement model described in chapter 3. This model is expressly designed to surface disconnects and promote analysis that will get to core dilemmas. The model, which is listed below, is designed to use data to generate knowledge that can guide action:

Aim
Reality
Root Causes
Improvement Options
Value-added Implementation
Evaluation and Continuous Improvement

Table 8.1 highlights the skill sets and mindsets associated with each step in the process. Notice the wide range of skills and different mindsets associated with this one model. This is just one such model—there are many problem-solving and process-improvement models in use. We present it here to illustrate this interweaving of mindsets and skill sets—and because it is particularly effective at surfacing disconnects in a constructive way.

The ARRIVE model can be very powerful in surfacing disconnects and driving continuous improvement efforts. This is just one example of the many ways that skill sets and mindsets combine together to reveal the full value associated with disconnects. Note, however, that the model alone is insufficient to ensure the core strategic dilemmas are surfaced if the new skill sets and the new mindsets are only being developed by front-line teams, which is exactly what happened in the chapter 3 case example.

In many ways, making disconnects visible is analogous to renovating an older building. Even small renovations—such as moving a wall—often reveal much deeper and more complicated underlying problems—such as faults in plumbing and wiring. One option is to patch up the holes in the old wall. Another is to take on the larger task of fixing the underlying problems. A third option is to reexamine the overall goals of all the parties associated with the renovation. The same is true regarding interpreting patterns in disconnects so as to surface key dilemmas. Core questions are raised regarding people's basic goals and interests around continuous learning. For example, many learning initiatives will surface disconnects that involve core dilemmas around whether employees should be viewed primarily as a cost to be monitored and controlled or as a resource needing investment and support.[13]

Building the skill sets and the mindsets that value disconnects is a never-ending process. While there are many barriers to success—such as leadership turnover, misaligned incentives, business decline, and others—there is a key turning point after which these and other barriers are seen in a neutral, nonblaming way as disconnects. They are still challenging, but there is great leverage in passing the point of no return—where disconnects do not instantly generate blame or knee-jerk responses.

TABLE 8.1 Skill Sets and Mindsets Associated with ARRIVE
Process-Improvement Model

Steps in the Process	Skill Set (with approximate time estimates)	Mindset
Aim *(The aim of the process—How are things supposed to happen?)*	• Brainstorm potential elements of the aim process. (15–30 min.) • Agree on the primary element or elements as your definition of the aim. (15–30 min.)	• Creative, "out of the box" • Compelling vision
Reality *(How do things actually happen?)*	• Brainstorm elements of reality. Include perceptions, numerical data, a process map, and other indicators that provide evidence of what actually happens. Place data in Pareto charts or other formats that aid analysis. (30–60 min.)	• Comprehensive • Accurate • Nonblaming • Seeing what was previously hidden
Root Causes *(What would account for any gaps or any alignment between the aim and reality?)*	• Assess the relationship between the aim and reality. Note places where there is close alignment and places where there are clear disconnects and divergence. Seek root causes—not just symptoms. Use the five "whys" to get at root causes. (30–60 min.)	• Analytical • Probing • Appreciative of core dilemmas
Improvement Options *(What are options that might help close the gap or maintain alignment?)*	• Brainstorm potential options that might help address some of the disconnects identified and sustain the "connects"— Be sure you are not just treating symptoms, but addressing root causes. (30–60 min.)	• Creative, "out of the box" • Attentive to multiple stakeholder interests
Value-added Implementation *(Of the many options, which ones will add value? How would they be implemented?)*	• Assess which of the many options will add value (5–10 min.) • Construct a plan for implementation— with tentative milestones and resource requirements (30–60 min.)	• Realistic • Strategic
Evaluation and Continuous Improvement *(What are the criteria for success? What is the evaluation plan? What mechanisms will help ensure continuous improvement?)*	• Brainstorm and agree on potential criteria for success (15–30 min.) • Construct an evaluation plan (15–30 min.) • Brainstorm mechanisms to ensure continuous improvement (15–30 min.)	• Consistent • Persistent • Open to learning

NEW MINDSETS AND NEW SKILL SETS NEEDED TO TRANSFORM A TRADITIONAL WORK SYSTEM

Autoco's Riverdale Assembly Plant dates back more than half a century. The plant population has fluctuated over the years with a peak of over 7,000 employees and a current payroll of less than 3,500 employees. This plant and others in the Autoco system face a challenge common across many established operations, a challenge involving the transformation of an existing culture and production system from a hierarchical, mass-production model to a team-based, lean-enterprise model.[14]

Historical Context
There is a long history of joint, union-management activities at the Riverdale plant, beginning with the joint-skilled-trades apprenticeship program and the joint safety program, which have been in place for many decades. In the early 1980s, joint activities expanded to include employee involvement and joint training. The Employee Participation Work Groups were voluntary, with one in each department of a plant. The joint-training activities were initially begun to serve displaced workers laid off from the auto industry, but quickly expanded to include training programs for active workers. In the early 1990s, the Autoco Total Preventative Maintenance initiative was also begun on a joint basis. The mid-1990s saw the first program to involve hourly production workers in the design and development of a new car model. This led to notable improvements for some components in the new car line, which is produced in this plant and one other.

At this stage, what was visible were key steps taken to operationalize the Bold Vision associated with each joint activity. The employee participation process had an eight-step problem-solving model as a structured way to harness employee knowledge in solving workplace problems. The initiative had its own Small Group Activity model aimed at channeling the knowledge of skilled-trades workers on preventative maintenance matters. The joint-apprenticeship program was a training and development initiative. These and other learning activities were all visible. Less visible were the employees who chose not to be part of all these joint activities. A key lesson learned by these employees during this same time was that participation in problem-solving and knowledge-generation activities was voluntary—which would later underlie a major disconnect as the organization began to move toward a wall-to-wall team system. There is a core dilemma here—if you launch the initiative on a voluntary basis, buy-in from employees is easier, but a transformation around total involvement of the workforce becomes more difficult.

A similar dilemma became evident during the mid-1990s, when there was a worldwide restructuring of the corporation. Under this banner, many of the distinct joint activities for safety, worker participation, preventative maintenance, quality, and other topics were centralized. This is what was visible and it had a clear logic around integration of the many activities. The separate joint–governing committees for each activity in this plant (and others in this company) combined their activities under the auspices of a single, plantwide joint–steering committee. Though there was a clear logic to support the move to foster greater integration, what was less visible was that most of the champions of the joint activities experienced the shift as a reduction in commitment to their individual initiatives. Ultimately, this led to a deterioration of the entire system of joint governance, which only became visible years later when there was a need for accelerated implementation of a lean-production system.

Also, the plant is located in an old industrial area, with a highly diverse workforce. In the late 1990s, a series of sexual harassment lawsuits served as a wake-up call to union and management leadership alike. In this case, the disconnect was very visible—with concerns that it would impact on the reputation of the corporation as a whole. Less visible to the external world were the resulting settlements, which involved extensive training in diversity and in respect for the entire plant population as well as the establishment of a plantwide diversity council. Interestingly, as the team-based work system began to be established, many people commented on how helpful the diversity training was. The same principles of respect and tolerance covered in the diversity training turned out to be instrumental for a team-based, lean-production work system.

Launching a Lean-Production System

It was during the mid to late 1990s that the plant first began implementation of the Autoco Lean Production System (ALPS)—Autoco's version of a lean-production system. In 1996, a set of union and management ALPS coordinators were trained. In 1997, the entire plant was shut down for a plantwide "town hall" meeting in which management leaders, projected on large video screens, announced the launch of the Autoco Lean Production System. The body shop was selected as the initial pilot implementation area, with extensive resources concentrated on the training of newly formed Continuous Improvement Work Teams (CIWTs). A central Plant Implementation Team was established with union and management representation.

In 1998, the plant sought to expand the effort to other parts of the plant, including the engine line, the paint shop, and the trim/final assembly areas. The central Plant Implementation Team was disbanded, with the members each assigned to separate departments. Unfortunately, there were a series of management personnel moves around the same time that led to a nearly complete turnover of the Plant Operating Committee, including the manufacturing manager, some of the area managers responsible for the production departments and managers responsible for human resources, quality, maintenance, finance, and material handling. What was visible, was all the fanfare in launching the new initiative. The focus was clearly on a range of improvement activities involving data, knowledge, and action. What was less visible was the loss of knowledge at senior levels and loss of commitment at middle levels as various leaders left the plant.

When a new plant manager arrived in 1999, he found newly forming Continuous Improvement Work Teams, but without many resources devoted to supporting them. For example, weekly team meetings would be held, but there were few mechanisms to handle requests for information, maintenance support, and other forms of assistance needed by the teams. Disconnects were accumulating in the form of open agenda items at the team meetings—

pending action by other parts of the organization. The many former joint activities had been combined into a single forum, but each only had enough time to give a brief status report before some "hot" issue would take over the agenda in the meetings. The members of the Plant Implementation Team were feeling isolated in their respective departments. Front-line supervisors and superintendents were told to become more participative managers, but the pressure to "make the numbers" in production were undiminished. Throughout the plant, people who had built up their hopes for the new initiative were disappointed by the results—a "hope/heartbreak" cycle all too familiar to management and labor alike. What was supposed to be a continuous learning process, was becoming fragmented learning and was even at risk of becoming oppositional learning.

Accelerated Implementation

Two related and pivotal events took place in the year 2000. First, the plant was awarded a new model to replace its current product—with the launch of the new model scheduled for 2003. Second, the plant was picked to be one of a select group of plants (spanning all the major product lines of the company) in which implementation resources would be concentrated to accelerate the implementation of the Autoco Lean Production System (ALPS). This would be a test as to whether a lean production system could be implemented in an accelerated way in a brownfield plant.

The first responses involved an intensification of previous activities. A training "bubble" of workers was hired to backfill for different areas of the plant as the entire workforce was trained in group process skills and basic equipment maintenance, and was given a reinforcement of the sexual harassment and diversity training.

While there were still many of the voluntary Employee Involvement groups in the plant, the focus shifted to Continuous Improvement Work Teams (CIWTs) with a mandatory half-hour meeting per week. The new plant manager was under pressure from some corporate executives to move the plant quickly to an entirely team-based structure. He resisted, however, stating that the maintenance and other support resources could only provide sixteen new teams with the level of support needed. Had the plant pushed the implementation of teams at a more aggressive pace they would also have had to face head-on the prior expectation that participative initiatives should be voluntary.

Working together on a joint basis, the union and management leadership reached an agreement to establish team leaders for newly established CIWTs. There were not, however, sufficient resources to hire additional team leaders for all the CIWTs. There were some new hires, but others moved into these roles from existing positions in the factory, such as repair and inspection positions. The need to establish the team leader role had long been recognized by union and management leadership, but there were always political pressures associated with this concept. Would the team leaders just become a "straw boss?" Would restructuring the existing positions take away highly preferable jobs? Here there were challenges to the mindsets of both the hourly and the managerial workforce.

The union and management leadership attended a lean "boot camp" run by the central corporate ALPS office that included various simulation exercises, briefings, and the chance to shadow team leaders for a few hours in lean-manufacturing settings. As one area manager reported, "the boot camp was a real eye opener." While "lean" skills were covered at the boot camp, it was the impact on mindsets that justified sending people away for the three-day sessions.

Value Stream Mapping In addition to accelerating previous activity, there were new initiatives. First, the plant conducted a value stream map in the motor line area. This highlighted certain "constraint" operations that were bottlenecks in production.[15] As part of this process, the hourly and salaried workforce conducted a series of "waste walks," identifying over $60 million in potential improvement opportunities. As the CIWTs began to address some of these opportunities, parts of the production line were changed—with in-process inventory removed and the overall "footprint" of the operation reduced. As the plant's manufacturing manager observed, "We soon realized that we had to redo the value stream map. With each improvement, the operation changed and the old map no longer applied. We ended up revisiting the value stream map every two or three weeks in some areas." Again, this was a shift in mindsets—from seeing a value stream map as a one-time "check-the-box" to an integrated change in the way the operations are managed.

As the value stream method spread to other parts of the plant, a growing number of suggestions emerged to change line-layouts—from hourly and salaried employees. Where the changes had a potential impact on jobs, the local union and management leaders became directly involved. Although a potentially controversial situation, the tensions were somewhat reduced when an early redesign effort ended up creating new positions in the plant in which it was established that the "kitting" of certain parts could be brought into the plant and done by employees on partial disability leave. This represented a net gain of jobs for the union, a constructive employment opportunity for certain employees, and an aid to efficiency for management.

A parallel set of value stream maps were conducted for the plant as a whole—covering external suppliers and delivery systems. The plantwide value stream map was integrated with the new product development efforts. It quickly became clear that the "lean" requirements of the new product were going to be difficult to achieve given the geographic spread of the supply-chain. This led to a unique plant proposal that would create a supplier park adjacent to the plant. Constructing the proposal was a delicate process. The corporate purchasing function initially resisted the idea as cost prohibitive. The plant and the new-product engineers had to construct a business case regarding the benefits associated with the additional lean capability. Concurrently they had to meet with city officials to address a range of tax abatement and site improvement issues. Key executive champions at the director, executive director and vice president levels were all involved in this effort, which culminated in the 2001 joint announcement with the city of the planned supplier park.

Bridging across the value stream were over a dozen design teams, many of which reached out to actively engage production operators and managers. The focus was on ensuring the manufacturability of the new designs. There was some variation across the design teams in the level of involvement of manufacturing, as well as some variation in the level of understanding of lean-production principles. While the level of integration does represent important progress, there is not an enduring set of mechanisms designed to ensure that this type of upstream manufacturing involvement characterizes all product development efforts.

Material Flow and Quality Systems   During 2001, the implementation of new material flow systems was significantly accelerated. This included the establishment of "marketplaces" for large components and commodity items, as well as line-side racks and other storage setups to ensure minimal in-process inventory and ergonomic presentation of parts and components. Pressure was also brought to bear on external suppliers to ship smaller batches on more of a just-in-time basis, with some even delivering parts using what is termed "in-line vehicle sequencing."

Unfortunately, there was not a direct correspondence between the suppliers who shifted their operations and the parts of the plant changing its material flow operations. As a result, some suppliers ended up having to sort through the increased cost of delivering many small batches that the relevant area of the plant couldn't fully utilize. As well, other parts of the plant were ready for this sort of support from suppliers, but the suppliers were not ready to provide it. Even where there was a match between the internal plant flow capability and the external supplier flow capability, it did not always match the areas where the new Continuous Improvement Work Teams and team leaders had been established.

Analysis of the complicated material flow situation reveals that a push for progress from the central material handling function was not fully linked to the specific plant realities. The concepts of material flow were integral to the plant's establishing a lean production system, but the implementation needed a better coordinated process of shared learning around capabilities and improvement opportunities.

Despite the many complications in coordinating material flow improvement efforts, the plant has made significant improvements in reducing the number of days of inventory on hand. It has also achieved the highest rating for material flow practices in an assembly plant—based on the internal, annual corporate-assessment process.

A key innovation in the plant has been the development of a systematic method for addressing quality concerns prior to making the shift to a full "andon" system, where workers can press a "caution" or a "stop" button to signal quality concerns. This is designed to enable a transition from having inspectors at the end of each production line to having line operators responsible for their own quality.

Although the focus of lean principles emphasizes customer "pull" and material/product "flow," there is a prior level of stability needed before either pull or flow can occur. The reduced inventory and other lean practices can become significant liabilities if the work system is unstable. Prior to stability, however, the parties identified the need to strengthen what became termed the joint infrastructure.

Joint Infrastructure   Addressing infrastructure issues was not easy. Both union and management leadership had to learn to see gaps or "disconnects" in a constructive, nonblaming way. In fact, sustained attention to these social infrastructure issues did not really begin until early in 2001—when the plant manager and the local union bargaining committee chairperson co-led a series of sessions on infrastructure. Participating in these sessions was the Plant Operating Committee, the Plant Bargaining Committee and the Plant Implementation Team.

For example, the parties learned at one of these sessions that there was no existing forum or process to ensure that requests for maintenance support from Continuous Improvement Teams were addressed. Both production and maintenance managers could have been blamed for this disconnect. Instead, the parties enlisted support from all key stakeholders to form a short-term "Kaizen Shop" to handle Continuous Improvement Work Team requests, with the focus then shifting to the overall alignment of maintenance support operations.

In this context, the plantwide joint–steering committee had to shift away from just being a forum for status reports on various joint activities. Instead, it had to take on responsibility for constructing joint visions, strategic planning, and coordination of implementation activities.

With maintenance and leadership support increasingly clear, the plant set about to ensure the placement of team leaders with Continuous Improvement Work Teams throughout the plant. During the year 2001, eighty-eight Team Leaders were appointed in the final assembly areas (forty-four on day shift and forty-four on afternoon/evening shift) and approximately one-half to one-quarter as many were appointed in each of the other production areas—such that most work areas in the plant are now team-based operations, with team leaders.

The importance of a reinvigorated joint infrastructure was illustrated by efforts to move from a containment approach to quality to more of an in-station approach. A group of external consultants with experience in Japanese transplant operations introduced a mechanism to improve the visual presentation of job procedures for quality, safety, and other matters. This was done with input from front-line workers, but did not involve the union's health and safety representative, quality representative, or job security/time study representative. Needless to say, this oversight temporarily halted forward progress on the new visual display mechanism and created a new set of trust issues for the parties to work through.

Midlevel Leadership Skills

Midlevel Leadership Skills   Another key aspect of the infrastructure and stability involved the capability of front-line supervision and middle managers. All of these individuals had been promoted to their managerial roles based on their hard-driving approach under a mass-production system. There were key gaps in their interactive skills, as well as in their substantive knowledge of lean-manufacturing principles. In response, the plant manager and the lean manufacturing manager began a series of thirty- to forty-five-minute single-point lessons for each area of the plant. The participants included superintendents, supervisors, union committee people, and team leaders.

Conducted at the shift-overlap time on a different day of the week for each area of the plant, they prepared these lessons on a range of relevant topics. In each case, there was the expectation that the material would be applied on the job and the participants would be able to return a week later prepared to discuss lessons learned. As the manufacturing manager commented, "these single-point lessons were like a Lear jet taking off—they really accelerated our efforts." She further reported that the participants would show up a week later with carefully prepared presentations summarizing their application efforts—motivated by hearing the single-point lessons from their bosses rather than from a specialized trainer.

Despite the reported value of these sessions, there are still significant challenges facing the plant. For example, in the early fall of 2001, the corporate vice president for vehicle operations conducted a regular visit to the plant and expressed concern about the continuous improvement efforts of a number of the teams—based on the lack of detail posted on the work area visual display boards and subsequent conversations with operators, supervisors, and middle managers. There was particular concern—shared by plant management leadership—around the capability of many of the front-line supervisors and superintendents to reinforce and drive the new work system.

Performance Outcomes

Performance Outcomes   During 2001, plant safety was the focus of a major case-management initiative, as well as other targeted safety improvement efforts. The results were dramatic, with a reduction of 378% in lost-time cases and 375% in what is termed the severity rate. Worker Compensation costs were also reduced by approximately 62%.

The J.D. Power quality metric improved by 14% from 2000 to 2001, which is an indicator of initial product quality assessed through customer surveys. Customer satisfaction numbers remained essentially unchanged during this time period, however.

A final, almost intangible aspect of the changes taking place in this plant has involved leadership—at many levels. At the corporate level, the vice president for North American vehicle operations conceived the accelerated implementation strategy and then reinforced the effort with regular visits and coaching support for everyone from the managers to front-line operations. The director for manufacturing operations championed the use of value stream and quality operating principles, as well as the supplier park. The international union has provided strong support for the efforts to create new jobs in the location, as well as appropriate caution in the need to link improvement efforts with the existing joint infrastructure. The plant manager has established the highest ethical standard on issues of integrity and respect, driving performance while valuing knowledge. The manufacturing manager has become a coach and mentor for people throughout the plant, reinforcing learning about lean principles and practices, while maintaining the discipline needed to run a large automobile assembly plant. The local union leadership has embraced continuous improvement in the work system as central to long-term job security and growth in this location. And a generation of new leaders is emerging across the plant.

The story of the Riverdale Assembly Plant is still unfolding. Substantial gains have been made in the way this work system operates. For many key stakeholders it would be unthinkable to go back to the older, mass-production approach. At the same time, there is much to be done before this transformation is complete. A key question remains—will a "brownfield" plant that completes the journey to becoming a lean-production system end up stronger than a "greenfield" plant that has operated this way all along? Whatever the final degree of success, it is clear that an appreciation for knowledge and learning is woven throughout this transformation process—involving new skill sets and new mindsets.

CONCLUSION

The shift in mindset is associated with valuing disconnects, engaging dilemmas, and appreciating divergence. The examples presented in this chapter are meant to be illustrative of the process, but are not the only way to do this. Many organizations have found that the use of simulations, benchmarking visits, and other interactive forms of learning, play key roles in shifting mindsets toward increased openness around disconnects. There is a key role here for leaders in taking a constructive, nonblaming approach to disconnects, seeking ways to display patterns of divergence for shared understanding, and naming dilemmas as they become evident.

Skill sets turn out to be a necessary complement. Without the skills associated with the convergent cycle, it is hard to constructively engage disconnects. On the other hand, only teaching these skills—without linking them to mindsets—invites difficulty and frustration. When the skill sets and the mindsets do come together, it is possible to contemplate transformation in the systems for learning and knowledge—which is the focus of our final chapter.

APPENDIX: ADDITIONAL SUPPORTING DEFINITIONS AND GUIDANCE ASSOCIATED WITH THE LEADERSHIP TRANSITION CURVE[16]

1. **Recognizing "Shock":** Surprise, in extreme cases panic and immobilization. Mismatch between expectations and reality.

Addressing Shock

- Treat the shock as valid and expected
- Use active listening, flip charts, and other means to recognize and record reactions
- Ensure people feel that their reactions and concerns have been heard
- Draw on your own experience—show empathy with analogies to similar situations you have faced
- Provide supporting data, but don't anticipate that it will all be absorbed

2. **Recognizing "Denial":** Denial that change is necessary. Retreat/withdrawal. False competence, "Blocking."

Addressing Denial

- Anticipate questions and challenges around supporting data
- Capture questions and challenges on a tracking matrix or "parking lot" and get back with answers
- Ensure chances to interact with peers who have faced the same issues
- Do not try to "argue" the person out of denial—that is their current reality—often rooted in past experience with similar changes
- Give people space and face-saving opportunities to begin a learning journey—on-the-job coaching may be needed to address issues in real-time

3. **Recognizing "Awareness":** Awareness that change is necessary. Understanding of own incompetence.

Addressing Awareness

- Recognize and appreciate points of growing awareness
- Encourage exploration of options and implications
- Build awareness in "bite-size chunks"—not everything at once
- Adopt a coaching/facilitating stance
- Be sensitive to the drop in perceived competence that comes with increased awareness

4. **Recognizing "Acceptance":** Acceptance of reality. Letting go of past comfortable attitudes.

Addressing Acceptance

- This is the point of greatest vulnerability—self-confidence is at its lowest point, the old way won't work, the new skills are not in place, and others may still be in denial
- Provide specific technical and social skills needed for success—single-point modules with chances to apply the skills on the job and see results
- Ensure the support structure is in place for improvement suggestions, which will begin to come

- Use accomplishment matrices for skills training and other activities to make progress visible

5. **Recognizing "Experimentation":** Experimentation and testing of new approaches and skills. Practice phase, trying to do things differently. Feedback of results. Success and failure.

Addressing Experimentation
- Create a learning laboratory environment—where new ideas can be tested, adjusted, and applied
- Establish boundaries within which it will be okay to make mistakes—so long as people learn from them
- Adopt a nonblaming, enthusiastic partnership stance—we all learn from experimentation—including both expected outcomes and unanticipated consequences (which always turn up)
- Don't change more than one or two variables at a time—so you can learn from the results

6. **Recognizing "Understanding":** Understanding reasons for success and failure. New models/ personal theories created.

Addressing Understanding
- Capture lessons learned—encourage sharing of understanding in work groups and with others
- Establish hand-off processes when people with new understanding move to other work areas or other locations—this is "knowledge management"
- Accept and embrace the fact that people know more than you do on key aspects of their operation—this is becoming a "knowledge-driven work system"
- Don't micromanage people with new levels of understanding, but don't abandon them either

7. **Recognizing "Integration":** Integration of new skills and behaviors into a new way of operating.

Addressing Integration
- Identify leading practices to standardize and replicate
- Ensure that people are able to serve as "boundary spanners" linking this part of the operation with others
- Focus on alignment with other parts of the operation—internal and external "customers" and "suppliers," support functions, etcetera.
- Protect against the "not invented here" syndrome—stay open to learning from others
- Anticipate factors that pull individuals and groups back to earlier stages in the journey—turnover in leadership or membership, changes in technology or policy, shifts in economic circumstances, etcetera.

Notes

1. Joel Cutcher-Gershenfeld, et al., *Knowledge-Driven Work: Unexpected Lessons from Japanese and U.S. Work Practices* (New York: Oxford University Press, 1998).

2. Peter Senge, *The Fifth Discipline: The Art and Practice of the Learning Organization.* New York: Doubleday, 1990).

3. Jim Womack and Daniel Jones, Lean Thinking: Banish Waste and Create Wealth in Your Corporation (New York: Simon and Schuster, 1996); and Earll Murman, et. al., Lean Enterprise Value: Insights from MIT's Lean Aerospace Initiative (New York: Palgrave/MacMillian, 2002), Chapter 4.

4. Murman, et. al., *Lean Enterprise Value,* 87.

5. Yoji Akao, ed., *Hoshin Kanri: Policy Deployment for Successful TQM* (Productivity Press, 1991); and Masaaki Imai, *Kaizen: The Key To Japan's Competitive Success* (New York: McGraw Hill, 1986).

6. Edgar Schein, *Culture and Leadership* (San Francisco: Jossey Bass, 1985).

7. This cycle has been widely used by the Ford Leadership Development Center. It also appeared in 1987 in an unpublished paper by T. Chapman and J. Jupp, entitled "A Cycle of Change: The Transition Curve." It was adapted for use as a tool on organizational development and change by Roger Komer. Of course, it has roots in the classic analysis of stages of loss by Elizabeth Kubler-Ross.

8. There is a long history in psychology of efforts to understand factors leading to perceptions of competence as well as the impact of those perceptions on valued outcomes. Work by Alfred Bandura and others focuses on how self-efficacy or perceptions of competence is a key factor in behavioral change. See Alfred Bandura, "Self Efficacy: Toward a Unifying Theory of Behavioral Change," *Psychological Review*, 84 (1977): 191–215; or Alfred Bandura, *Social Foundations of Thought and Action* (Englewood Cliffs, NJ: Prentice-Hall, 1986).

9. Timothy Aeppel, "Tricks of the Trade: On Factory Floor, Top Workers Hide Secrets to Success" in *Wall Street Journal* (July 1st 2002): A1, A10.

10. Personal conversation and class presentation by Mark Duffy, former executive vice president of operations for this firm (1999).

11. Kochan, Tom, Wanda Orlikowski, and Joel Cutcher-Gershenfeld, "Beyond McGregor's Theory Y: Human Capital and Knowledge-Based Work in the 21st Century Organization," (Prepared for MIT Sloan School 50th Anniversary, 2002).

12. Bailyn, Lotte, *Breaking the Mold* (New York: Maxwell MacMillan, 1993).

13. See Tom Kochan, et. al., "Beyond McGregor's Theory Y."

14. This case study was drafted in 2002 based on a period of two years in which one of the authors served as a consultant to the parties on the accelerated implementation of the new work system. In preparing the write-up, an additional series of interviews were conducted with senior union and management leaders and a cross-section of midlevel and front-line leaders involved in the implementation. The write-up was then reviewed by the parties, though any errors are our sole responsibility.

15. A creative way of discussing constraints and bottlenecks is from a novel by Eliyahu Goldratt and Jeff Cox, *The Goal: A Process on Ongoing Improvement*, 2nd ed. (Croton-on-Hudson, NY: North River Press, 1992).

16. These additional definitions and considerations were developed by Joel Cutcher-Gershenfeld when operationalizing the Leadership Development Cycle for use in training.

Sustaining Learning Systems

W e have a dilemma. In our final chapter we want to provide clear, succinct, actionable guidance around valuing disconnects and enabling
organizational learning. We also must remain true to the reality that we have
surfaced throughout the book—that such changes are complex and they do
not happen quickly or easily.

Our resolution? We will distill succinct guiding principles, but we will
also attend to the "story behind the story" when it comes to organizational
learning systems. This doesn't resolve the dilemma—as dilemmas are never
fully resolvable—but at least we all enter this final chapter with the tension
clearly defined. We can't provide simple solutions, but we can strive for crisp
insights and telling examples that speak to the opportunities embedded in
this learning dilemma.[1]

BOLD VISIONS AND HARSH REALITIES IN REVIEW

There is increasing pressure in the system. As we saw in chapter 1, there is
pressure to transform traditional work systems into ones that are more
knowledge driven. Work, for many individuals and teams, requires more
than just the mastery of repetitive tasks. Jobs require new learning, such as
learning from data on quality or learning how to improve operations or
learning how to value the different skills of coworkers or even just learning
how to foster mutual respect. For many organizations, responsiveness to customers and shareholders is a moving target—requiring constant adaptation.
Lessons learned this year may not deliver the same results next year

Learning and knowledge are strategic priorities. The Bold Vision—
linking data, knowledge, and action—highlights the learning process that
underlies numerous initiatives aimed at continuous improvement. Some initiatives may employ approaches that range from training trainers to engaging multiple stakeholder models to forming strategic partnerships to investing in intellectual capital to changing systems overall—all approaches
highlighted in chapter 2. Most often, these are combined in various ways—
all aimed at integrating learning and knowledge into the core functions of
the organization.

No matter how compelling the Bold Vision, disconnects are inevitable. There are countless ways that things will fall short of what is expected or needed. As change efforts are accelerated, the likelihood is that the number of disconnects—visible and hidden—will increase. Too often the Harsh Realities dominate and learning systems begin down the slippery slope introduced in chapter 3.

Faced with learning disconnects, the first instinct is to try to "solve" the problem or to assign blame. Such efforts will, at best, achieve some measure of containment. At worst, they will create additional disconnects and trigger downward spirals of distrust and negativity that exacerbate the divergence in the organization. Far more constructive is an entirely different approach—one that values disconnects for the data they represent. As we saw in chapter 4, this begins with labeling, classifying, and analyzing the patterns of disconnects—ideally in advance rather than after the fact.

By looking across multiple disconnects and asking hard questions, it is possible to see underlying dilemmas. Surfacing underlying dilemmas is easy to say and hard to do. Most of these dilemmas are enduring organizational challenges—such as balancing cooperation and competition or centralization and decentralization. Seeing the dilemmas does not promise easy or quick solutions. In fact, the lesson from chapter 5 is that it more likely will reveal just how hard the choices are. Properly understood, these dilemmas are genuinely painful—because they highlight what can't be done given the constraints of time, resources, history, and other factors. Many leaders are humble in the face of dilemmas. This is not because they lack ambition, but because they have honestly faced this immutable part of reality—in taking certain actions, they foreclose others. It is humbling to face up to what can't be done—even when many other valuable things are being accomplished. Still, there is something cathartic about accurately naming a dilemma. There is often a deep sigh of recognition that comes with saying aloud what has been previously sensed, but not stated. Making the dilemma visible thus increases the likelihood of shared appreciation of the dilemma across stakeholders—so they will understand (even if they don't always like) the dilemma, analyze it, and generate creative ideas for handling it (rather than seeing it only as an either-or proposition).

Taken together, there is learning that occurs as people pursue the Bold Visions and there is learning that occurs as a result of disconnects and the dilemmas. As we saw in chapter 6, the result will be many concurrent forms of learning taking place at the same time within an organization. In particular, we highlighted six types of learning—all of which are important. First, there are specific technical tasks, demanding routine forms of capability made possible through *incremental learning*. Second, there are more complex combinations of tasks involving adaptive capability achieved through *continuous learning*—provided there is sufficient alignment among stakeholders. Third, there is the deep engagement that can come with *experimental learning*, which involves the interactive process of posing questions and finding answers. Fourth, *synergistic learning* is similarly interactive and brings the additional engagement associated with seeing system-level connections—provided there is sufficient stakeholder alignment. Finally, *entrenched learning* and the *revolutionary learning* are found when stakeholders are opposed. Both are often overlooked, but require recognition and even appreciation.

Our injunctions to foster divergent learning or to embrace divergent learning really require that no one form of learning dominate organizational strategies for learning and knowledge. Instead, it points to a learning architecture that encompasses multiple forms of learning. It also points to the importance of understanding the divergent thinking associated with each type of learning—not just the convergent thinking that is typically emphasized in the Bold Visions. Reality quickly becomes complex and at the same time more open to alternative perspectives and solutions. Further, there are dynamic connections across types of learning—synergistic learning may depend on skills developed through incremental learning or revolutionary learning may evolve into continuous learning. Some of these connections reinforce the Bold Visions and some reveal Harsh Realities.

Success in the face of this divergence requires the building of new skill sets—particularly the skills around treating disconnects as data, building knowledge from dilemmas, and taking action among many divergent forms of learning. Sample tools for doing this were highlighted in chapter 7—are illustrative of the much-needed discipline associated with any skill building.

Equally important, as we saw in chapter 8, are the mindsets associated with simultaneously appreciating Bold Visions and Harsh Realities. Mindsets do not change easily or quickly. There are often stages of shock and denial that precede awareness, experimentation, acceptance, understanding, and integration. But such change is possible and therein lies the key to success.

This unblinking, constructive look at disconnects, dilemmas, and divergence can be very powerful. As one plant manager commented after the accelerated implementation of a team-based, knowledge-driven work system, "we are seeing more rocks than we had ever seen before—things that were hidden below the surface—but the plant has also not ever run as well as it is running now."[2] He was referring to the growing number of teams surfacing significant issues around work flow, information requirements, skill gaps, and related matters. These were all "rocks" hidden by the mass-production system and by only focusing on the Bold Vision. Although this required him and the other leaders to do substantially more work, he was also reflecting a growing can-do spirit in the organization and the tangible results that are possible with new skill sets and new mindsets. Achieving such gains is not, however, a guarantee that they are sustainable, which is the central focus in this concluding chapter.

Sustaining organizational learning initiatives is not easy, but the following case provides some insights into the dynamics that are involved. The case provides a window into how embracing both Bold Visions and Harsh Realities can lead to truly remarkable changes.

INTEGRATING HARSH REALITIES WITH BOLD VISIONS IN A CUSTOMER SERVICE OPERATION—A CASE EXAMPLE[3]

Valuing disconnects has been elevated to the status of business strategy in the case of information technology services at the Fujitsu Corporation in the United Kingdom. Indeed, this approach has helped this organization gain increasing recognition for, as they put it, "doing for service operations what Toyota has done for manufacturing operations."

Stephen Parry, the architect of this approach and head of strategic change and development, has focused on Fujitsu IT customer support call centers. This is a part of the business that is more often treated as an unwelcome internal support responsibility or as a cost-center to be outsourced. Instead of seeing the volume of complaints as burdensome, Parry's approach centers on a process of what is termed "sense and respond" that involves interacting with and learning from the people on the phone.

The focus goes far beyond solving the stated problem by asking a set of simple questions that elicit the caller's underlying needs and priorities. These data are then analyzed across multiple callers, generating responses, such as identifying root causes and preventing future problems or even surfacing new business opportunities. As Parry commented, "Why should we try to reduce the average handle time [for an incoming call] on work that we shouldn't even be doing."[4] Fujitsu has applied this approach to its own IT support function and has now made it a business line in its own right for call centers dealing with a wide range of products across public- and private-sector client organizations.

The operations of most call centers are characterized by numerous disconnects. Metrics emphasize maximizing the volume of calls handled, which created pressure for shorter conversations that only addressed the immediate problem stated by the caller. Contracts for call centers give them incentives to seek ever greater numbers of calls, making it in their interest to have customers make multiple calls to deal with piecemeal aspects of their problems. The work is often oppressive, resulting in high turnover and reduced capability on the part of the workforce, increasing the likelihood of incomplete solutions to problems. Moreover, valuable information embedded in the problems themselves is lost.

Instead, the staff in the Fujitsu call centers is trained to ask callers not only what they saw as their problem with the information technology, but also how this was impacting their business operations. They quickly learned that understanding the larger context for the problem enabled them to better prioritize recommendations and action. It also yielded valuable insights into potential preventative actions. For example, a regional airline client had numerous staff members calling in with problems attaching some types of files to e-mail correspondence in their internal IT system. When executives were told internally that staff members were having this kind of problem, there was no response—it was seen as low priority. As a result of the Fujitsu data collection, however, they surfaced the fact that the most problematic attachments involved messages around new customer bookings and passenger transfers making connecting flights. Fujitsu was then able to calculate a cost of as much as four lost bookings per flight and delayed information hand-offs on as many as seven hundred transferring passengers a day. Suddenly, this was seen as a high-priority issue. It took probing by Fujitsu's operators to understand the consequences and then translate it into terms that would motivate and guide action. It is truly a case of using data to generate knowledge, which then guides action—where the focus is on disconnects as data.

The concept may sound simple, but the operationalization of the concept represents a revolutionary change for any business utilizing this approach. Initially referred to at Fujitsu as Interactive Management Methodology (IMM), the term "sense and respond" crystallized in 1999. It involves a spiral of activity, which begins with the front-line staff being trained and supported in collecting data not just on the problem, but on the implications of the problem for the client. Then, staff is supported with tools, resources, and time during the day to examine the data. Periodically, there will be interventions scheduled where multiple operators dealing with a client will be brought together to bring data and interact with client representatives. Through these sessions, improvement opportunities are identified—often yielding insights in the business that would not have otherwise been visible.

The term "sense" refers in particular to sensing "what matters to customers." This is comparable to the way the Toyota refers to customers as "true North"—providing orientation for the efforts of the enterprise. The term "respond" refers in particular to actions such as "adapt, evolve, inform, and innovate." This is what emerges from the periodic interventions, based on the data collected. In between these two concepts, Fujitsu emphasizes "people." In particular, they highlight three stakeholder groups:

1. the client and their customers;
2. the front-line staff; and
3. the support organization.

The focus in their improvement efforts involves all of these groups. Summing up this approach, Parry states, "we are in the business of adding value." Disparaging the traditional call center model, he adds, "We are not a corporate waste disposal unit." Mark Kell, a manager in the strategic change and development group, notes that some people in the call center were operating in ways consistent with the "sense and respond" approach, but "they were doing it in spite of the system, not because of it." He adds that "people often say that this approach was what they thought would be the way to work and they are pleased to see that this is how we do work. It is not this way at other call centers." The "sense and respond" approach is illustrated in figure 9.1.[5]

To support the "sense and respond" approach, Fujitsu negotiates very different contracts with its clients compared to typical call centers. Normally,

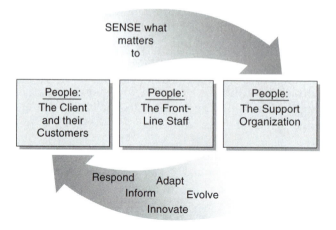

Figure 9.1 "Sense and respond" at Fujitsu, UK

payments are based on the volume of calls handled and similar metrics. By contrast, Fujitsu's contracts emphasize the number of end users supported, with a commitment to improve the quality and lower the cost of this support on a year-over-year basis. As a result, the Fujitsu staff is focused on finding ways to solve problems to prevent the need for future calls, rather than on how to increase the efficiency with which they handle the existing volume of calls. Through this "sense and respond" approach, Fujitsu has found that between 50% and 70% of the call volume is preventable. Moreover, as the volume goes down, their staff and staff in the client organizations are able to spend increasing amounts of time on prevention, which produces a positive, self-reinforcing dynamic. Instead of trying to force clients into one narrow set of performance metrics that are the same across all clients, the company establishes unique metrics for each client and then adapts these metrics to reflect value-creation opportunities as they emerge.

Fujitsu has reached a degree of mastery over this process. They can, for example, look at disconnect data for an initial period of time and then make accurate predictions of how the sense and respond approach will directly translate into improved customer satisfaction. Part of the mastery involves a systematic approach to the "demand" of calls that flows into the centers. The concept of demand here is unusual, in that there are some forms of demand that are to be valued and sought, while others are discouraged or eliminated. As Gwenda Connell, a strategy and change consultant at Fujitsu, noted, four types of demand are tracked.

The first type of demand involves interactions that create value for the users of the service, which they term "value demand." The goal with these types of calls is to ensure a flow of these kinds of interactions—particularly interactions that provide insight into the way the IT systems provide value to end users.

The second type of demand concerns interactions that trigger new ideas, which they term "opportunity demand." Demand for services not currently supplied within the scope of the existing contract is traditionally ignored. The goal here is to innovate based on these interactions to provide new products or services to end users.

The third kind of demand is for information or support that is preventable, which they term "failure demand." The goal here is to eliminate this kind of demand—it stems from a failure in the IT design or service process. In other words, don't optimize the flow of requests for information that could be designed into the software, IT systems, or other support services in the first place. In discussing an example along these lines with a British regional airline company, Roger Sandell, Fujitsu's client director, noted that they are "now getting the business value that [they have] been looking for as a result of our management of the IT Helpdesk. One specific example was that [they] replaced the airport ticketing printers that [Fujitsu] had identified as causing end user and customer dissatisfaction."

The final type of demand is "institutionalized demand"—where the demand can be traced to external causes that would need institutional responses. If, for example, end users on a truck fleet service are constantly contacting a call center with reports of flat tires in a given area, the response may be an intervention with local highway authorities to explore needed road repairs. By classifying the types of calls, the appropriate types of responses can then be supported. Summarizing the key components to this approach, Steve Parry highlights the importance of:

- Understanding customer business objectives
- Continually identifying, analyzing, and responding to customer demand depending upon its "value" type
- Enabling the call center advisor, through proactive measures, to continuously review the service against customer business objectives
- Capturing knowledge to resolve issues quickly
- Generating business results, including call demand reduction, improved customer satisfaction, reduced total support costs, and proactive eradication of predicted problems to improve the overall IT infrastructure.

In building capability to operate in this way, Fujitsu has established four developmental levels. At the first level, an individual develops mastery over how to conduct a telephone help session in a new way. This involves initial skills training and then a great deal of on-the-job coaching. The second level involves being able to teach others to work in these new ways. The third level involves being able to identify opportunities to redesign the work process itself to better support the "sense and respond approach," while the fourth level involves being able to rethink overall organizational systems along these lines. To explain this, Parry uses a very simple analogy: At level 1 you know how to tell time, at level 2 you can teach others to tell time, at level 3 you know how to build a watch, and at level 4 you know how to design a watch. In progressing to the higher levels, there is an increased need

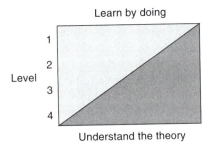

Figure 9.2 Skills and knowledge developmental levels at Fujitsu

to understand underlying theory, not just applied practices. Figure 9.2 presents this concept in a chart.

This "sense and respond" approach represents a substantial improvement in working conditions for the employees. The typical attrition rate in comparable call centers is around 40%, while Fujitsu has an attrition rate of 8%. Walking around in the call center, the evidence of this new approach is visible in countless ways. Workstations are relatively large, open desks, not closed cubicles. There are many personal touches—pictures, plants, and the like. More than half of the people don't even have headsets on—they are examining data on their computers or doing other tasks—not just the forced march of customer call handling. As Mark Kell put it, "it is people working on the system, not the system working on them."

The organization has received recognition for having one of the best European people development programs, even though they point out that this is not a program at all. In fact, Beverly Evans, also a strategic change consultant at Fujitsu, points out they are careful not to use words such as "empowerment" or "quality" since these terms are associated in this industry with "add-on" programs that are separate from the work process itself. By contrast, the developmental value of the "sense and respond" approach is central and inseparable from the way the organization operates. It is also an approach that is delivering solid business results. Even conservatively measured, this business unit in Fujitsu can point to over £200 million in new business, including "upselling" that can be directly attributed to the "sense and respond" approach.

Diffusion of the approach is reaching other parts of Fujitsu on a global basis, as well as numerous service organizations in different fields. For example, Keiko Nakayama, vice president, OSC Customer Centre, Fujitsu Japan, is cited in Fujitsu UK presentations as stating: "Fujitsu Services has been successfully delivering the solution services to customers through Sense and Respond. It is quite natural that Fujitsu and Fujitsu Services have started collaborating to evaluate and implement Sense and Respond in Japan. Fujitsu sees that this approach can upgrade the skill and motivation of support staff, thereafter causing the innovation of Customer Satisfaction."[6] In fact, this approach has catapulted the company to number two status in the

EU market and number three status worldwide, with steady progress still being made relative to their competitors.

Aspects of the approach work particularly well in the IT context given the short cycle times associated with new product development—what has been termed a rapid "clockspeed" by scholars. As a result, there are many opportunities to translate the sense-making data into new services and product features. At the same time, the larger principles clearly apply to any service operation that has clients who have their own customers or end users. Orienting around value delivery to these customers and then building capability along these lines elevates knowledge and skills into a core business strategy. A recent study of over one hundred call centers, commissioned by the UK Government Department of Trade and Industry (DTI), concluded that "Fujitsu's DTI Help-Desk was by far the highest performing unit in terms of call-handling quality and customer satisfaction." The study further observed, that "the revolution encapsulated in the 'Sense and Respond' model creates customer intelligence and a highly sophisticated frontline capability delivering increased revenue, lower staff turnover and reduced costs. Without Fujitsu's inspirational leadership and courage the future of the European call centre industry would be bleak. And it still could be if we don't have the sense to listen and respond'."[7]

Parry concludes "this is a different management principle, rooted in a new theory of management." Interestingly, at the outset he did not seek top management support. "I only wanted tolerance," he notes, since he knew that this had to begin with front-line operations and demonstrated results before he could expect full support. "Now that the CEO is being called up by the press since we are a finalist in the 2002 National Business Awards for Customer Focus, the response is, 'keep doing this.'" It is a change strategy that is consistent with the "sense and respond" mindset—Parry knows that support by the senior executive was only possible through understanding priorities at that level and then responding with demonstrable results on metrics that would motivate deeper support.

Woven throughout the Fujistu story is an appreciation of disconnects as central to business success. Rather than being ignored, the dilemmas embedded into the traditional call center have been acknowledged and the shared understanding has been used to analyze the system and come up with a new approach—a new way of thinking about what call centers could be like. The guiding principles have been operationalized in ways that are particularly appropriate for this business context. The Bold Visions and Harsh Realities are woven together and form the core of the overall business strategy of the firm.

A FRAMEWORK FOR SUSTAINED, TRANSFORMATIONAL CHANGE

So how can other organizations take the core guiding principles and combine them to produce the sort of sustainable transformation that we see in the Fujitsu case? Certainly, there is no cookbook or how-to manual. As we have noted earlier, no two organizations begin with the same ingredients or sit in the same context. This is critical, since the particular way to interpret the learning process of a given disconnect, dilemma, or divergence must always be in context. One size will not fit all.

Further, the challenge is large. Transformation requires more than just a significant change at any one level of a system. It requires an aligned set of changes at all levels. This includes the strategic level, the governance level, and the level of daily operations.[8] Progress at each level involves a series of initiatives aimed at supporting learning, combined with the skill set and mindset to constructively engage the predictable disconnects, the enduring dilemmas, and the divergent learning.

Given this challenge, consider the elements of most traditional models for systems change, including learning systems. Most models begin with the concept of a "shared vision."[9] Then, there are various ways to treat the concepts of "strategy," "structure," and "process."[10] The concept of "continuous improvement" is also featured as a key part of most systems change models. We have taken these generic elements of systems change models and combined them together in figure 9.3, where we characterize these as parts of a "Front Stage" perspective on implementing a learning system.[11] We do not offer this as a definitive model for systems change, just as an illustrative example. This will allow us to then make the link between the Bold Vision and Harsh Realities.

This Front Stage perspective will touch on the Bold Vision for organizational learning in many ways. First, the learning vision itself will typically feature a Bold Vision that involves some variation on the learning process where data is interpreted to guide action. Strategies are then built on this concept—assuming that a flow of data, knowledge, and action will drive the organization. Learning structures are established to nurture this flow and the cycle shows up again as the actual learning process. Continuous improvement is the intended result.

This Bold Vision is what is most visible in a systems change initiative centered on organizational learning (though it would apply for other systems changes as well). It is what you see—held up as the aim or vision for the change effort. It includes the stages that must be addressed to become a learning organization. Nevertheless, the reality of becoming a learning organization reveals a much more complex set of dynamics.

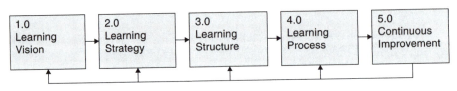

Figure 9.3 Implementing a learning system: Front Stage—What you see

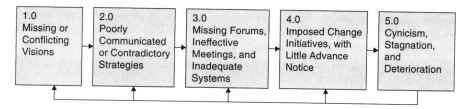

Figure 9.4   Implementing a learning system: Back Stage—What you don't see

With any change effort there is the "story behind the story." This story is one of the Harsh Realities associated with the systems change effort. Figure 9.4 provides one way of portraying these less visible, but no less important Harsh Realities.

This Back Stage perspective highlights key disconnects on the road to organizational learning. These disconnects include conflicting visions, poorly communicated strategies, inadequate building of learning systems, and imposed change mandates rather than a focus on the learning process. As we have stressed in this book, it is not a question of "if" these disconnects will occur—in fact they are predictable given the dilemmas that all organizations face and the dynamics of divergence around learning. Instead of "if," it is how well the organization deals with these types of disconnects during the change initiative that will tell whether the organization realizes the Bold Visions, or is doomed to fall down the slippery slope toward increased cynicism and stagnation.

In most organizations the Bold Visions for systems change are visible—they are even highlighted. One might say they are in the foreground—Front Stage. The Harsh Realties are less visible—indeed, they are often concealed. One might say they are in the background—Back Stage. Keeping the Harsh Realities of learning and knowledge out of sight isn't just unfortunate—they will ultimately undermine the Bold Visions. What is needed is the development of the skill set and mindset to be comfortable moving between the Bold Visions and the Harsh Realities—ultimately integrating these two worlds into daily work activities at all levels of the organization.

This integration of these two worlds is not easy to do. Organizing stimuli into things that are in the foreground and things that are in the background is basic to the way we perceive patterns in the world.[12] The foreground gains our attention, while the information available in the background is generally ignored or not actively processed. For example, the words on this page are to readers the foreground while the white space is perceived as the background. With the can-do and "get things done" attitudes in many organizations moving toward organizational learning, the tendency to see the Bold Vision as the foreground is strong. Skill sets are developed and mindsets are changed to focus on the data-to-knowledge-to-action model.

It is also well documented that what is perceived or seen as the "figure" and what is seen as the "ground" can shift. There are numerous examples of reversible figure and ground objects.[13] There are a number of factors that determine what is perceived as a figure against the ground. Perceptions depend not only on the features of the object in question but also on the context and past experience. Context and experience matter in what we see as the figure and what is shunted to the background. This means that much work must be done to change skill sets and mindsets relevant to disconnects, dilemmas, and divergence.

Ultimately. we see that the two cycles are actually two sides of the same coin. Disconnects, dilemmas, and divergence always accompany data, knowledge and action. Disconnects are data. Dilemmas are visible based on knowledge. Action generates divergence. Bold Visions and Harsh Realities are always occurring simultaneously. This integration is represented in figure 9.5, where the linear charts from figure 9.3 and Figure 9.4 have been wound together in a helix format.

Once someone "sees" that the cycles are two sides of the same coin, he or she can at any given time "choose" which object to view as the figure and which to view as the ground. Thus, once a person sees the dual perspectives, what is figure and what is ground can change or jump back and forth between the two perspectives with little effort. There can also be a balance between figure and ground where both are seen as equally likely. A vivid example is a woodcut by M. C. Escher called *Heaven and Hell* in which angels and devils alternate in our mind but neither seems to dominate the other. The goal of this book is to encourage the development of skill sets and mindsets that facilitate moving between these two worlds—between the

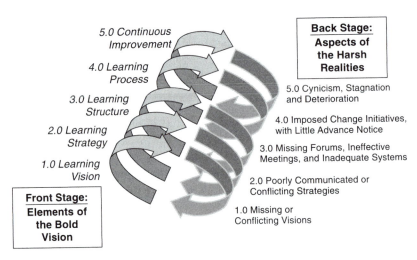

Figure 9.5 Integrating Bold Visions and Harsh Realities in the learning systems change model[14]

Bold Visions and the Harsh Realities of organizational learning at the same time.

Given this frame or way of thinking about organizational learning, let us return to each stage of the Front Stage model. The six core principles highlighted at the outset of this chapter can be applied to each step in the change model. The application of these core principles leads to the identification of learning guidelines that can aid the transformation to organizational learning. By following these learning guidelines, the aim of moving to organizational learning can be enhanced. At the same time, we also highlight how appreciating the Harsh Realities of the Back Stage model leads to the identification of additional and crucial aspects of organizational learning that are often undervalued or overlooked.

This is a generic model for the implementation of an organizational learning system. But its value is not in being adopted as is. Rather, it is most useful as a template for asking comparable questions that are tied to a specific context of a given organization.

1.0 Learning Vision   As we noted earlier, virtually all change models begin with the concept of a common or shared vision. The aim is to begin at the end—identifying what success would look like and ensuring that this vision of success is widely shared. This is critical in any change initiative. Indeed, an appreciation for shared, Bold Visions is woven throughout this book. In the context of systems for learning and knowledge, a subset of the learning vision is:

> Learning Vision 1.1: Create a vision that clearly articulates the aim or aims of the organizational learning systems.

For example, such a vision might read as follows:

> *We are committed to continuous learning at all levels of our organization, with the just-in-time delivery of training and full support for knowledge-based improvement in our operations.*

Of course, just articulating this sort of a Bold Vision invites disconnects. Training will not always be available on a just-in-time basis, knowledge-driven improvement efforts will not always be supported, and so on. Therefore, a second corollary that goes hand in glove with Learning Vision 1.1 is:

> Learning Vision 1.2: Ensure that the vision for the learning system clearly acknowledges the Harsh Realities that the organization will have to face in order to achieve the articulated aim or aims.

Based on this guideline, a second sentence might be added to the vision:

> *When we encounter Harsh Realities that fall short of this vision, we are also committed to learning from these disconnects in a nonblaming, constructive way.*

2.0 Learning Strategy   Organizational strategies that depend on and integrate learning or knowledge are more important than the specific model or approach to organizational learning. Thus, a learning strategy that might follow from the learning vision would include the following learning corollaries:

Learning Strategy 2.1: Ensure that organizational/business strategies value increased capability.

To increase capability, organizations must build capability for learning (data → knowledge → action), especially in "constraint" or bottleneck operations—with capability expanding as current constraints are addressed and new constraints become the focus of investment and effort.

Learning Strategy 2.2: Establish stability in operations and effective feedback with measurable data on safety, quality, cost, and schedule performance as a baseline, and then drive continuous improvement in each dimension.

Again, these are all aspects of a learning strategy that is focused on the Bold Vision and that has great potential. Tied to the Bold Vision, however, is the likelihood of increased disconnects in each dimension. To anticipate disconnects, consider the following additional strategy element:

Learning Strategy 2.4: Foster the skill sets and mindsets to learn from disconnects, value divergence, and surface underlying dilemmas

3.0 Learning Structure
The learning structure includes physical structures, such as classrooms, team meeting rooms, information technology, and other physical forms of support for learning and knowledge. The learning structure also includes more intangible structural features such as career paths, reward systems, and communication systems. Other terms for the learning structure are the learning "infrastructure" or the learning "architecture." In this respect, visible aspects of learning structure might emphasize the following:

Learning Structure 3.1: Emphasize role definitions for managers/leaders that include coaching, teaching, and valuing knowledge

Learning Structure 3.2: Develop a network of training professionals organized to provide just-in-time training

Learning Structure 3.3: Integrate team-based learning into daily operations

Learning Structure 3.4: Build information systems that provide timely, understandable feedback on safety, cost, quality, and schedule performance, with access to back-up data needed for root-cause analysis

Learning Structure 3.5: Ensure that reward and reinforcement systems value investments in learning and knowledge

Learning Structure 3.6: Develop methods to track skill acquisition and capability at the individual, team, and business unit levels

Learning Structure 3.7: Create forums for key stakeholder groups to engage in learning dialogue and action

Again, these are all valuable and important aspects of Front Stage learning structure, but these alone are incomplete as a robust model for organizational learning. The following are also important:

Learning Structure 3.8: Develop information systems that track progress and gaps associated with skill building

Learning Structure 3.9: Create new appeals systems for open issues associated with continuous improvement efforts by teams and others in the organization

Learning Structure 3.10: Ensure that dispute-resolution systems provide basic levels of respect and fairness in organizational operations

Learning Structure 3.11: Remove disincentives in reward and reinforcement systems, such as rewards that emphasize "local" or "sub" optimization of one part of an operation at the expense of others in the system

Learning Structure 3.12: Establish forums that bring together stakeholders who are interdependent and who otherwise do not have opportunities to engage in constructive dialogue

4.0 Learning Process

The learning process encompasses all the learning and knowledge-related interactions that take place within the learning structure—in service of the learning strategy and the learning vision. The convergent part of the learning process includes the many instances where individuals, teams, and other groups are working through the process of examining data, generating knowledge, and taking action. These include:

Learning Process 4.1: Target root-cause analysis at "constraint" or bottleneck operations

Learning Process 4.2: Develop supervisors, managers, and other leaders in areas of coaching individuals and teams in knowledge-generating and continuous improvement skills

Learning Process 4.3: Align support functions (finance, human resources, material handling, engineering, maintenance, information systems, and so on) so they can learn how to better serve "internal customers"

Learning Process 4.4: Utilize data to generate knowledge and guide action for senior management and at other leadership levels to model and value the learning processes they seek to foster across the organization

These and other processes are at the heart of operations in any organization employing strategies linked to learning and knowledge, but additional processes involving divergent learning are just as critical:

Learning Process 4.5: Surface data on disconnects encountered from frontline operations and seek to identify and implement continuous improvements in operations

Learning Process 4.6: Review patterns of learning and knowledge disconnects to identify issues addressable at that level and system barriers requiring the attention of middle and senior leadership

Learning Process 4.7: Seek data on system barriers that are undermining learning, knowledge, and continuous improvement—to generate knowledge and guide action

5.0 Continuous Improvement Continuous improvement is the final stage of the change process. It occurs when the procedures, polices, and systems that emerged as a result of the change effort formally replace the old methods of performing. This stage involves systems alignment, codification of new behaviors, and the transfer of knowledge to others so that continuous improvements can be a reality. Alignment occurs when the organizational structure (for example, roles and responsibilities, accountability, communication patterns), operating systems (for example, budget and time allocation), and human resource systems (for example, rewards, training, selection criteria) are consistent with the vision for the change effort. Codification occurs when old polices and practices are replaced with new systems and methods of operation and those new behaviors become standard procedure. In addition, new employees are trained in the organization's new approaches to work and knowledge is systematically transferred from incumbent employees to new employees. Only then can continuous improvement become the reality. This leads to the following learning principle:

Continuous Improvement 5.1: Develop systems for monitoring the change effort by quantifying progress, identifying gaps, and developing new action plans

In addition, for continuous improvement to continue, one must also take into account the Harsh Reality cycle:

Continuous Improvement 5.2: Acknowledge and appreciate divergent learning approaches as ways to continually adapt to changing circumstances and situations

We have offered a total of twenty-seven learning principles, which together represent a blueprint for making this journey to continuous improvement. They do not provide the actual recipe for success but they are the appropriate ingredients. The actual recipe is different in each organization and, in fact, surfaces from the learning associated with each of the principles—this is not a passive process!

The yield from the combination of Front Stage and Back Stage learning will be continuous improvement, but only where there is integration of the Bold Visions with the Harsh Realities. Consider a detailed case example of the learning vision (1.0), with the Front Stage and the Back Stage both visible. We then provide ways to integrate Bold Visions and the Harsh Realities in the other four parts of the Learning Systems Change Model.

FRONT STAGE AND BACK STAGE ELEMENTS OF A LEARNING VISION (1.0)—A CASE EXAMPLE

Most processes for constructing a shared vision involve brainstorming potential elements of a vision (generating data). Then there is a process of clustering the elements of a vision and distilling a succinct and compelling statement or illustration (interpreting the data to create knowledge). This is followed by an interactive and often iterative and emergent process with key stakeholders—where others develop awareness and appreciation for the draft vision, as well as where the vision evolves to take into account stakeholder input (applying the knowledge to guide action).

In each stage of the process—brainstorming elements of a vision, distilling them into a vision statement, and the iterative adjustment of the vision so that it can be a shared vision—there are disconnects that will be revealed or are predicted. If they are ignored or smoothed over, there is the risk of a superficial vision that is not truly shared. If they are engaged, it is possible to then see underlying dilemmas and divergence—which then make the construction of a true shared vision feasible. It will also likely reveal the importance of that vision over time—since many of the dilemmas will be enduring and require different responses as circumstances change.

To illustrate the weaving together of the convergent and divergent learning processes, consider a strategic planning retreat that was recently held for a group of people associated with a nonprofit fund devoted to issues of AIDS education and related matters in the Jewish community. This is intentionally a very different context than the industrial or public sector examples used in other parts of the book, but the principles are equally applicable. The intent of the strategic planning retreat was to form a freestanding tax-exempt corporation to expand the scope and impact of the efforts. A key part of this process involved constructing a mission/vision statement. To begin, the group reviewed language on the fund that had been incorporated in past brochures associated with the effort, which read as follows:

> The Peter Daniel Clark Fund was established in memory of Peter Daniel Clark who died of AIDS-related lymphoma in 1992 at the age of 34. The Foundation is dedicated to increasing awareness and understanding of AIDS in the Jewish community. Peter's desire was that one day there would be open and responsive communication within and between Jewish families about the stigma and tragedy of living with HIV and AIDS. The Fund collaborates with other agencies in the greater Boston area that partake in AIDS education and awareness, including Jewish Family and Children Services, AIDS Jewish Voices, The Boston Living Center, and the AIDS Action Committee. The Foundation supports a myriad of AIDS education programs and the Annual Peter Daniel Clark Seder of Hope and Healing.

Brainstorming for potential elements of a vision, the group produced the following list:

- Peter Daniel Clark Fund represents a uniquely Jewish voice in dialogue and education on AIDS
- Issues of "acceptance" for individuals, families, and communities on broader issues of sexual identity
- Issues of "hope and healing" more broadly in the Jewish community
- Social action that embraces an entire community—the entire world—t'kun olum—from awareness to action

- Partnership with other organizations—in the Jewish community, AIDS community, and the civic community
- Open issue on the use of the word "progressive"
- Open issue around the phrase "sexual identity" as it impacts fundraising and public perception
- Underlying issue around addressing the feelings of isolation that can come from AIDS, sexual identity, and other matters

This was then distilled into the following draft of a vision/mission statement.

> Peter Daniel Clark Fund represents a uniquely Jewish voice for dialogue, education, acceptance, and action on AIDS, sexual identity, and broader issues of "hope and healing" for individuals, families, and the community— on its own and in partnership with others.

In drafting this statement, many potential disconnects began to be visible. Some of the participants felt that issues of sexual identity, for example, had to be stated explicitly, while others surfaced concerns about being so forthright. The specific religious focus—on the Jewish community—was understood to be a defining feature of this effort, but there were different views around whether such wording would be seen as somehow unwelcoming to many non-Jewish participants in activities sponsored by the fund.

Rather than sidestep these and other issues, an analysis was conducted comparing the draft mission statement with the earlier brochure language. This analysis was specifically intended to prompt constructive dialogue on areas of potential disconnect—to make the gaps more visible. Thus, following contrasting phrases were noted:

"... is dedicated to ..."
> or
> "... represents a uniquely Jewish voice ..."

"... increasing awareness and understanding ..."
> or
> "... dialogue, education, acceptance, and action"

"... AIDS ..."
> or
> "... AIDS, sexual identity, and broader issues of 'hope and healing'"

"... within and between Jewish families"
> or
> "... for individuals, families, and the community"

"... with other agencies ... including ..."
> or
> "... on its own and in partnership with others"

After both statements, the brainstorming and the analysis were circulated to all key stakeholders, a subsequent meeting was held to reconcile the issues.

Instead of a simple review of the points of comparison, however, two alternative vision statements were introduced. These were as follows:

Alternative A:

The Peter Daniel Clark Foundation represents a Jewish voice in the HIV/AIDS epidemic. The Foundation's mission is to openly address this disease within the Jewish community and its varied organizations and institutions. Through education and increased awareness, we hope to decrease rates of transmission and destigmatize HIV. In addition, we will continue our work via such forums as the AIDS Passover "Seder of hope and healing" to comfort those infected and affected by HIV/AIDS.

Alternative B:

The mission of the Peter Daniel Clark Foundation is to promote education, spiritual guidance, and social support for Jewish people living with and affected by HIV/AIDS, to maintain collaboration with JCFS, AIDS Jewish Voices, Boston Living Center . . . and to develop Judaic HIV/AIDS programs that can be replicated within other Jewish communities.

While this may just seem to be an endless iteration around different ways to word a vision/mission statement, its importance goes far beyond the careful selection of the right words. In debating the different options, additional disconnects were revealed. For example, Alternative B prompted an important discussion on identifying the relevant stakeholder organizations, and it became increasingly clear this was an underlying dilemma: By signaling a unique focus on the Jewish community it reaches out to a target population in need of support, but it also risks being seen as exclusionary by the non-Jewish community. Some issues were not disconnects or dilemmas, but just technical choices—such as whether it was more appropriate for the new organization to label itself a "fund" or a "foundation." In the end, a single vision statement emerged.

The Peter Daniel Clark Fund is a unique Jewish Voice in the HIV/AIDS epidemic. The Foundation's mission is to promote open dialogue, education, and spiritual guidance across the Jewish community. The Foundation is deeply committed to addressing the critical challenge of acceptance among individuals and families directly affected by issues of HIV/AIDS.

What is important about the statement is not just that it is clear and compelling, but also that it emerged from a process such that it is shared among all key stakeholders. Some key issues, such as the role of the fund in addressing issues of sexual identity are implied by the text, but not made explicit—with the view that the words would need to be revised at the point that the fund begins to support programming and other activities along these lines.

Most change efforts involve some sort of future state or desired state or "blue sky" vision. It is important to embed in such visions, concepts such as constructive conflict, valued disconnects, enduring dilemmas, and divergent learning. In other words, even an optimistic future vision should be rooted in reality—not fantasy. The reality is that there will always be conflicting as well as common interests. The reality is that disconnects will always emerge. By constructing a vision of success that contemplates these parts of reality it is not only more likely to be achievable but also more likely to succeed.

LINKING THE LEARNING STRATEGY (2.0) TO THE OVERALL ORGANIZATIONAL STRATEGY

At the outset of a transformation journey—and at key stages along the way—it is essential to assess the overall alignment of the organization's learning strategy. This advice is central to nearly all change models. Our own experience, however, is that full alignment is elusive and a false ideal. The real priority is to avoid major misalignments.

An organization can simultaneously seek to serve customers, shareholders, and society. It can also insist that people are its most important resource. Will it ever be possible to articulate a single set of goals and objectives that optimizes all of these dimensions? We think not. Is it essential, however, to avoid directly conflicting aims? Absolutely. The key is to look for areas where the interests of customers, shareholders, the workforce, or society are directly threatened.

This means that periodic strategy alignment efforts must feature stakeholder analysis—who are the major stakeholders and what are their key interests or concerns? Not all stakeholders will necessarily have been directly involved in constructing the shared vision. Just listing the full set of stakeholders and interests, will in itself often highlight misalignments. It also means that a broad cross-section of stakeholders should be involved in this analysis—since learning about misalignments by some stakeholders and not others will be a disconnect.

For example, an organization that is overly preoccupied with quarterly returns to shareholders will have a bias against long-term investments in workforce capability or around other societal objectives. The solution is not an indistinguishable mass of goals, objectives, and metrics that tries to be everything to every stakeholder. Instead, it involves directly identifying the associated disconnects, appreciating the divergence they will generate, and naming the underlying dilemma or dilemmas. Here, the core dilemma centers on the way short-term performance priorities undercut needed long-term investments. There is no "solution" to this dilemma (otherwise it wouldn't be a dilemma), but there are constructive options to consider. For example, there may be ways to convert long-term workforce and societal investments into factors that can be valued by shareholders. This might involve demonstrated stability in a volatile stock market, or indications that you are the employer of choice in a tight labor market, or clear ways of linking brand loyalty with corporate citizenship. The point is not to seek unrealistic consensus across all stakeholders—but to anticipate and address mis-alignments in a dynamic way.

LINKING THE LEARNING STRUCTURE (3.0) TO OVERALL ORGANIZATIONAL STRUCTURE AND SYSTEMS

Many aspects of an organization's overall structure and systems will not have been established with the aim of supporting learning and knowledge-related change initiatives. These include social structures and systems for communications, performance feedback, rewards, recognition, training, dialogue, visioning, negotiations, agreement, learning, and more. For example, reward systems may center primarily on individual performance, while many learning and knowledge-related initiatives involve the effort of groups and teams.

The technical systems in an organization are equally likely to feature various disconnects. Technical systems include computer information systems, material handling systems, physical facilities, new technology, and other related matters. For example, computer information systems may have been designed primarily to provide an upward flow of data to higher-level decision makers—not a direct feedback loop to individuals, groups, and teams at all levels.

In most cases, there are additional disconnects between the official or Front Stage systems and the way things actually get done. That is, most social and technical systems will have countless "work-arounds" where people have found it easier or more efficient to not follow the official system. This in itself may be a disconnect in some ways and a "connect" in others. For example, a group of workers may cover for someone who is temporarily away from the job attending to a family emergency. Someone is not on the job when they should be. At the same time, a work/family crisis may be avoided, the bonds among these individuals may deepen, and a genuine social need may be addressed. An honest look at such disconnects may point to a reaffirmation of policies that prevent people from covering for each other or it could lead to more flexible work/family policies. The key point is that such informal practices are woven throughout organizations and are properly part of the analysis of organizational systems and structures.

Examining potential disconnects in organizational systems and structures is essential as a form of "error proofing" new learning and knowledge initiatives. This is a way of anticipating disconnects in support systems. It involves going through each element of the social and technical systems and considering what stresses and strains are likely to take place as people strive toward the various elements of the future vision.

Structure and systems are not generally highlighted by short-term, high-profile change initiatives. They are slow to change and rarely earn center-stage attention. Yet the analysis of disconnects almost always surfaces breakdowns in the social and technical systems. Just communications processes and information systems alone account for a massive number of disconnects in most organizations.

Many support functions have responsibilities for aspects of the infrastructure. These vary across manufacturing and service organizations, but might include human resources, quality, finance, information systems, purchasing, material handling, facilities, maintenance, and other functions. Under the mass-production and bureaucratic models, each of these functions is primarily focused on a mix of monitoring/compliance activities and service-providing activities. Not included in this mix is a third category, enabling change.[15]

For example, the finance function might split its time between ensuring compliance with financial accounting principles and budgetary targets, on the one hand, and providing services to managers and executives in the form of analysis and reports, on the other hand. It is quite another matter to add to this mix the periodic restructuring of the financial accounting system to remain aligned with the needs of the organization, as well as to reorient the service activities to focus as much on providing understandable, timely cost-performance feedback for the front-line operations. Indeed, this represents quite a culture change for many finance organizations.

Similarly, the human resource function has to ensure compliance with dozens of employment laws and regulations, as well as corporate policies and collective bargaining agreements. It also provides many services including administering pay and benefits, delivering training, maintaining dispute resolution procedures, and the like. It is quite another matter to add to this mix responsibility for effective workgroups and overall organizational development support.

Embedded in the alignment of support functions is a core dilemma. The same organizations that have traditionally focused oversight and control, down through the organization, and service, up to middle and senior managers, must now simultaneously shift directions. They must continue in their existing roles while also providing services to the front lines and facilitating change—both of which involve an enabling and facilitating stance that is the opposite of that associated with the traditional roles.

Thus, an appreciation for disconnects highlights the critical importance of systems and structure. Attention to systems and structure makes new demands on support functions, which then surfaces deep dilemmas for these parts of the organization. Addressing these issues involves a role renegotiation, new skills, new goals, and new objectives, and leadership that simultaneously embraces this vision and anticipates the many twists and turns that will arise in pursuing the vision.

An example of issues around structure and systems can be found in the link between what are termed lean implementation efforts at the Boeing Corporation and the structure of the company's cost accounting system. The lean initiatives place a high premium on continuous improvement efforts by work groups in the manufacturing operations. This surfaced a major disconnect with respect to the company's cost accounting system. Under the existing system, manufacturing managers had budgets that mostly consisted of direct headcount costs and various indirect labor charges. Most of the costs associated with raw materials and components were on separate procurement budgets. Time spent in training was a direct claim against time spent in production. Gains in long-term sustainability of the aircraft did not show up at all. As a result of these and other factors, there were strong incentives for managers to focus on ways to reduce headcount and much weaker incentives associated with savings in materials, investments in capability, and the enhancement of life-cycle value for the product.

In response, Boeing has initiated a variety of pilot experiments with activity-based costing systems, life-cycle value design initiatives, and related efforts to restructure the cost accounting system. A preliminary assessment of these efforts suggests that they do have the desired effect of shifting management behavior—but the challenge of restructuring these systems across the enterprise are vast.[16]

LINKING THE LEARNING PROCESS (4.0) TO OVERALL PROCESS CHANGE INITIATIVES

Some change initiatives focus on top-down restructuring—which is at the heart of many reengineering initiatives, corporate mergers and acquisitions, and strategic alliances. Nearly as many change initiatives focus on bottom-up process improvement—which is at the heart of many employee involvement, total quality, team, lean, and other such initiatives. Top-down restructuring primarily involves forcing dynamics, while bottom-up process improvement primarily involves fostering dynamics. In addition to the top-down and bottom-up processes, there are other change initiatives, such as the use of pilot experiments, followed by planned diffusion; the establishment of new, "greenfield" operations to take a clean slate, wall-to-wall approach; implementation across a given product line or value stream; and many other variations.

All of these change initiatives involve data, knowledge, and action—though the learning is by a different mix and sequence of stakeholders in each case. A top-down reengineering initiative generally concentrates what we have termed incremental learning among senior leaders. There may even be some revolutionary learning where the changes are sufficiently bold. It will simultaneously generate some entrenched learning and possibly even some revolutionary learning on the part of those who are threatened by the initiative.

A bottom-up initiative may also involve some incremental learning, as well as continuous learning if the front-line efforts are well established. Where there are "in-groups" and "out-groups" with respect to the bottom-up activities, it is also possible to set in motion entrenched learning.

Pilot-diffusion initiatives are premised on experimental learning. If careful attention is paid to the diffusion process, it can also include a mix of incremental learning and continuous learning. Too often, however, the high-profile pilots are threatening to other parts of the organization, triggering entrenched learning.

Given all the different types of learning that may be associated with these various change initiatives, how can we anticipate what learning will actually occur? The key, of course, is to appreciate the way that the intentional, Front Stage learning is interconnected with the Back Stage, divergent learning.

Each change initiative is notable for the dilemmas that it embodies. Top-down change can produce rapid results, but often at the expense of commitment. Bottom-up initiatives build commitment, but may be slow to deliver results or may be hard to focus. Pilot-diffusion models often produce successful pilots, but just as often struggle with the subsequent diffusion.

Any systems change initiative will involve the skillful sequencing and blending of these many strategies, which virtually guarantees many associated disconnects. It can be very difficult to trace the links between the disconnects and the underlying dilemmas when so much is occurring simultaneously. Yet that is precisely the task since it is in understanding these dynamics that synergistic learning is most likely.

Change initiatives don't exist just because leaders have announced such intentions. Such announcements are merely strategic intentions or wishes. Actual initiatives emerge based on numerous tactical choices. Sometimes there are highly vivid pivotal events, in which the strategic choices are thrown in sharp relief. Just as often there are less visible choices that take shape over time.

Even though all initiatives have embedded dilemmas, there are tactics that increase or decrease the ability to effectively engage the dilemmas. For example, insisting on strict command and control obedience or relying only on the knowledge of a few high-profile experts will mean that it is only a handful of leaders and experts who will be wrestling with the dilemmas. It will be a spectator sport for everyone else. Similarly, a short-term tactical focus will remove from consideration many options that are attentive to a wider range of stakeholder interests.

By contrast, tactics that are inclusive of a wider mix of stakeholders increase the degree to which the dilemma is shared—with the hard choices more likely to be appreciated and understood. Similarly, a longer-time horizon allows for trade-offs and sequencing of options that can substantially mitigate the intensity of the dilemmas. Of course, new dilemmas are introduced when the mix of stakeholders is widened or the time horizon is lengthened, but we have consistently found that these and other related tactical choices facilitate the simultaneous engaging of the Front Stage and Back Stage dynamics.

Appreciating reality involves setting expectations about both the active learning cycle and the divergent learning cycle. People should be expected to spend time in formal problem solving and in other forms of data analysis—as part of the Front Stage learning process. So part of the expectations should be to provide the resources to support such learning—including meeting spaces, facilitation resources, skills training, and time for such activities. Also involved is follow-through with the support functions that are often needed to implement suggestions and recommendations that come from such efforts.

As well, senior leaders must anticipate and embrace a steady diet of perceived systems barriers. People at front-line and middle levels of organizations should be focused on documenting system barriers as they encounter them. These are more than just lists of disconnects. Once surfaced, the disconnects have to be analyzed to assess the degree to which they can be resolved at front-line levels. Issues that require higher-level attention should be accompanied by data and options based on the data.

Organizations that have "good news" cultures will find this particularly challenging. Surfacing disconnects and perceived system barriers invariably casts a negative shadow on particular individuals and parts of the organization. Dr. Deming, the quality guru, frequently admonished, "don't blame people, fix the system."[17] It is advice that should be embraced and repeated often by leaders at all levels.

LINKING CONTINUOUS IMPROVEMENT IN LEARNING SYSTEMS (5.0) TO OVERALL CONTINUOUS IMPROVEMENT IN THE ORGANIZATION

A core measure of success is the generation of new knowledge that then enables action. This is a very practical standard—if the process seems valuable or helpful, then this will have been a worthwhile undertaking. But what if the process seems to have gone flat—what if there is not any real new learning taking place? What if there are no helpful or new action implications brought to the surface?

If nothing new is revealed, then it is possible that existing actions are well directed. Or, it is possible that the analysis has not been well-focused. How do you know which is the case? Simply put, an analysis of disconnects that yields no new insights must be met with its own analysis—why was that the case? As was noted earlier, the Japanese process of asking the "five whys" is a methodology oriented at getting to root causes. It is a way of converting data to knowledge. We are suggesting here that some of the "whys" concern not just the disconnects, but the ability to interpret the disconnects. It is all part of the larger picture.

Continuous improvement in the learning process is often called for. Our analysis suggests that it is only possible with the simultaneous appreciation of the Front Stage active learning process as well as the Back Stage dynamics.

A CONCLUDING THOUGHT

In this book, we have presented two distinct cycles that each contribute to the establishment of effective systems for organizational learning. One learning model is built around data, knowledge, and action. Many books on organizational learning have focused attention on these elements of what we have called the Bold Vision—as well as their application to continuous learning in organizations. Many organizations that are attempting to become continuous learning organizations benchmark successful companies and try to emulate these key elements of the learning model.

Organizational learning theorists and practitioners have not focused as much attention to the cycle featuring the 3Ds—disconnects, dilemmas, and divergence. Yet, these Harsh Realities have as much centrality as the Bold Visions. Unfortunately, many people in organizations focus only on the Bold Visions as "real learning" while the disconnects, dilemmas, and divergence are lost as part of the background—something that you know is there, but not something that the organization is actively "looking at" or trying to learn about.

What can possibly guide individuals and organizations in dealing with disconnects, dilemmas, and divergence so that wise choices can be made? First, it is important to see each dilemma as consisting of three elements—each of which requires attention. Thus, it is not just a matter of guidance in dealing with a dilemma, but guidance in dealing with that fact that the dilemma has more than one plausible solution, dealing with the implications of the different tradeoffs, and dealing with the irreversibility of any particular choice. The intensity of the dilemma might be primarily a function of any one of these elements, or some combination of the three. Regardless, the journey to becoming a learning organization requires not only the Bold Vision but the ways to learn from the Harsh Realities of organizational life.

We leave you with this final thought on appreciating the realities of simultaneous convergent and divergent learning—even if the ultimate result transforms that reality. The spirit of this undertaking can perhaps best be conveyed not through analytical narrative but through the poetic art of this passage from a classic children's book, *The Velveteen Rabbit*:[18]

"What is REAL?" asked the Rabbit one day . . . "Does it mean having things that buzz inside you and a stick-out handle?"

"Real isn't how you are made," said the Skin Horse. "It's a thing that happens to you. When a child loves you for a long, long time, not just to play with, but REALLY loves you, then you become Real."

"Does it hurt?" asked the Rabbit.

"Sometimes," said the Skin Horse, for he was always truthful. "When you are Real you don't mind being hurt."

"Does it happen all at once, like being wound up," he asked, "or bit by bit?"

"It doesn't happen all at once," said the Skin Horse. "You become. It takes a long time. That's why it doesn't often happen to people who break easily, or have sharp edges, or who have to be carefully kept. Generally, by the time you are Real, most of your hair has been loved off, and your eyes drop out and you get loose in the joints and very shabby. But these things don't matter at all, because once you are Real you can't be ugly, except to people who don't understand."

Notes

1. Note that we offer a number of ways to integrate Bold Visions and Harsh Realities in this chapter, but view these as only illustrative—not definitive. Enterprising readers are encouraged to find additional, inventive ways of linking these thoughts.

2. Ron Reeves, plant manager, Ford Chicago Assembly Plant, personal conversation, October 2000.

3. Write-up based on site visit (May 20, 2003) and subsequent e-mail correspondence.

4. "Fujitsu Models Itself After Toyota with 'Sense-And-Respond' Strategy" in *Lean Manufacturing Advisor* (Productivity, Inc., Portland, Oreg., June, 2003).

5. Steve Parry, Fujistsu Corporation, internal manuscript on "Customer Knowledge-Driven Organization, Based on Lean Services Principles, Systems Thinking, and Leadership" (2003).

6. Ibid.

7. Gary Fisher, research fellow, London School of Economics—cited in Parry, "Customer Knowledge-Driven Organization."

8. This is the key thesis advanced by Thomas Kochan, Harry Katz, and Robert McKersie, in *The Transformation of American Industrial Relations* (New York: Basic Books, 1984).

9. See, for example, the discussion on "shared vision" in Senge, Peter, *The Fifth Discipline: The Art and Practice of the Learning Organization* (New York: Doubleday, 1990).

10. The classic treatment of these concepts derives from Raymond Miles and Charles Snow, *Organizational Strategy, Structure and Process* (New York: McGraw-Hill, 1978). This framework is developed in the context of negotiated change in Richard Walton, Joel Cutcher-Gershenfeld, and Robert McKersie, *Strategic Negotiations: A Theory of Change in Labor-Management Relations* (Boston: Harvard Business School Press, 1994).

11. The approach echoes the analysis by Ray Friedman on the Front Stage and Back Stage aspects of negotiations. See Ray A. Friedman, *Front Stage, Backstage: the Dramatic Structure of Labor Negotiations* (Cambridge, Mass. MIT Press, 1994).

12. Gestalt psychology has focused on how people organize their world through patterns of stimuli to produce a perceptual experience. A favorite phrase of Gestalt psychologists is that the "whole is different from the sum of its parts." For earlier work on Gestalt psychology see Wolfgang Köhler, *Gestalt Psychology* (New York: H. Liviright, 1929); Kurt Koffka, *Principles of Gestalt Psychology* (New York: Harcourt, Brace and Company, 1935); and Kurt Lewin, *Principles of Topological Psychology* (New York: McGraw-Hill, 1936). For more recent work see David Murray, *Gestalt Psychology and the Cognitive Revolution* (New York: Harvester Wheatsheaf, 1995). One example of the application of Gestalt principles to improving organizational effective-

ness is by Edward Nevis, *Organizational Consulting: A Gestalt Approach* (New York, NY: Gardner Press, 1987).

13. There are numerous examples of how we tend to perceive a pattern as the foreground against a background. Patterns are often seen this way even when the stimuli are ambiguous leading to reversible foreground-background relationships. For example, one demonstration of a figure-ground reversal is where the light portion of an image is a goblet, while the dark portion is two profiles of people that can be perceived as a figure against a background. Another example is the picture that can be viewed as if it is a young women or an old women. Once people "see" both figures embedded in the picture, they can easily move from seeing one figure as the foreground and the other figure as the background.

14. This visualization is adapted from a model that was developed for the UAW and the Ford Motor Company by Joel Cutcher-Gershenfeld, based on the Front Stage and Back Stage ideas in this book.

15. This framework derives from analysis by Russ Eisenstat, as adapted by Janice Klein.

16. Betty Barrett, "Fostering Workplace Innovation and Labor-Management Partnership: The Challenge of Strategic Shifts in Business Operations—Pratt & Whitney (United Technologies) and IAM Local 971, West Palm Beach, Florida" (Cambridge, MIT Labor Aerospace Case Study, 1999).

17. W. Edwards Deming, *Out of the Crisis* (Cambridge, MA: MIT Center for Advanced Engineeering Study, 1986).

18. Margery Williams, *The Velveteen Rabbit* (New York: Simon and Schuster, 1983).